PIRATES

IN THEIR OWN

WORDS

Eye-witness accounts of the 'Golden Age' of Piracy, 1690-1728.

Edited by E.T. Fox, M.A., PhD.

DEDICATED TO O AND L,

WHO MAKE LIFE WORTH LIVING.

FOR ALL OF THE USERS OF PIRATE-HISTORY INTERNET
DISCUSSION FORUMS AND GROUPS, WHOSE HUNGER FOR
ORIGINAL SOURCES INSPIRED THIS BOOK.

ABOUT THE EDITOR

E.T. Fox is an historian specialising in social history, crime and rebellion in the early-modern Atlantic world. He received his Master's degree and Doctorate from the University of Exeter, focussing on the political and social history of piracy during the 'golden age'. He has appeared in numerous television documentaries and worked as an historical advisor on many more; he has also acted as a consultant to more a number of film productions. He is a prolific lecturer on historical topics, and is the author of *Pirates of the West Country* and *King of the Pirates*, a biography of arch-pirate Henry Every, and numerous articles. He lives in Devon, England, with one wife, two children, three dogs and two cats.

CONTENTS

INTRODUCTION

There has, over the last century or so, been published a large number of collections of primary source documents, from church records and collections of wills to the letters of great men and women. Many of these collections have been thematic arrangements drawn from several different sources, such as letters from historical war-zones or documents relating to a particular event, but the subject of the so-called 'Golden Age' of piracy has received scant attention. Only two works have made primary source material relating to piracy of the late seventeenth and early eighteenth century generally available, both superb in their own right, but neither without drawbacks.

The first of these works was John Franklin Jameson's *Privateering and Piracy in the Colonial Period*, published in New York in 1923, and covering the history of American piracy and privateering from 1638 to 1762. For the student of 'golden age' piracy the broad scope of the book inevitably means that the amount of material relating to their study is limited to 69 documents of the 203 that the book contains. Nevertheless, the selection of documents and their arrangement is excellent. Despite being reprinted in 1970, Jameson's book was rare and fairly hard to come by for many years, but recently it has become freely available on the internet as an eBook, and can be purchased from more than one print-on-demand publisher. Jameson mostly, though not exclusively, drew his material from American archives, making it a useful companion to this book which is a collection mostly, though not exclusively, drawn from British sources, and with only one exception [**doc. 63**] I have not reproduced any documents published by Jameson.

More recently, in 2007, Joel Baer's *British Piracy in the Golden Age* collected numerous printed sources relating to British (in the largest sense of the word) piracy from 1660-1730. At 1,760 pages spread over four volumes it is a marvellous work containing 36 complete facsimile reproductions of pamphlets, trial accounts, religious texts, and other printed publications, as well as dozens of newspaper accounts relating to piracy. Baer's work, magnificent though it is, is beyond the means of many people, retailing at £350 for the four volumes in 2014. With its focus on the printed word, Baer's work naturally does not include any manuscript sources. I have included a number of printed sources not found in Baer's volumes, and have only included two newspaper articles [**doc. 59**] and a part of one document [**doc. 22**] previously published by Baer.

The first four chapters of this book consist entirely of eyewitness accounts of piracy in the 'golden age'. In the first and longest chapter the documents were all written or dictated by the pirates themselves, that is to say, voluntary participants in the act of piracy. In many cases these are the depostitions given by pirates before trial or during investigations, some given voluntarily, some the result of interrogation following arrest. In either case they were given at a time of extreme stress and the deponent was naturally keen not to incriminate himself, and this must be taken into account when reading them. To illustrate this point, a striking difference can be seen between the pre-trial deposition and the pre-execution confession of Walter Kennedy [**docs 24, 25**], the former made while he was trying to save his life, the latter made when he had nothing more to lose. The other documents in thiş chapter written by pirates are the stuff of everyday life: a will, letters, even a reference. The second chapter consists of the testimony and memoirs of forced men, mostly captured seamen impelled against their will to serve on board a pirate ship. Estalishing a man's forced status is made difficult by the fact that claiming to have been forced was one of the commonest ways pirates tried to escape the noose. In selecting the testimonies for this chapter I have included only those who voluntarily surrendered themselves and informed against their former captors, actually rose up and overpowered their captors, or managed successfully to convince a court of their innocence. Accounts written or dictated by the pirates' victims make up Chapter 3, including some of the most detailed accounts of life aboard a pirate ship. One of these accounts [doc. 57] is the only abridged document in this book. Recognising that what I find interesting in a document might be different to what someone else would find interesting about it, I have resisted the temptation to shorten any other document. In this case, however, the text reproduced here is part of a much longer one, too long for complete inclusion in this book, but the extract I have chosen is (in my opinion) so rich in fascinating detail as to be worth including. Chapter 4 contains three trial accounts. There are many surviving accounts of different pirates' trials, many of which were published in time to be sold at the guilty pirates' executions, and some of which have been reprinted since, such as Captain Kidd's and the notorious female pirates, Anne Bonny and Mary Read's. The complete trial of Bartholomew Roberts' company was included in the pseudonymous Captain Charles Johnson's 1724 *General History of the Robberies and Murders of the Most Notorious Pirates*, a must-have book for any pirate researcher, which is available in various reprints, and there are several printed trial accounts included in Baer's *British Piracy in the Golden Age*.The three trial accounts transcribed here have been selected for a variety of reasons: the trial of William Gibbens was chosen because it highlights areas of pirates' life not covered elsewhere and because if is one of the very few documents to provide information on the pirate company commanded by James Fife; the trial of Weaver and Ingram, of Anstis' company, is one of several documents relating to that company transcribed here [**docs 26, 32, 42, 43**], and because it is one of the few printed 'golden age' piracy trials not included in Baer's *British Piracy*; and the trial of Nicholas Simmons and his companions has been chosen as a example of a piracy trial held with the intent of proving the defendants not guilty, and as a companion piece to **doc. 48**.

The fifth chapter is the only one not made up entirely of eye-witness accounts, but includes a variety of documents which nevertheless shed some light on the life of the pirate. The deposition of Adam Baldridge [**doc. 63**] relates the experiences of a man who was not a pirate himself but was instrumental in creating the 'golden age' of piracy. Other documents include first-hand accounts of battles with pirates, official documents such as a certificate of pardon, and financial documents that shed light on the economy of the pirates. Perhaps the most poignant of all is the undelivered letter to a pirate from his wife, signed with loving kisses [**doc. 66**]. Following Chapter 5, I have included a glossary of terms and an extensive bibliography.

In editing the documents I have tried to change as little as possible. I have retained the original spelling and included footnotes to explain difficult words, and I have done little to modernise the grammar. I have used the modern convention of italicising ships' names, and placed inverted commas around speech, but no other major changes have been made. I have also included footnotes to explain place names which have changed in the last three centuries, references to people, and cross-reference the documents with one another. I have also included short introductions to most documents so that they can be placed in their proper context. Many

12

of the documents contain common abbreviations which were to some extent standard, such as 'sd' for 'said', 'yr' for 'your' or 'his Maties' for 'his Majety's, and a list of common abbreviations can be found in the glossary.

One question which comes up frequently in discussions about the 'golden age' of piracy, is when exactly the 'golden age' was. Different authors have given different answers, ranging from a couple of centuries from the mid-sixteenth to mid-eighteenth centuries, down to a period of only a decade or so from the mid-17teens to the mid 1720s. I have chosen to limit the period covered by this book to the four decades between 1690 and 1730, because pirates at that time were unique in the level of impact they had on global trade, and because it is the only time in the history of Anglo-American piracy that different groups of pirates can be said to have formed a larger and semi-independent community. English pirate companies had banded together before 1690, but had remained tied to bases very close to legitimate society such as the ports of southern Ireland. From 1690, however, pirate ships were able to remain cruising thousands of miles from their 'home' port for indefinite periods, particularly in the Indian Ocean in the 1690s and 1720s, using St. Mary's Island, Madagascar, as a base, in the 17teens in the Caribbean using the harbour of New Providence in the Bahamas, and into the 1720s using a series of less stable bases on the West African coast. Furthermore, pirates operating thousands of miles apart knew one another through these shared bases. Marcus Rediker has calculated that over 90% of the Anglo-American pirates active in the 17teens and 20s were members of one of two groups of interrelated pirate companies, the largest group, known as the 'Flying Gang', originating at New Providence in around 1716.[1] Given this definition of *what* the 'golden age' of piracy was, it is possible to say with some precision *when* it was. The establishment of St. Mary's Island as a viable pirate base in the Indian Ocean began with the arrival of former buccaneer turned trading-factor Adam Baldridge on 17 July, 1690, and really took off with the arrival of the first pirate ship there on 13 October the following year [**doc. 63**]. From then on pirates operated in the manner outlined above until the extirpation of the last of the 'Flying Gang' pirates, John Philips, in mid-June 1724 [**doc. 47**]. Although Anglo-American pirates, especially the gang originating at a chance meeting of George Lowther and Edward Low, carried on operating for two or three years after 1724, they never again had the same cohesion as earlier pirate companies, nor did they have the security of a regular base to which they could return between cruises.

---

[1] Marcus Rediker, *Villains of All Nations, Atlantic Piracy in the Golden Age* (London, 2004), pp.80-81

1. PIRATES

So much has been written about pirates of the 'golden age', both factual and fanciful, that it is hard to recognise now that these larger-than-life characters were real people. They grew up as members of a society which was familiar to them, and in many respects familiar to us, they loved, had friends, in some cases had children, they left wives and parents at home, they worried about the future, they feared death and injury, they had aspirations and desires. At a distance of some 300 years, their voices have long since fallen silent, but pages and pages of documents either written or dictated by them have survived, giving us a glimpse into their world.

Most of these documents were dictated to the scribes present at their interrogations following their arrest, a stressful time to say the least and a scenario in which they cannot reasonably be expected to have told the whole truth. Nevertheless, self-serving though their testimonies can be, they are our best source for understanding what it meant to be a pirate in the 'golden age'. Another potential source of the true voice of the pirate is the many 'last words' publications, which purport to be the dying confessions of pirates on their way to the gallows, but many of them were written without the supposed author's input at all, and many more were written by memers of the clergy who attended condemned pirates and who, presumably, heavily edited the pirates' words to suit their own moral purposes. A small number, however, have a ring of genuine truth about them, or a level of detail which suggests the pirate's own input, and some have been included in this chapter [**docs 7, 25, 27**].

Other documents included here represent the commerce of everyday life as it applied to the pirates. Like everyone else, pirates died, and knowing that death awaited them they sometimes sought to put their affairs in order by compiling a will, one of which has survived [**doc. 14**]. The death of a pirate, and his desire to see to his widow's comfort, is also at the root of a letter written by pirate captain Robert Collover to a shipmate's widow [**doc. 17**], and thoughts of mortality perhaps drove one anonymous pirate to write an agony letter to a popular newspaper [**doc. 19**].

In this chapter the pirates speak for themselves, they tell us only what they want to tell us, not necessarily what we would like to know. At times they were uncommunicative, but the documents selected for this chapter are generally noted for the loquaciousness they display. At times they were dishonest, but we must accept that dishonesty and try to look through it. At other times they were selectively honest, only telling the parts of the story that made them appear most innocent, and it is not always possible to guess at what they might have kept back. Still, we cannot ask them in person, so we must content ourselves with what they left us.

1. Samuell Burgess.

The Case of Samuell Burgess. SP 34/36, f. 35

Samuel Burgess was a member of the crew of the Blessed William, *commanded by Captain William Kidd who would later find fame as a pirate himself, and was involved in the mutiny led by William Mason. The mutineers sailed to New York and there exchanged their ship for a prize named the Jacob, in which they sailed to the Indian Ocean and embarked on a career of piracy. After returning to New York Burgess went to work for Frederick Phillipse, the merchant who financed Adam Baldridge's trading post on St. Mary's Island, and eventually had command of the* Margaret, *a trading vessel sent by Phillipse with supplies for St. Mary's* [**doc. 67**]. *On his return journey, Burgess gave passage to a numer of pirates who wanted to retire* [**docs 10-13**], *but while anchored at the Cape of Good Hope the* Margaret *was seized and Burgess and his passengers were arrested for piracy. One of the other mutineers of the* Blessed William *was Robert Collover* [**doc. 17**], *who was instrumental in Burgess's trial in London. Burgess was found guilty, and it was while awaiting his execution that he wrote a petition begging for a Royal pardon, accompanied by the brief memoir which is reproduced here. The petition was success, he was pardoned in 1703, and joined a privateering expedition along with a number of other former pirates. Burgess eventually returned to the Indian Ocean and for a short time had command of a pirate vessel, before settling comfortably ashore in Madagascar, where he was reportedly still alive in 1716.*

Hee was bred to the sea and [in 1689] served as a foremast Man, on Board the good ship *Blessed William*, and being at Antego[2], the Officers carried away the ship and left the

Captaine on Shoar, and having so done chose one William Mason (who was a part owner) Commandr and then sailed on the Coast of Crocus where they took two Spanish Boates, but what was in them, or what taken out, I know not haveing had no share thereof.

Wee then made the best of our way for New Yorke,

In 1690 Wee arrived at New York, where the said Mason our Commandr obtained a Commission from the Governour[3] against the French and by vertue thereof wee took six prizes which wee brought into our Commission Port where they were condemned as Lawfull Prize.

One of these Prizes[4] proved a Much Better ship than our owne, shee was fitted and with the same Commission put to sea (as I thought) to Cruise upon the Enemies but after wee had been some time at sea and gott to the southward of the Line many of us suspected wee were going about the Cape of good Hope. But it being put to the vote whether thither or to the Westward it was carried for the Westward, which the Officers were all against, and when wee steered Westward they refused to take Charge of the ship, so that we were forced to submitt to them, and our Course was directed round the Cape and so to Madagascar where wee arrived in August 1691.

At Madagascar I went ashoar and left the ship, with a full Resolution never to see her more, but there waite the first oppertunity to gett to some English Port.

---

[2] Antigua
[3] Jacob Leisler
[4] The *Jacob*

Thence our ship went out on a Cruise and I remained ashoard among the natives untill April 1692, destitute of Cloaths and the very Necessaries of Life and without any meanes to obtaine a reasonable sufficiencie the want of which Impaired my health, and brought me very Low and no Oppertunity in all that time offering, in March our ship returnd to Madagascar, and I was constrained to go on Board againe or starve on shoar and in June 1692 I did re:enter in the said ship, and in her sailed to the Gulph of Mocca, where shee took two ships and return'd to Madagascar and from thence to New Yorke, where wee arrived in Aprill 1693.

Soone after my Arrivall I applyed myselfe to Collo[5] Fletcher, then Governr of that province, and gave him a full Narrative of all I had seen and done in which he was so fully convinced of my sincertie therein, that he gave me his protection which Originall protection is now in the hands of Mr Crawley Register of the Admiralty.

That since he hath been in Merchants Service, and Commanded many ships in severall Voyages to Barbadoes, Jamaico, Newfoundland, Lisbon and other places, and Discharged the said Trust, to the Intire satisfaction of the owners and Employers.

In 1698 when the Lord Bellamont came over Governour of New Yorke (where is my habitation and Family) I applyed myselfe to his Excellency in May 1698 and gave his Lordship an ample and sincere account of all my Circumstances as afore is mentioned, and so much to his Satisfaction that he wrote to England to the Secretary of State to obtaine of his

---

[5] Colonel

19

Matie a Grant for my Free pardon and his Excie did receive orders as I have heard to grant me one[6].

But the Command of a good ship Offering for a Tradeing voyage to Madagascar for slaves I accepted thereof and had his Excellencies pass and sailed in 1698 for the said Island where I arrived in the year 1699, and there I mett with his late Maties Proclamation of free pardon to all that would lay hold thereof brought by Capt Warren which I did Cheerfully accept, and Publiquely declared, I did so, and that I would surrender myselfe the first opportunity, which I can fully prove.

That in my returne home to New Yorke at the Cape of Good Hope on the 19th Day of Decembr 1699 Capt Louth seized me and my ship alleadging I had Pyrates on Board, and that he had a Commission to take Pyrates and their Effects and did take all from me and also his Maties said Proclamation, and brought me a prisoner into England where I have Laid in Irons near a Year and on the 29th of June Last was Indicted at the Admiralty Session in the Old Bailey upon four Indictments, Vizt.

Two for takeing two Spanish Barques in January 1689 on the Coast of Crocus 60 Leagues from Barbadoes. To which I pleaded the truth, that I had not any share thereof.

The two other Indictments were for takeing two Moorish ships in the Gulph of Mocco in August 1692, to which I pleaded I was forced to go with them or starve on

---

[6] This was perfectly true, Bellomont had received an order for Burgess's pardon. [John R. Brodhead, Berthold Fernow and Edmund B. O'Callaghan (eds), *Documents relative to the colonial history of the State of New York*, Volume 4 (New York, 1854), p. 412]

Madagascar, as is before related, and that at both, I was but a private mand and Could not help it.

The Evidence against me was Robert Collover and one Browne, the former so Notorious a Wicked man as scarse a Worse, and Browne not much better, however the Jury found me Guilty and I am in Law a Dead man, and now with a Mortification not to be Exprest throw myselfe on Your Maties royall Goodness and Mercy which on my Bended knees I begg for Christ sake.

Samll Burgess.

2. William Phillips

The Voluntary Confession and Discovery of William Phillips, 8 August, 1696. SP 63/358, ff. 127-132

Henry Every's spectacular pirate cruise [**docs 2-5**] *of 1694-1696 began with a mutiny at Corunna when unpaid sailors from the 'Spanish Expedition' seized the expedition's flagship,* Charles II, *renamed it* Fancy, *and sailed for the Indian Ocean. Of the coast of India, Every and his pirates captured the* Fateh Mohamed *and* Gang-i-Sawai, *ships filled with wealthy pilgrims returning from the annual Haaj to Mecca. The seizure of the two ships, the latter of which was actually owned by the Grand Mogul of India himself, caused uproar in India and the East India Company representatives at Surat found themselves under house arrest for several weeks as a result. One brief cruise was enough to provide Every and his men with enough financial security to retire from* *piracy, so they made their way to the Bahamas where they split up, some returning to England via Ireland, others disappearing in the colonies. Henry Every and most of his crew were never caught, making Every, whose personal share was perhaps as much as £3,000, one of the most successful pirates who lived to tell the tale. Of the pirates who did meet the authorities, some voluntarily surrendered while others were arrested. Only six were executed: William May, Edward Forseith, John Sparks [doc. 3], William Bishop, and James Lewis following a highly publicised series of trials in 1696, and James Cragget a few years later. One of the principal witnesses at the first trial was a young apprentice, Philip Middleton [doc. 36], who probably gave more voluntary depositions in pirate cases than anyone else in the seventeenth century.*

In August 1693 (as I remember) I went on board the *Dove Galley* Capt Humphreys Comr in Compa[ny] with the *Charles the 2d* the *James* and a Pink bound for Coruna from thence to the Spanish West Indies.

At Corunna the men demanded their pay which was to be paid them by contract every six months, which not being paid them, and hearing the Spaniards and Irish design'd to turn all the English on shore, and take their Vessels from them, they were obliged to keep a very strict Watch, whereupon Henry Every master of the *Charles the 2d* went up and down from ship to ship and perswaded the men to come on board him, and he would carry them where they should get money enough. About forty men came accordingly on board the said ship by night, upon which they cut the cable and losed the sails having a fair wind to go out. The Spaniards hearing it

22

fired severall shott from the Town at us, but did no damage. When we came out of the reach of the Castle and Forts we gave the Captain his Pinnace which carried him and about seventeen more Spanish and Irish ashore.

When we were thus got to sea after about three weeks sail finding ourselves short of provisions having but one barrell of beef and a small quantity of fish (but bread and water sufficient) we went to the Island of May being a Portugueze Island near the coast of Guinea where we took in salt and about Twenty Bullocks. Here we met with three English ships which we did no injury to but paid them for what we had of them, and seven of their men came voluntarily along with us.[7]

From thence we went upon the Coast of Guinea thinking to make a Voyage there. But meeting with no Prize we went away for Princes[8] being another Island belonging to the Portuguese near the Line, missing the Island we fell in with an Island called Felandopo[9] being about 150 Leagues distant from Princes, sending out boat along shore to discover the Inhabitants, and get some knowledge what the Island was, they being unacquainted with Trade ran away: but we finding a convenient place cleaned our ship, but in all this time we could not speak with one of the Inhabitants.

From thence we steer'd again for Princes where we arrived (being about six months after our first departure from Coruna) we took in here some rum and Sugar and fresh Provisions which we bought of the Inhabitants and paid them

---

[7] See **doc. 4**
[8] Principe
[9] Fernando Po, now Bioko

23

for. Here we met with two Danish men of war that had been redeeming a Danish Factory upon the Coast of Guinea, we sent to them that if they would give us what provisions we had occasion for and what money they had on board, their ships should go free, which they refusing telling us we were a thin schut and they did not fear us, we attack them both together, and after an hours dispute they yeilded, upon which we took from them about fifty tons of Brandy, and about 640 ounces of Gold dust. We lost one man and kill'd four of them and one of the Captains. We gave the Men their arms and provisions and a long boat and set them ashore at Princes, thirty Dutch and Swedes took party with us and one of the Chiefe Merchants. We had a report at this time that we had a War with Denmark, and they thought so too.

From thence we went back to Felandepo with the two Danes where not knowing what to do with them we burnt the biggest and sink the other at Cape Lopez. One of them had 26 Guns and 80 men and was much bigger than us, the other 24 Guns and 40 men. At the time our ship, wch was called the *Phancy*, had 44 Guns and but 80 men, and was about 300 tons.

From thence we went for Cape Lopez about 100 Leagues from Princes where we took in Wax and honey in exchange for small arms.

From thence we went for Annabar[10] a Portuguese Island about 150 or 200 Leagues distant from Cape Lopez (being about a month after our departure from Princes) there we took in more water and Oranges and about fifty hogs which we paid for part money, part small arms.

---

[10] Annobón

From thence we sail'd away for Madagascar in the East Indies, we arrived there in twelve weeks or thereabouts. There we bought about 100 bullocks for powder and small arms. After about a months stay we sail'd for Johanna[11] an English Island being about 300 Leagues where we arrived in about fourteen days. There we bought some hogs and paid for them; during our stay there three East India ships came in sight, upon which we made up to them under English Colours, and finding them to be English we made the best of our way to the Red Sea.

In about three weeks we made Babs key[12] which is at the mouth of the Red Sea; before we arrived there we met two saile, which came up with us and prov'd to be upon the same account. We ordered them on board us, Capt Ferrar (who landed in the ship at Dunfanaghy) commanding one called the Old Bark, and one Capt Want the other, the Vessel being his own, called the Spanish Bottom. They gave us two Barrells of Flower, and desired to go share and share with us, they were both but small Vessells of 80 and 90 tons and about sixty men each. (They told us two more upon the same account were at Madagascar coming for these seas, one a Brigantine Capt Meese Comandr, living in Rhode Island near New England, the other a Vessel of about 100 tons Capt Wake called the New Bark.) We sail'd all night together and being bad weather lost one another and our ship lost her foretopmast: when we came to Babs key as aforesaid we found Capt Ferrar there, we asking him for his consort he said she was a bad Sailor and he fear'd she could not get up.

---

[11] Anjouan, now Ndzwani
[12] Bab-el-Mandeb

Here we got a new top mast up and the Spanish bottom coming up told us she met with a French man a small Junk upon the same Account with about twenty two men. They were almost starv'd in the seas, and the Spanish Bottom took them on board, and at Babs key we took them on board having more room. About three days after came up the New Bark and the Brigantine (and a sloop one Capt Tue) which Ferrar had told us of. When being five of us together and sloop we agreed on and signed articles to share and share alike. During our stay here we sent out Pinnace to Mecca being about 25 Leagues distant to see what ships they could see there. At their return they told us there were about 40 Sail, which we knew by a prisoner as well as by their seeing them in harbour. We askt the prisoner what ships they were and what money they had, he told us six sail of them were Juda ship and very rich. We waited at Babs key 14 days before they came down yet they escaped us in the night. The next day we took a small junk which told us they were all gone. We made what hast we could after them. Our Vessel being the best sailor we took the Brigantine in Tow, Capt Ferrar being a good sailor kept us company. We sunk the Spanish bottom and took the men on board us and the Brigantine, the other two we left behind making after us. We sail'd thus 14 days and got before them then staid for them and met with a ship of 6 guns which we took without resistance. She had a pretty quantity of silver and gold on board. We took her within 10 Leagues of [Surat] where we have an English Factory. He told us the Juda ships were all gone another way, only the Admirall of Mecca a very rich ship was still behind. The next morning we saw a sail which we took to be the New Bark: standing up to her a prisoner we

26

had on board told us it was the Admirall of Mecca a ship of 70 Guns and 700 men. Our Vessel agreed to fight her with guns, and the Brigantine and Ferrar were to board her; but they seeing her so big a ship durst not come near her (this was in about August 1694). When we came within shott she fired two chase guns of 18 pounders at us. They grazed our Missen mast but did us no damage. We not intending to fire at them till we came board and board they fired the first broad side at us, and overshott us being so large a ship, upon which we gave them Eleven broad sides in all and boarded her, they then immediately surrendered, so we were Masters of her in about two hours. They fired very warmly upon us all the while and threw fireworks into us to set our sails etc on fire, but we lost never a man only one wounded in boarding. When we were on board, they being all run into the hold, we called them up and gave them good quarter. We askt the Captain what money he had on board he told us he had one basket of about £2000 that belonged to him, the rest belonged to Turkish merchants which we found in the hold in baskets, there might be in the whole about £150,000. The next day Wake came up leaving Tue in the sloop behind him. After two days we gave them the ship again taking the money out and we sail'd all four together to Roger Poole[13] about 30 Leagues from [Bombay] where we have an English Factory. There we watered and shared the money. We gave Capt Wake no share not being there and having taken a Vessel by the way and shared about £100 a man. Ferrar in the Old bark and four of his men we gave shares to being concerned in taking the first ship. The Brigantine Capt Meese shewing a great readinesse to assist us in the fight shared with us. Capt

---

[13] Rajapur

27

Want in the Brigantine after his own Vessel was sunk went on board Ferrar's Vessel, who the men turn'd out for a Coward, and they are gone for the Gulph of Persia to make a Voyage there. There were about 160 shares at £700 a piece of thereabouts, but it was not very equally devided. The Brigantine and we sail'd together towards Madagascar. In the way our men desiring to change their silver for the Gold the Brigantine's men had for the conveniency of Carriage, and finding the Brigantine's men clipped the Gold before they exchanged with us, we sent for the Captain, Meese, on board and commanded all their money on board, and took it from them, but we gave them £2000 among them and a small cable and anchor and they told us they would go for Madagascar and if they could get men go to sea again, if not they would load Negroes there and so come for Rhode Island to which Capt Meese belonged and we have heard no more of her.

Wake told us he would go to St Maries in Madagascar expecting to meet a ship there of force of 22 Guns, which he designed to buy and so go into the seas again. We heard no farther of him but that the ship he expected did go and that she was built somewhere in New England on purpose.

We thinking to go to Madagascar fell in with an Island called Dunmasquereen[14] belonging to the French, and is about 50 Leagues from Madagascar. Having two and twenty French men on board we sent some of them and some English to the factory to know if they would let us victual there, upon which the Governor of the Island came on board and entertain'd us very kindly. We bought 80 bullocks of him and salted them there, going ashore every day and being well treated by the

---

[14] The Mascarene Islands

Inhabitants. The Frenchmen on board us would have perswaded us to have gone to Martineco[15] and to have broke up there, which we would not consent to, so they would not go farther with us and perswaded 15 or 16 of our men to stay with them, designing to buy a small vessel that was building there and go into the seas again.

Having cleaned our ship we came away for the West Indies designing for New Providence where arriving within six Leagues we sent a letter to Coll[16] Trott the Governor, and three men, Hollingsworth, Chinton and Adams by name, Capt Every read the Letter to us which was to this effect, That we were soldiers of fortune and had done no Christian Nation any damage and were the King's subjects and to know whether he would entertain us, we sent a present of £500 with the letter. Adams came back in the Governor's own sloop with some Gentlemen of the Island and brought us from the Governor a Cask of Wine, a hogshead of Beer and a Cask of sugar and told us we should be very welcome, whereupon we weighted anchor for Providence; where coming we fired all our Guns and the Governor answered us Gun for Gun, so the Captain went ashore and some other Officers and delivered the Vessell to the Governor to take care of her for the Owners in England.

When all the men were gone ashore we sent some Negroes and others to look after her, who being careless suffered the ship to run ashore where she was staved, which we supposed was done on purpose, he[17] having first taken out the rigging and some of the Guns, and he took the rest up before we

---

[15] Martinique
[16] Colonel
[17] Trott

came away. Whereupon Capt Every who now goes by the Name of Capt Henry Bridgman bought a sloop which now came to Dunfanaghy Capt Ferrer commander. Hollingsworth bought another sloop in which we came to Westport.

In our sloop were

Hollingsworth Ma[ste]r who is now at Galway

Rob. Richee ma[ste]r of ye *Phancy*. Gone for Scotland

Rob. Ogilby ditto

Patrick Lawson ditto

Tho. Johnson ditto

James Stevenson ditto

Ed. Forsight was seizd and dismist, if gone for England lives near Newcastle upon Tyne

Trumble, he is only a passenger from Providence and did not belong to us

Tho. Castleton, lives in York and gone thither

Wm Bishop, gone to England, lives about Plymouth or Biddeford

Jacob Game, a Dutch man, here in town

Richd Chope married here, but gone for Engld being married in Wapping

Dennis Merick, gone for Bristoll

John King, if in Engld about Oxford, his wife lives near Windsor

Edward Sevill here in Town

John Miller here in Town

In the ship that came to Dunfanaghy were Ferrar the Cat[18], gone with the sloop for Bristoll

Capt Every goes by the name of Capt Henry Bridgman, his wife lives in Ratcliffe Highway [and] sells periwigs. A tall well sett man aged about 40 wears a light coloured Wigg most commonly, pretty swarthy, grey Eyes, a flattish nose. I believe he is gone for England saying always he would make the best of his way to England, his mother lives near Plimouth[19] where he had formerly some Estate.

Hen Adams Q[uarte]rma[s]t[e]r to the Phancy. I believe he is yet in Ireland brought a Woman over with him from New Providence. Goes Lame, his friends are in Deptford

Tho Johnson, Cook to the *Charles ye 2d*. I believe in Ireland, his wife lives in East Smithfield, London.

Joseph Dawson gone to Yarmouth in Suffolk

Samuel Dawson here upon baile

John Danne here, his friends in Essex

James Craggett, here lodged in Castle Street, his wife in Ratcliffe highway near Capt Every's

Nathaniel Pyke in town, his Wife lives at Chattham

John Strousier, in the Country. One in Castle Street can tell of him, born in Yarmouth

Rob. Silly somewhere with Strousier, his father is a Chimney Sweeper near St James's market

[18] Captain
[19] At Newton Ferrers

James Lewis, in town, a Weaver, his friends in London

Mr Gause in prison here, one of Ferrer's men

James Murray, his father lives about Ardmach, is married to one Rea's niece near Derry.

Sommerton I think is come over too, his friends at Chattham.

For the Rest left behind:

Prince the Boatswain and Chinton went for Carolina with others, some continued upon the place and married there.

Some gone for New England

Some for Jamaica

We killed about fourteen or fifteen of the Admirall of Mecca's men, but there were no women of any quality on board nor any ravished as is reported, therefore if any thing of that kind was done it was done by some of the ships that are still out.[20]

Dublin, August 8th 1696

This is a true account of the said ship's proceedings from her first going out to this time, to the best of my knowledge and remembrance, which I am ready to testify on Oath, and if any other circumstances shall hereafter be remembered by me, I shall be ready to declare the same. And I humbly pray your Ex[cellen]cie that I may not only have the benefit of his Ma[jes]ties most gracious Pardon of Life and Estate for my self and Edward Sevill (in case he shall deserve the same by

---

[20] Rumours of atrocities meted out to the Arab and Indian women found on board the *Gang-i-Sawai* abounded, some more fanciful than others. Philip Middleton, in one of his many depositions, claimed that several women were abused by the pirates, but did not go into details.

his ingenious confession), but also if the said Every be taken by means of my description or information, that I may be intituled to the £500 promised by the proclamation or such share thereof as shall be thought reasonable, I being perfectly drawn in to this affair and had not sooner any opportunity of getting clear of it, which I always intended to do as soon as I could, having serv'd his Ma[jes]ty from his first accession to the Crown in England and at Dundalk and the Boyne and other places in Capt South's Troop in the Duke of Schonberg's Regiment of horse, from which I was fairly discharged by reason of sickness as my said Captain can testifye.

3. John Sparks.

The Examination of John Sparks, 10 September, 1696. HCA 1/53, f. 18

The Examinate saith that he went out of England with Captain Charles Gibson of the ship the *Charles the Second* as his cabin boy abt three years ago and sailed with him as such to y Groyne[21] where the ship lay abt nine months and then several of the mariners of the said ship agreed together and carried away the said ship that the Examinate was then sick in his hammock and knew nothing of their design but when it was put in execution there were three persons… set over him as a guard but he should get away. That Benjamin Gunning belonging to a pirate then at Corunna , Robert Richey, Henry Adams , and Anthony Track belonging to y *James* and Henry Every mate of the sd ship the *Charles ye second* were the Ringleaders as he afterward heard when they came to sea. That after they got out to sea Capt Gibson and several others were put ashore in the pinnace but the Examinate being sick continued onboard and was told that the ship was going for England and the Examinate would be soon be at home. That the said ship was carried away from the Groyne on y 7: of May 1694 and had then onboard abt 44 guns and 84 men, that from Corunna the said ship (being now named the Fancy) sailed to y Isle of May where she met with three English ships and took from them a cable and an anchor some salt salt [*sic*] beef and linen for which they made y inhabitants pay them double, from there the said ship sailed along the Coast of Guinea and putting out English colours invited ye Natives

---

[21] Corunna

to come and trade with them and thereupon abt 14 or 15 negroes came abd and brought with them abt three pound wt of gold dust and when Capt Every and the comp had got them onboard they took y gold from the negroes and made them slaves nine of which they afterwards sold at Princess[22] Island when they voyaged there. And coming thither they there met with two Danish ships one of 36 ye other of 22 guns whom they fought and took and they put y men on shore at Princess except abt 24 who were willing to go with them to try their fortune, that they took one of the said Danish ships some elephants' teeth and seven or 800 cases of Brandy and what other things they thought fit and then burnt y biggest of the two and fitted out the least which they carried with them to Cape Lopez where the men onb[d] her disagreeing Capt Every and y rest of y men caused her to be sunk and then sailed abt the Cape and went to Madagascar and from thence to Johnanna Island where they put on shore a Moorish grab[23] which they plundered taking out of her Cotton cloth some pieces of eight and other things and then sailed to and landed at several places and at ye Isle of Comoro met with a French which they took and plundered laden with rice and took onb[d] two French men and so returning to Johanna met there and took another Moorish grab which they plundered and sunk and then went to ye Red Sea and met there five or six English pirates and sailed to Bob's Key where they waited in expectation to meet the Moorish fleet coming down from Mocha but the said fleet happened to pass by in ye night time undiscovered but abt two or three days after they took a Moorish grab which informed them the fleet was before

---

[22] Principe
[23] A type of local craft

35

passed by and thereupon they made what sail they could after them and on ye 3: of September 1695 abt 20 leagues from ye high land of St. John's and off Surat they came up with a Moorish ship which after abt an hour's fight they took and out of her great quantities of gold and silver to ye value of least 20 thousand pound and on ye 5: of the same month came up with another Moorish ship called the *Gunsway*[24] of abt one thousand tons with whom they fought abt three hours and a half and they took her and after having plundered her and taken out great quantities of gold and silver they sent ye two Moorish ships into Surat and so ended their voyage. That he believes there was taken away and plundered out of the last Moorish ship to ye value of abt one hundred and thirty thousand pounds, that this Examinate was kept onb^{d} by ye comp but as a kind of slave to wash their clothes, sweep the decks and light their pipes and had but upwards of one hundred pounds for his share when others of ye Company had above nine hundred pounds a man.

4. David Evans.

The Examination of David Evans, 27 January 1696(7). HCA 1/53, ff. 27-28

Evans was tried in London in July 1697 but managed to secure an acquittal, after which he travelled to New York where he was arrested a second time but, having been tried once already was released.

---

[24] Anglicized version of *Gang-i-Sawai*.

This Examinate saith that being a mariner onbd an English ship belonging to Plymouth called the *James and Thomas* whereof Paul Bickford was mstr and being with the said ship at the Isle of May in company with two other English ships y one called the *Rebecca* of Plymouth y other a pink belonging to Lond[on]. A ship whereof one Capt Every was comr then called the *Fancy* and he hath heard before called the *Charles the Second* did abt the month of July 1694 come into the Road of the Isle of May and they of the *James and Thomas* being a ship of sixteen guns supposing her to be a French ship prepared and resolved to have fought her she having out at her coming in her upper tier of guns only. And saith that after the said ship the *Fancy* was come into y Road and at an anchor she commanded the other ships boats to go onbd her and they of the *James and Thomas* refused to man out their boat and go onbd and thereupon the *Fancy* run out her lower tier of guns and some in her said that if they of the *James and Thomas* did not man out their boat and come onbd they would fire at her whereupon finding she was stronger than they at first expected manned out their boat and went onbd the *Fancy* who took away all the men of the *James and Thomas* onbd the said ship the *Fancy* and afterwards put again so many of y men as they thought fit onbd the said ship the *James and Thomas* but kept this Examinate and five others of the said ship's company onbd the *Fancy* and put a guard over them till the said ship the *Fancy* sailed from the Isle of May and then by force and constraint carried away this Examinate along with them. That from the Isle of May they sailed along the Coast of Guinea and there they took some Negroes who came onbd to trade with them and made

37

them slaves and took also some gold dust, from thence they went to Principe where they took and plundered five Danish ships, from Principe they sailed to Fernando and so afterwards to Madagascar and round the Cape and then to Johanna where they took a Moorish grab laden with rice and upon y same coast they run ashore another Moorish grab and plundered her, and then some time after went to Bob's Island[25] at the entrance into the Red Sea where they lay for some time in expectation of the Mocha fleet which passed by them in y night undiscovered but some time after taking a grab belonging to that fleet were informed they were passed by and thereupon the sailed after the said fleet and off of the highlands of St. Johns they came up with and took a Moorish Merchant ship burthen abt 300 or 400 tons after a short fight which they plundered and took out of her both gold and silver to a considerable value and the next day after they came up with and fought and took a Moorish Man of War of abt 70 guns mounted called the *Gunsway* belonging as was said to the Great Moghul and manned with abt one thousand men and after they had taken her they took and plundered out of her very great quantities of gold and silver in pieces of eight and Chaquins and then let them go and so made the best of their way for Rajipoore but before they come thither the said Every and his company divided the spoil and plunder they had so taken as aforesaid and they gave to this Examinate to y value of abt 400: which he durst not but take for fear they should have put him on shore upon the Indian coast for they having forced this Examinate and the other five they were jealous of them so that the Examinate could never get any opportunity of making his escape till they came to

---

[25] Liparan, now Perim

Providence and from there the Examinate shipped himself for Pennsylvania where he discovered the whole matter to the Govr who told this Examinate that the mstr of the Plymouth ship y *James and Thomas* had been at Maryland and made known y matter to ye Councll there and that he the Govnr had this Examinate's name before from the Govnr of Maryland and so at Pennsylvania the Examinate shipped himself for England onbd the *Pennsylvania Merch*[ant]: and English man of war called the *Tiger* Capt Tuckey Comr who at King Road at Bristol seized upon the Examinate and from him took ten ozs and ten achyes (sixteen to an oz) of dust gold and also took from him several Chaquins and bills upon some English merchants to y value of abt 200:

5. Thomas Joy.

The Information of Thomas Joy, 16 August, 1699. HCA 1/53, ff. 55-56

This informant saith that on abt the year 1694 he was signed in London by Capt Gibson Commander of the ship *Charles* to sail in the said ship as Cooper upon a voyage from this port of London to some port or place in the Spanish West Indies. That in prosecution of the said voyage this informant sailed in the said ship in company with the *James*, the *Dove Galley* and a pink which were bound with them upon the said voyage to the Groyne, where they said ship the *Charles* lay for abt 9 months and the informant being ashore at y Groyne working for the English Consul he was sent for aboard the

said ship *Charles* by Henry Every Chief mate of the said ship
to trim some Casks whereupon he came aboard the said ship
and having trimmed several Casks he was going ashore again
but was stopped by the said Every to trim another Cask,
which the informant did, but it being almost dark he designed
to lie aboard the said ship all that night, that abt 9 o'clock that
night the informant being between decks at supper heard a
great noise above upon the deck and going up the scuttle to
see what was the matter he found upon the deck one John
Guy, the carpenter of the said ship with a broad axe in his
hand cutting the cable and this informant going to put his foot
upon the Windlass the said John Guy said he would cut his
leg off if he came there, and this informant then went to the
Gangway and asked the men where they were going wth the
ship and they made answer to him that they were going home
wht her to the Owners and the said ship being under sail and
he seeing Capt Gibson go into the boat and fearing that the
seamen had some ill design, he he made to go into the boat
wth the Captn, but there being two men placed one in the
stem and y other in the stern of the boat to see who came in,
and seeing the informant coming in they asked of Every the
Chief mate whether the cooper, meaning him the informant,
should go wth the Capt and the said Every replying 'no' and
bidding them turn him into the ship again he was accordingly
turned into the ship and forced to go in her and the informant
saith that he well knoweth one James Cragget who was a
foremast man aboard the said ship *Charles*, and that he joined
wth y said Every and the other men in running away wth the
said ship from y Groyne, and he hath lately seen the said
James Cragget at Norwich, and he further saith that the said
ship Charles afterwards sailing upon the Coast of Guinea

40

they found two Danish ships at the Island of Principe, whom the said ship *Charles* fought and took and sailing afterwards to Bob's Island near the Gulf of Mocha, they tarried there abt six weeks in order to intercept and take the Mocha fleet, and being informed that they were gone by in the night they sailed after them that next morning, and off the high land of St. Johns near Surat the said ship *Charles* came up wth a great ship whose name he knoweth not and took her and they afterwards divided the plunder of the wch came to abt 7 or 800l[26] a man and he saith that the said James Cragget assisted in the taking of y sd ship and had for his share of the plunder of her 7 or 800 sterling. And at a day before the said ship *Charles* also token[27] a small Moorish pink of little value and the informant further saith that they afterwards sailed the said ship *Charles* to Providence and there left her, and that he was carried in the said ship by force all the sd time, and did endeavour to leave her at the Isle of May before they took any ship but was prevented.

6. Richard Sievers.

Deposition of Richard Sievers, 19 December, 1699. HCA 1/98, ff. 11

Richard, or Dirk, Shivers seems to have arrived in the Indian Ocean as a mate on one of Every's consort vessels, the Portsmouth Adventure. *He was later to be found as Captain of the pirate ship*

---

[26] L: pound sterling
[27] too

Resolution. In 1698, in company with Robert Collover, Chivers captured the Great Mohammed, one of the richest prizes taken in the Indian Ocean [**docs 8, 9**]. *He returned to St. Mary's where he eventually accepted a pardon and returned to Europe.*

Richard Chivers Declares yt he belongeth to Hamburgh seaman by trade hath beene from Hamburgh Eighteen years Constantly In ye English service both of Kings and merchants. In December 1695 hee Come from Roade Island on ye Coast of New Englande; In a Vessell Call'd ye *Portsmouths Adventure* alias ye Old Barke Burthen Ninety tonns Intending to Cruise on ye Moors had six guns Joseph Firra[28] Commander; In Aprill 1696 they Come about ye Cape good hope; at Mayotta they Left the sd Vessell being disabled and Embarqu't on ye *Resolution* Robt. Glover Commandr belonging to New Englande Burthen neere two hundred tons Eighteen guns and one hundred and ten men they went to ye Red Sea but no Vessells Coming yt year could make no prize, ye same year they come out of ye Red Sea and tooke two Moors shipps one wth some Rice ye other Empty; thence went to Madogascar to new fit; and off Mascorine Lost all theire Masts after wth Jury Masts got St. Maries where their men died constly but they refitted ye shippe and 7br 1698 they tooke a Moors shippe off Judah; off St. Johns.

---

[28] Joseph Farrell

7. James Kelly on two decades at sea.

A full and true Discovery of all the Robberies, Pyracies, and other Notorious Actions of that Famous English Pyrate, Capt. James Kelly... Written with his own Hand, During his Confinement in Newgate; and Delivered to his Wife, the Day of his Execution; Published by her Order and Desire (London, 1700)

James Kelly's career is best told by himself, the only worthwhile addition being that he was positively identified in 1699 by a surgeon and a Jew who examined him to see whether he was circumcised, which was extremely unusual in the seventeenth century and was proof that he had, during captivity in India, converted to the Muslim faith.

In or about the Year 1680 I Shipt my self with Capt. Tho. Arnoll, my first going out of England in the Ship Viner about 330 Tuns, bound for Ginua[29]. That Voyage I proceeded till I came to Germany, where lay the *Norwich* Man of War, who seiz'd upon our Ship, and made a Prize of her. Then I Shipt my self on Board of the *Dolphin*, Capt. Yankee Commander upon the Privateer account; the Ship was then lying in Bull-Bay, between Port Royal and Galliss[30], so the Ship having occasion of Sailes, Riging and many other necessaries, we sent a Ship into Jemaco[31] loaded with Sugar, for to purchase the necessaries, that we had occasion of the Sugar taking from the Spaniards; But the Man that was put in trust with the Ship was seiz'd on and Man'd, and fitted out for to take our

---

[29] Probably Guinea
[30] Yallahs
[31] Jamaica

43

Ship, or our Consort; that was the Ship *Buneto*: Capt. Jacob, he came out on the Sunday Morning, which was a thing not usual, and when he came near the Ship, he show'd us the Sign, which he was ordered to do if all was well; the Sea Breese then setting in, he could not fetch the Ship, so he fetcht a Trip off, and our consort then riding to Windward, the other Ship tackt, and when he came within small Arm, that of our consort, he hoisted the Kings Jack[32] upon his Insignet Staff and call'd his Men upon Deck, which were about 70 Red Coats; then laid our Consort on board, their Men for the most part being Drunk. So our Consort was taken, and when the Men see they were betrayed, they tumbled into the Canoe till their was so many that overset her and put them all to swiming, the Soldiers Fired at them and killed them most in the water, but them which were on board; they seiz'd on the Ship and abused them inhumanly, in somuch that if a Man had a Ring on his Finger, they would bite the whole Finger off: from thence we took our departure; not being willing to Fight against English Colours, and arrived at high Spainyolo[33]. Then we met with a Privateer Capt. John Williams Commander, whom we Joyn'd with, so we Sail'd toward the Coast of Cathergeen[34], and in our way our Consort spying a Leak so he was forc'd to bear away to the Desambilloes[35], and a Day or two following our Ruther[36] unhung, but mannaging her with her head Sails, we fetch the Island Forto[37], and when at Anchor we hung the Ruther

---

[32] The Union Jack, at that time reserved for Royal Navy vessels
[33] Hispaniola
[34] Cartagena
[35] Sambalas Islands
[36] Rudder
[37] Isla Fuerte

again, from thence we Sail'd to the Frinds Islands, which lyes off of Point Pickeroon, there we set a Man to look out upon a high Tree, he spyed a Spanish Pereoago[38], so the Canoa went out for to take her, but could not come up with her, so came on board again, and a fresh going went in, and one Man being acquainted with the Creek where the Pereoago went in, and lay all Night, and took her the next Morning, she had on board Magazeen Goods and Brandy, from thence we Sailed to the River of Grandee[39], and from thence we Sailed to Senego and took it from the Spaniards, from thence we went to a great Indian Town near St. Mark[40] and took it, and one of our consorts meeting with the Beef Stantion, left 20 Men to secure the Castle; and while we were in the Town we were disguis'd at Sankto Mark; and raising all they could they Assaulted us and fell upon the Men that kept the Beef Stantion, and Slew all but 3 or 4, and they all were wounded save the Docter, so we hearing Guns Fired, we assailed out of the Town and came to the Beef Stantion, and found all the Men Dead save them 3, or 4 above mention'd, so return'd again to the Town; we made all ready to return to our Ship, and coming down the Spaniards lay in Ambush, but the Prisoners we then had, we kept in the middle of our Company, so marching down we took an Indian, who inform'd us that an Ambush was laid for us in such a Place; so when we came near the Ambush we Fired a Valley, and they answer'd, so when they were discharg'd, we Sallyed in upon them and broke their Ambush, but having several Men Wounded but none kill'd, we then marcht down into the Ship

---

[38] Periagua, a canoe
[39] Rio Grande
[40] San Marcos

45

with no more Damage. From thence we took our departure intending for Sand Bay, where we arrived and ride for some days, then spyed a Ship, she proved to be a Spaniard coming from Sancktoago on Cuby[41], loaden with Sugar, Sweet Meats and Tobacco bound from Cathergeen, but coming up with her Fired at us, and we at her again, we had 120 Guns and 8 Patareerers[42], she had 80 Men or more each double Armed, we between 40 and 50, but having a long dispute with her till each of our Men Fired two Cattuch Boxes[43] away, doing much damage on each side, but at length took her and went to Royal a Hatch[44], there we put the Capt. and all that was living on Shore, so took our departure for High Saniously[45] at the Isle of Ash[46]. We met a Dutch Ship and put the Kings Tents on Board of her, desiring a Commission, which they granted, the French there living, then went towards the Coast of Cathergeon where we soon arrived, and there met a Dutch Man lying off Point Canoa, we Fired a Shot thwart his fore Foot, but he did not mind it, then we came on his Broad-side, and he Fired a Broad-side upon us, and Shot out a Head of us, but we kept him Company all that Night, and in the Morning about 10 of the Clock we took him; then Sailing to our Commission Port with the loss of a great many men, there we put on Shore the Kings Tents our men then being English, French and Dutch gave the French our share of the Man of War; for their share of the Prize, some Men going a Shore to get Water and get Ballence[47], were seiz'd on by the

---

[41] Santiago, Cuba
[42] Pattereroes, small swivel guns
[43] Cartridge boxes
[44] Rio Hacha
[45] Hispaniola
[46] Ile a Vache

French, who likewise Man'd the Man of War and a Bark of Longer[48], and came off and took our Ship from us and turn'd us ashore, [illegible] or provisions we knew not, But we were forced to Grabble pattatoes out of the Ground with our Fingers; then Capt. Trustan came to me being formerly acquainted, he was Capt. of the Barko Longo, he asked me if I would go on Board with him, if he did give me any Arms and what I had on Board, only my part in the Ship he would not, to which I consented, then he desired me to get him some able Seamen, which I did, so came on Board, then Capt. Yankee Ordered Capt. Trustan in the bark of Longer, and Jacobs in the Prize to go to Potty Guavos[49], and going about we met with a North Wind, and the Prize was put to Leward as we thought and we got into Caimcetus[50], when the weather broke up, we went to Neepe[51] there our Capt. went on Shore, and said he would send me a Bumboat with Brandy, Lime-Juice and Sugar, accordingly she came and we bought Brandy and Sugar, then the Frenchmen made a Bowl of Punch by the Main Hatch, and we by the Binacle, but before we concluded to take the Vessel, only waited for an oppertunity, now we thought no better time could present, so I and Randal Hicks was pitch't upon, to secure their Arms in the hold it fell to my turn to go first down, then I Provided Arms for him and my self, then out did People rise against them on the Deck, having no Arms only Hand Spikes and Billets and such like, the Frenchmen seeing our Men Fierce Jumpt down the Hold thinking to get their Arms, but we

---

[47] Possibly ballast
[48] Barco Longa, a long boat.
[49] Petit Goave
[50] The Cayemites
[51] Nippe

47

prevented them and handed the Arms upon the Deck, and carried them aft, then cut the Cable in the Horse[52] and sent Hands up to lose the Sails, having but little Wind and could not get off Shore, we call'd the Frenchmen upon Deck, and made them Ship all our Ores and Bank her off, then having a fine Breese of Wind, we put the Frenchmen on shore to Windward of Rantan[53], then made the best of our way to the Isle of Ash, but meeting an English Ship belonging to Jemaco sent the Cornoa[54] on Board Sam. Cemthan Commanded her, John Cook then being Commander of our Ship; I being well acquainted with Capt Cemthan went on Board of him with his Canoa, and I acquainted him how our business was, and how our English Men were turn'd on shore and likewise desired him to go in with his Kings Jack Ancient[55] and Penant, and to demand the Men on Board, I going my self in with him, so Captain Cemthan went on Shore and demanded the English Men that was left heir by Capt. Yankee, his request being granted 2 or 3 came on Board with Capt. Cemthan, and then I showed my self to them and Certified them how all things was so, so one of them went on Shore and acquainted the rest how all things were, and they all came on Board: From thence we went up to Meriso[56] and there met a French Ship about 200 tunn loaden with Wine; then went to Statia[57] and took a Dutch-man in the Road lying unrig'd, loaded with Sugar and much Brandy; from thence to the Rimagodose[58], there lay a new English Pink who was

---

[52] Hawse, the hole through which an anchor cable passes through the ship's side
[53] Possibly Pointe a Raquette
[54] Canoe
[55] Ensign
[56] ?
[57] St. Eustatius

48

beat over a Reefe into a Pond by bad Weather, Bound for Jemaco, so Man'd the Long-Boat to search out a Channel, we found a narrow Channel about the breadth of the Pink; the Men then belonging to the Pink were delighted to go on Shore, but we coming on Board, Clapt a Spring upon her Cable and Cast her, then lose the Sails and Cut the Spring, but going through the Channel, we stuck at length, with great trouble we got through, then we sunk our back of longer off Turteloy[59], then sailed for Virginia in the Pink: my Lord Culpepper then being Governor we sent our Master to him for admittance in, then said my Ld. if you can show any thing from any Port for what done, I will grant your request, we then show'd him our French Commission, and then sent him a present and remained there some time, then took our departure in one of our Prizes for Cape Deverde Islands[60], but meeting the *Portsmouth* Pink, who was taken by the Dutch in the last Holland Wars, where we plundered her, soon after arrived to Cape Dorvord, from thence to Suraclone[61] Guinea, there took 2 Dutch ships, of one we made a Man of War, mounting 36 Guns in her, our own ship we burnt, the other we gave the Dutch Men. From thence toward the South Sea, where we soon arrived; the first Ship met with us was Capt. John Eaton in the Ship *Nicholas* with 20 odd Guns, but he had French Colours and we English up changed several shot, she not being our English Colours, we being downing upon her she made our Colours, she made Friends and Joyn'd Consorts, then we Sailed to Wanfanandus[62], from thence to

---

[58] Virgin Gorda, Virgin Islands?
[59] Tortola
[60] Cape Verde Islands
[61] Sierra Leone
[62] Juan Fernandez, now Robinson Crusoe Island

49

the Coposses[63], here see a Sail and took her, and Chandler held our Ship by her, lying here some time. Came 3 Spanish Ships, then we took 2 being deep loaden the other light, but all with Provisions and Sugar, then Sailed to Gulipillos[64] there laid up Provision for store. From thence to Port Dela Vallice[65] then Waterred from thence to Amipolo[66]. There made a hulk of the Prize and lay Guard Ship while Capt. Eaton Careen'd;. Then he for us, from thence to the Southward, but not agreeing parted, then sailed to Plato[67], Eaton meeting us there would have joyn'd us again, we would not; then we went to the Southward, but finding no Purchase went to Pene, now riding there came a great many French Men, some English with them, the French we gave a Prize that we took, but the English we took on Board our Ship, the mean while the Spaniards fitted out a Fire Ship from Poneman[68] but coming off about the Dead time of the Night, we made our Potterague[69] and met her, demanding her to come to Anchor, they would not, but coming nigh to their Ship went into their Cannon and set the Ship on Fire, but she fell in between our Ship and the Fireship and did no damage. Then came over 500 English Men, and some time afterwards came the Spanish Almado[70] to take us, we fought the Almado from Sun rise to Sun Set, they being 9 Sail, we 2. Then meeting about 4 Sail, whom the English Men met and took, we joyn'd and Sail'd to Rialaba[71], and landed and took the

---

[63] Lobos?
[64] Galapagos Islands
[65] ?
[66] Amapala
[67] Isla Plata
[68] Panama
[69] Periagua
[70] Armada, fleet

City Legam[72] lying some time in the City, but getting little or no Purchase we return'd again, for we were depriv'd, for they had carryed the Money and Goods into the Country.

From thence I went to Barbados, from thence to Jemaco. In a small time after King William was Proclaimed, and were with the French; so I shipt myself in a Privateer, Captin Thomas Harison Commander: But he and his people not Agreeing, they would not go were he would have them, they having some shares in the Ship, would go were they Pleased Themselves; the Captin not willing to go with them; left this ship, went on board the Dimond Slupe. We went toward the Mederas[73], I James Kelly being then Commander, where we arrived, then took Poosa[74] but did no harm, only taking Provision; from thence to the Canarys, where came the Vice Consul, who we detained as a Prisoner, till such time as he had confest the strength of the Town and how we should take it, and what quantity of Men there was, which he agreed, but we could do no good, so from thence to the Cape Deverds, and took a Portagees out of Sancto Oago[75], lying in the Road bound for Brasel. Loading with Reime; then Sail'd to Fogo, and put the Prisoners Ashore from thence to the Island Boare[76] , made a Hulk of the Prize, and Creen'd the Ship. And then Sail'd for the East Indias, arived at Madages[77].

And From thence we Sail'd toward Chaney[78], expecting to Touch at the Chean Sumar[79], but the night before we made

---

[71] El Realejo
[72] Léon
[73] Madeiras
[74] Porto Santo?
[75] Sao Tiago
[76] Brava
[77] Madagascar

Achean[80], we lay by; then the Men Rose, and took the Ship in there owne Possesion and kill'd the Captain. The Conspiracy was first made by his own Men, he using them so Cruely formerly; then being told the new comers which being 9 consented, but I understanding they had a mind to kill the Captin would not consent, when the Ship was going to be taken, by perswasion I took the Gunroom, not thinking they would kill the Captin, I being a Commander formally, some would have had me Captain; but by reason I would not consent to kill Captain Eachcom, others would not. The next Morning made Sail toward the Chean, when Night, we ask'd who would go Ashore them that would, only 2 or 3 detained on force, when the Boat went on Shore them that was on board, took up Armes; then Sail'd for Merga[81] in the King of Syams Country, came to an Anchor at an Island, the Commander going on Shore with some Men; but when on Shore, happened to meet with some of the Men we left at Achean, our Captain then went to the Governer, who being very Inquisitive to know from whence we came, the Captain Resolved him, and askt him whether we might have the liberty to Clean our Ship there, the Governer said, he could not, but desired to go to the Vice Roy, where he went, who granted him necessary leave to clean our Ship; then Departed Sailing toward Lincombar[82] Island, there we Wooded and Wattred, and got such necessarys as the island afforded. From thence we Sail'd to the Coast of Pumatra[83], there we

---

[78] China?
[79] Chain Sumar? The Sumatran archipelago?
[80] Aceh
[81] Mergui
[82] Nicobar
[83] Sumatra

took a Portugalls Ship Bound to Chancnoako[84] with the Vice King on Board, then met with Captin Hide bound to China, company Trading Ship came from Bumbay, so Sailing up to him, he asked what we wanted we said what he had; but neither Ship nor he, then he said you must Fight for it, so we did, doing much Damage on both sides, parted; after took several Chanseeses[85], one great Ship, we Carried to the Negrese in the King of Peguse Country, there Detained two English Ships belonging to Madeross[86] till our Ship was Careened; mean time come on the King of Syames Ships, then fitted the Bregaten[87], and took her, and put the Men on Shore, from thence to Cape Cormerans[88], and there met two Portugese Ships from Chaney, took one, the other fled; then took Captain Wilicks belonging to Bangal and Sunk her for fear of being discovered, detain the Men on board till our Cruse was out, then took a Moars Pink, the Captin went on Shore, at the Kings Island, Desiring to Trade with them, they would not, then took several of the Island, and then to the Coast of Sumatra, for to look for a watering Place, but met a Mallayan Privateer, we clapt them on board with the long boat, but they kill'd all our Men, but three, and two of them were Wounded, so left her making the best of our way to Madegascar then we left the Ship, and Dwelt on Shore, till Captain Kidd came when his Men left him we went on board the *Moekoa*[89]; so I went Home along with him and then was put in Prision, where I remaind till I was call'd to my Tryal at

---

[84] ?
[85] Chinese
[86] Madras
[87] Brigantine
[88] Cape Comorin
[89] Mocha

the old Baily, before the Court of Admiralty the 21th of June last; where I was found guilty of Pyracy, tho I deny'd it, by Endeavouring to insinuate, that I was then at the Isle of Rhode in new England, but justice taking place, I received Sentance of Death. I made all the Intrest possible for a Repreeve to both the Sheriffs, and other Magistrate, but finding all hopes of a Pardon inefectual; I applyd my self to Devotion in order for my Souls Welfare. I do Confess I was on board when Captain Edgcomb was kill'd, and did consent to the Seizing the Ship, but not to his Death, tho I knew he was kill'd while I was below Deck; I had something more to say; but tomorrow being the Day of my Execution; my thoughts are took up on things of a higher moment; I desire that this Paper may be Printed and Published, to prevent all false and Sham Accounts that may (perhaps) be set forth in my Name, to Impose on the Publick.

And I hope this my sad Fate, will be a warning to Lude Sea Men, and notorious Pyrates, whatsoever.

I am the unfortunate,

James Kelly

July the 11th 1700.

8. Theophilus Turner.

The Information of Theophilus Turner, 31 January, 1700. HCA 1/53, ff. 76-77

Theophilus Turner was a carpenter and member of Richard Shivers' company at the taing of the Great Mohammed. *He left*

Madagascar for America but was arrested in the Chesapeake Bay.
Transported to England for trial, he gave the deposition
reproduced here, and was fortunate enough to secure a pardon
and returned to his trade as a joiner ashore.

This informant saith that he knows and is well acquainted
with one John Edlridge, a well made squatt man fairish of
complexion and as he supposeth abt 40 yeares of age, that he
became acquainted with the said Eldridge in the East Indies
neare two years and a halfe ago and saith that when he the
Depon[en]t became acquainted with him he the said John
Eldridge belonged to and was the Captain's Quarter M[aste]r
of a pirate ship called the *Soldadoe* whereof one Richard
Sivers was Comander and the informant then belonged to
another pirate ship called the *Moco Frigot* whereof one
Robert Culliver was Com[mande]r which said two pirate
ships consorted together and this Informant further saith that
abt the month of September 1698 the said two pirate ships
comanded by the said Capt Sivers and Capt Culliver did off
the highland of St Johns upon ye Coast of Suratt in ye East
Indies meet with a large Turkish ship called the *Mahomet* or
the *Great Mahomet* which the said two pirate ships sett upon
and after a fight wherein the Turkes had severall men killed
and wounded the said Capt Sivers boarded the said Turkish
ship and tooke her in the company and by ye assistance of
the other pirate ship called the *Moco Frigot* and saith that the
said Turkish ship was very richly laden and computed to be
worth abt one hundred and thirty thousand pounds sterling,
having on board greate quantityes of Chaquins and Arabian
gold pieces of Eight and dollars but the exact quantity this
Informant doth not remember, all which said gold and silver

was taken and seized by the Captains and Companyes of the two pirate ships aforesaid and saith that all the Turkes and Moores which were onb[oar]d the said Turkish ship when taken were sett ashore at several places in ye East Indies and the sd Capt Richd Sivers and some of his comp went onbd the sd Turkish ship and ye rest of the sd Sivers's Company went onbd the Moco Frigot and sunck their owne ship that the treasure of the sd Turkish ship was divided at times between the Captains and Companyes of the two pirate ships aforesaid that each seman say his share came to abt eight hundred pounds a man and so much the sd John Eldridge had and rece[ive]d for his share and Capt Robt Culliver and Capt Rich. Sivers had double shares to whit abt sixteen hundred pounds apiece. And this Informant further saith that he severall times saw and conversed with ye sd John Eldridge after the seizure of the sd Turkish ship who showed no manner of dislike to the action and this Inform[an]t came in the said Turkish ship with the said John Eldridge from the Coast of Suratt to Madagascar where they left the sd Turkish ship and after having been at Madagascar some few days the said John Eldridge, this Depon[en]t and severall others got a passage in a merchant ship called the *Nassau* Giles Shirley Com[mande]r belonging to New Yorke then trading at Madagascar and went in her from thence to Cape May off of Delawar Bay where the Dep[onen]t left the said ship.

9. John Brent.

The Examination of John Brent, 21 May 1701, HCA 1/53, ff. 33-34

This Examinate saith that in ye year 1695 the Examinate sailed from Plymouth to Corke and there took in provisions and so sailed for Barbados but in sight of that Island they were met with and taken by a French privateer and carried to Martinico. That from thence ye Examinate went to Barbados in a transport sloope that at Barbados the Examinate entered himself Gunner onbd a sloope called the *Loyall Russell* whereof one Arthur French was Comr which sloop when ye Examinate entered himself onbd was said to be bound to Newfoundland and the Maderas but before they sailed out the voyage was altered by the order of Governor Russell, Captain Bull and her other Owners and so was fitted out for Madagascar and accordingly abt the 19th of July 1696 they sailed from Barbados and in their passage touched at Cape Bona Esperanza[90] where they watered and so sailed to Madagascar for Negroes where they arrived abt the 4th of March fall and there met with Capt Kid in ye *Adventure Galley* and from thence they sailed with Capt Kid to Johanna and afterwards to Mahila where Kid put some of his guns onbd their sloop ye *Loyall Russell* and then ye sd Kidd Carreened his ship and afterwards tooke his guns out of ye sd sloope onbd his owne ship and so they sailed away together to Johanna and that ye sd Kid left their sd sloope but got away Hugh Parrot their boatswain by his owne consent, that one Hatton a p[ar]t owner dyed and severall of the men were sick and indisposed at Johanna. That from Johanna they sailed with their said sloope again to Mada[ga]scar to trade but by misfortune lost their vessel upon the Rocks abt 8 or 10

---

[90] Cape of Good Hope

57

Leagues from Madagascar but all ye Company got onshore in the boate that they lived at Madagascar abt nine months and then travelled away to Fort Augustin where they got onboard a ship called the *Soldados* whereof one Shivers was Comr and so sailed away to St Maries where where they got onbd a ship called the *Nassau* whereof Capt Shelley was Comr. That in their going to Ft Augustin they travelled abt two months along ye sea shore in a very miserable condition without either money provisions or necessaries and if they had not happened to have met with Capt Shivers he the Examinate must have been starved. That at St. Maries he entered himself with Shelley to go to ye West Indies and was to give Shelley abt twenty pieces of eight for his passage. That when he came onbd of Capt Shivers he was forced to go with him to the Coast of India and off of Bombay in between Bombay and Surat the sd Shivers met Capt Culliver Comr of a ship called the *Mocha Frigat* and the sd Shivers and Culliver sailing together they met with and took upon ye Coast of Suratt a greate Moorish ship wch he thinks was called ye *Mahomet* that there was onbd the sd Moorish ship some horses, a pretty handsome quantity of money, some Coffee, Cochineale and other goods which was shared amongst the Company's of the said Capt Shivers and Capt Culliver, that ye Examinate had some share given to him to ye value as he believes of 100l but did not desire to have had any of it nor would not have gone upon that designe if he could have subsisted onshore and w[ha]t he did was perfectly to preserve himself from perishing and having taken ye sd ship they made the best of their way to Madagascar and so ye Examinate went then onbd of Shelley as aforesd. That ye Examinate went with Shelley to ye West Indies and was set onshore at Kian[91], a place belonging to ye French and from thence the Examinate went to Barbados and so to England and hath been here abt two years since wch time he hath made a voyage to Guinea in ye Companies[92] service as Mr[93] of a ship to their satisfaction. That when they met with Kidd at Madagascar Kid would very fain have had the Examinate gone along with him and offered to French, Mr of ye sd sloope, three men for this Examinate but the Examinate would not go along with him, that if he the Examinate had had a mind to have gone upon a pirating account he might have gone with Kidd and been Welcome.

10. Thomas Bagley,

The Examination of Thomas Bagley, 27 August, 1701. HCA 1/53, ff. 96-97

Thomas Bagley, Michael Hicks, Richard Roper and John Barrett [**docs 10-13**] *were four of the pirates who shipped aboard Samuel Burgess's* Margaret *for the return voyage from Madagascar to New York* [**doc. 1**]. *One remarkale feature of these depositions is that many of the passengers were arrested in possession of large sums of money but none of them appear to have obtained it by piracy. Three of those whose testimonies are reproduced here won all their money gambling (though nobody on board the* Margaret *admitted to losing money gambling) and the very enterprising*

---

[91] Cayenne
[92] Presumably the Royal African Company
[93] Master

Richard Roper managed to accumulate the equivalent of around 35 years' worth of wages for a seaman in a comparatively short time by doing sewing repairs and nursing favours for his shipmates. Money acquired through piracy could, of course, be confiscated, but money that was come by legitimately could not, and this may or may not have had a bearing on the pirates' keenness to explain the source of their income. The fact that they all told the same unlikely story suggests that it was something they had discussed together beforehand.

This Examinate saith that abt 4 years since he went from Rhode Island in a Ship called the *Pellican* (Capt Robt. Cully Commandr) of the burthen of upwards of one hundred Tonns mounted wth ten Gunns bound to take Kayan a French Island in the West Indyes there being then Warr between England and France, and he saith that ye said Ship sailed from Rhode Island to one of the Cape de Verde Island, and there the Major part of the Ships Company being for going to Madagascar, the said Ship went thither accordingly and there they watered and cleaned the ship, and from thence went to the Mouth of the Red Sea to cruise and there tooke a Moorish ship wth Rice in her, and having taken out of her some of the Rice they left her, and afterwards they sailed to the Coast near Cape Commoroome[94], and there in or abt the month of Dec: 1698 they found a Moorish Vessel abt 200 Tonns towing a shoare with boates, whereupon some of ye said ship the *Pellicanns* Company went off in their Boate and brought her off, the said ship having some Opium and Cotton aboard, and because their owne ship was leaky they burnt her and

---

[94] Cape Cormorin

went all aboard the sd Moorish ship, and they sold the goods abd her to the Natives of the Coast of Commoroome, and this Examinate had abt Fifty peeces of Eight for his share, and soone after the said ship sailed to Madagascar, where he left her and entred himself a Passenger aboard the *Margaret* (Samuell Burgis Mr) then lying at St. Maryes and bound for New Yorke, and the said Samuell Burgis being first bound to the Northward of the Island of Madagascar to trade for slaves he put this Examinate and sevll other Passengers ashoare at St. Augustine's Bay for them to tarry there till his Returne, and whilst they were ashoar there, there came to an Anchor abt 2 Leagues off of the shoare Commadore Warren with 4 or 5 of his ships along with him[95], and sent three of the King's Proclamations ashoare together wth a Letter from himself and the other Commds[96] offering pardon to all such Pyrates as would come in and submit but in about twenty four hours afterwards sailed from thence, so that this Examinate and the other Passengers could not go aboard him or any of his ships, but gladly imbraced his Maties said pardon and resolved to tarry for the returne of the *Margaret* from the Northward, and to go in her to St. Hellena, and there waite for the arrival of the Men of Warr, and afterwards there came into the said Bay of Augustine Capt. Evan Jones Commander of the *Beckford* or *Bedford Gally* a Pyrate ship

---

[95] Commodore Warren had first visited the Indian Ocean in 1696-7, and on his return recommended offering the Madagascar pirates a pardon and destroying their base at St. Mary's. He was appointed to lead a second squadron to the area for that purpose, but after briefly visiting mainland Madagascar he sailed for India where he died. He was succeeded by Commodore Littleton who did sail to St. Mary's and persuaded some pirate to accept the pardon, but failed to destroy the pirate stronghold and was instead accused to over-friendly relations with the pirates.
[96] commanders

and offered this Exate and the other Passingers ashore considerable shares and advantages if they would go with him, but they showed him the King's Proclamations and the Letter under the hand of Commadore Warren and the other Commrs for his Maties pardon and told him that they had imbraced his sd pardon and refused to go along with him. And shortly after came into the said Bay the *Margaret* from her Trade of purchasing slaves and the Examinate and the other Passengers ashoare went aboard her and agreed with Samll Burgis the Master to carry them to St. Hellena instead of going to New Yorke as they first designed and the said ship *Margaret* afterwards meeting with a storme as she was going to weather the Cape of Good Hope which damnifyed some of the provisions the Master thereof came with her to an anchoer within the said Cape near to the Fort in order to recruite, and then Capt. Lowth then also lying at an anchor there sent his pinnace abd the *Margaret* to invite the said Samll Burgis the Mr to dine with him and the sd Master went accordingly, and then his pinnace returned abd the *Margaret* againe with some of his Officers who examined the Passenger abd who they were and they said they were Passengers and had imbraced his Maties pardon, and they invited three of them aboard and advised them to bring wth them the King's Proclamation for pardon and also Commodore Warrens Letter, which they did accordingly and were all seized by Capt. Lowth, who afterwards caused the said ship *Margaret* and all the goods abd to be seized together with the Ship's Company and the rest of the Passengers and he saith that he had aboard the said ship the *Margaret* at the time of her seizure in gold and silver to the value of Two Thousand one hundred and Fourty peeces of

Eight together with his Chest and Cloaths, and saith that he wonne the foresd mony at play.

11. Michael Hicks

The Examination of Michael Hicks, 27 August, 1701. HCA 1/53, ff. 97-99

This Examinate saith that on or abt the 26 Janry 1696 he went aboard the Ship *Pellican* (Capt. Robt. Colly Commander) of the burthen of abt 160 Tonns mounted with Tenn Gunns lying at Rhode Island and going with a designe to take a French Island called Kayon in the West Indyes there being then Warr between England and France and he saith that he sailed in the said ship from Rhode Island to St. Vincent one of the Cape de Verde Island to water, and there the major part of the ships Company voting to go round the Cape of Good Hope, carryed this Exate with them agt his will, and after they arrived at Madagascar they went to the mouth of the Red Sea, and there meeting with a Moorish Ship they stopt her for three or four days and after they had taken out some of he Rice they let her go, and then went away to the Coast of Mallaber to the high Land of St. johns, and there meeting with Capt. Culliford Commander of the *Resolution* abt October 1698 he left the ship *Pellican*, and got a Passage with him to Madagascar, and whilst he was aboard him one Capt. Shivers Commander of the *Soldadoes* his the said Cullifords Consort tooke a great Moorish Ship upon the Coast of St. johns, there being mony and other goods in her, and after they had shared the said prize between them, they gave the Examinate to the value of Four hundred pounds sterling, and he afterwards sailed in the said ship the *Resolution* directly for Madagascar and arrived there abt the middle of December 1698 and there meeting with the *Margaret* Samuell Burgis Mr bound for New Yorke he did in Febry following agree with him for his passage thither for one hundred ps of Eight and abt the 6th of March afosd he sailed in the sd ship *Margaret* from St. Maryes to St. Augustine to take in slaves and no slave Trade there presenting the said ship sailed to the Northward to get slaves and left this Exate and sevll other Passengers ashore there, and was to take them in again upon her returne, and abt the 19th day of July 1699 there arrived off of St. Augustine Commadore Warren with four Men of Warr and a Mercht ship in his Company and sent a shoare three of his Maties Proclamations and a Letter under his owne hand and two other Commdr promising pardon to all such Pyrates as would come in and submit, which was readily imbraced by this Exate and the other Passengers ashoare, but the Men of Warr making no stay there they could not get aboard them as they would have done if they had. And abt ten days after the *Beckford Gally* a Pyrate ship commanded by Evan Jones came into St. Augustine's Bay and offered this Exate and the other Passengers a shoare a share of all that was aboard her of goods and moveables if they would go along with them, but they refused so to do showing them the King's Proclamations for pardon and telling them that they had imbraced the same and that they meaning the Company of the *Beckford Gally* might also have the benefit of it too if they would come in and submit but they refused so to do, and a short time after the *Margaret* returning into the Bay of St. Augustine this Exate and the other Passengers went aboard her and acquainted Samuell Burgis the Master of her that they having recvd the King's Proclamations for pardon did designe to tarry a shoar where they were in expectation of the Men of Warr's coming thither, but upon the sd Master's disswading them from it and telling them that in regard they were there among heathens they could not remain there wth such security as they might at St. Hellena among Christians and therefore advised them to go thither to waite for the Men of Warr, which they resolved to doe and so sailed with ye said Samuell Burgis to the Cape of Good Hope, where he put in because some of the provisions for his slaves were damnifyed, and to get some refreshmts and upon their coming in to the Cape they found Capt. Lowth Commander of the *Loyall Mercht* at an Anchor there, who sent his Mate abd the said ship *Margt* and desired that three of ye Passengrs of the said ship would come abd and show him the King's Proclamations and then he would have nothing to say to them whereupon this Examinate and two others of the Passengers went abd the said Capt. Lowth carrying the foresd three Proclamations and Letter in their Pockets, but as soone as they came aboard they were put in irons being not brought to the Capt. and the sd Proclamations and Letter were taken out of their Pockts and the said Capt. Lowth did afterwards seize upon the said ship *Margaret* her goods and all the ships Company and Passengers and he saith that he had aboard the said ship *Margaret* at the time of her seizure as aforesaid abt the value of one hundred pound sterling in silver and in gold abt the value of six hundred pounds sterling, great part of which mony he won at play.

12. Richard Roper

The Examination of Richard Roper, 27 August, 1701. HCA 1/53, ff. 100-101

This Examinate saith that about five years since he went out with Capt. Wm. Kidd Commander of the *Adventure Gally* from England to New Yorke, and from thence to Madagascar, and there they tooke in water and provisions, and sailed from thence to the Red Sea and from thence to the Coast of Carawar as he remembers and then tooke a small Moorish ship, and after they had taken some pepper out of her let he go againe, and afterwards went upon the Coast of Mallabar and there tooke a Moorish ship of abt 200 Tons having a greate deale of Cotton and 2 horses aboard her, and Capt. Kidd afterwards put this Exate who was then a Boy and sevll of her men aboard her to carry her to Madagascar, and afterwards the Exate arrived in the said ship at Madagascar in Company of the said Capt. Wm. Kidd, and then he left Capt. Kidd and went with Captain Culliford in the *Resolution*, to Cruise off of St. Johns, and there they tooke a Boate called a Grab with some Bales, and after they had taken out some of them they let her go, and they met with Capt. Shiver Commander of the *Soldadoes* and they went in consortship together a cruising off of Surat, and there Capt Shivers did in the Company of the said Capt. Culliford take a great Moorish ship with a great deale of mony and other goods aboard, and afterwards this was divided amongst the said two ships companies abt 6 or 700l. a man, and this Exate being then a Boy together wth four other boys had but one mans share.

66

And afterwards they returned to Madagascar and then the Examinate left the said ship the *Resolution* and went ashoare at St Maryes where he lived for abt two months and then the *Margaret* Samuell Burgis Mr Coming in there and being bound to New Yorke he entred himself a Passenger aboard her, and went in her to St. Augustine and from thence to the Chimonotta's[97] to purchase slaves, where having bought one hundred and odd slaves the said ship returned to St. Augustine to take in the Passengers she had left there, by whom this Exate was informed that during this time ye said ship was upon the slave Trade there came off of St. Augustine Commadore Warren with sevll King's Proclamations and a Letter under his own hand and two others of the Commrs promising pardon to all Pyrates that would come in and submit, whereupon this Exate gladly embraced the said pardon and designed to go to St. Hellena to tarry there for the Men of Warr and afterwards the said ship the *Margt* sailed from St. Augustine for St. Hellena but meeting with bad weather and the Negroes provisions being damaged she put into the Cape of Good Hope to recruite, and there found the Loyall Mercht. Capt. Lowth Commander at an Anchor, and then Capt. Lowth sent his boate aboard the *Margt* and invited the Mr of her aboard him, and the Master accordingly went, and then the said Capt. Lowth sent his boat againe aboard the *Margt* for three or four of the Passengrs to come aboard him and shew the Kings Proclamation of pardon wch they had, whereupon three of the Passengrs went abd Capt. Lowth and carryed three Proclamations wth them and a Letter from Commadore Warren and the other Commrs, and when they came abd they were seized and

[97] Comoros Islands?

sentinels placed over them and shortly after the said ship and goods and all the Passengrs and ships Company aboard were seized by Capt. Lowth and he saith that he had aboard the said ship *Margaret* when she was seized as foresd abt the value of four hundred pounds sterling in silver and gold and Cloaths and other things to ye value of ten pounds, most of the sd mony being given him for tending upon sick people working of Cloaths and other services.

13. John Barrett

The Examination of John Barrett, 27 August, 1701. HCA 1/53, ff. 102-103

This Examinate saith that in the yeare 95 he sailed from Rhode Island in a privateer called the *Jno and Rebecca*[98] (John Hoare Comdr) bound to the West Indyes to Cruise agt the French, but when the said ship came out to sea the said Captain Hoare and the Major part of his men did against the will of this Examinate saile the said ship to Madagascar, where they cleaned and victualled their ship and from thence went to the Red Sea and there they tooke two Moorish Ships and after they had taken out of them some mony, Almonds, Beads, provisions and water they burnt them and then divided what they so tooke out of them amongst the said ships Company, the Exate having for his share abt 30 ps of Eight in mony and in Beads and Almonds abt the value of one piece of Eight, and afterwards they sailed for the Gulph of Persia, and there they tooke sevll Boates with Provisions

---

[98] *John and Rebecca*

abd them and some of the boates they let go after they had taken out the Provisions and others they broke to peeces for firewood and then went out of the Gulph to looke for water along the Coast, and then in November 96 they met upon the sea a Moorish ship abt 90 Tonns with East India goods aboard, which said ship and goods they tooke, and carryed them to Madagascar and in Febry last they arrived there and then divided the said goods aboard the sd Moorish ship amongst their Company, this Examinate having for his part ¾ of a mans share, but what it was worth he knows not, he making no other use of it than to buy provisions and the Exate then left the said ship the *John and Rebecca* and went and lived ashoare at Madagascar till Aug[us]t last at which time he having spent all his share of the said goods as aforesd, he then went out with Capt. Richard Shivers Commander of the *Resolution* and they sailed from Madagascar to Nicobar Island where they careened and victualled their ship, and then cruised off of that Island and tooke a Moorish ship, and after they had taken out of her abt two hundred pounds in mony and some provisions, they let her go, all ye said mony being paid to the men that bought provision at Madagascar and Nicobar to proceed upon this voyage so that this Exate had no share of it, and afterwards they sailed to Cape Commorin and watered and bought some provisions, and afterwards sailed to St. Augustine upon the Island of Madagascar and there they cleaned and victualled their ship, and then went to the Coast of India, where meeting with Capt. Culliford in ye *Resolution* they sailed together in Consortship the ship the Examinate belonged to being now called the *Soldadoes*. And he saith that the sd ships sailing together did in the month of September 1698 take a large Moorish ship having aboard her a great deale of mony and some goods. And afterwards there was divided what was taken aboard her amongst the two Companyes of the said ships, this Exate having ¾ of a mans share which came to the value of abt four hundred pounds sterling, and the Soldadoes being leaky they sunck her and went aboard the said Moorish ship, and carryed her to the Island of St. Maryes near Madagascar and the Exate them left her, and went to live at Madagascar at a place called Bonovolo, where he continued till Aprill 1699, and then went aboard Peter Ripley Master of a Brigantine and sailed in her to St. Augustine, where he was put ashore, and then entered himself a Passenger aboard the *Margaret* Samll Burgis Mr and went with him to Mattabial[99], where the sd Master bought a hundred and twenty slaves and then returned to St. Augustine; and the Examinate then going ashoare he met with Joseph Wheeler and Michll Hicks and others, who showed and handed to him the Kings Proclamation of pardon and the Letter from Commadore Warren and the other Commrs which he readily accepted, and sailed with them aboard the said ship *Margaret* bound for St. Hellena where they were to tarry for the Men of Warr, but wanting provisions and having sick men aboard, and the Negroes provisions being damnifyed they put into the Cape of Good Hope where they found the *Loyall Mercht* Capt Lowth Commander, who sent his boate abd them to inquire from whence they came and being informed that they came as Passengers from St. Augustine and had his Maties pardon with them and Commadore Warrens and the other Commrs Letter, and were going to St. Hellena to wait for the Men of

---

[99] ?

70

Warr and receive the benefit of the said pardon, the said Capt
Lowth sent for some of them aboard with orders for them to
bring the Kings Proclamation and the Commrs Letter, and
Joseph Wheeler, Michll Hicks and Wm. Gould went abd the
Loyall Merchant carrying the said pardon and Letter with
them, and when they came aboard they were confined and
the said Capt Lowth did afterwards seize the said ship the
Margaret, goods, Passengers and company aboard, and
brought home this Exate a prisoner with him, and he saith
that he had aboard the said ship when she was so seized one
and twenty hundred Lyon Dollars[100], thirteen hundred ps of
Eight, in plate and small mony to ye value of one hundred ps
of Eight and in corrall and amber to the value of one hundred
peeces of Eight more, a great part of which mony he won at
play.

---

[100] A Lion Dollar was a large silver coin bearing a depiction of a lion rampant,
minted in Holland in the 17th and 18th centuries for overseas trade. Like the
Spanish "piece of eight" it became common currency all over the world.

14. The Will of Joseph Jones

The Will of Joseph Jones, 9 May, 1698. HCA 1/98, f. 108

This last will and testament is a remarkable survival, probably the only pirate's will from the 'golden age' still in existence. It seems likely that other pirates made wills leaving their property to their shipmates or family [doc. 17], but sadly, they have all since been lost.

In the Name of God Amen.

This ninth day of May in the Year of our Lord God one Thousand six hundred ninety and Eight, I Joseph Jones being very sick and weak of body, but of perfect mind memory thancks be given to God: I doe make and Ordaine this my last will Testament in manner and forme following. That is to say: First and Chiefly, I give my Soule into the hands of Almighty God who gave it me and my body I comment to the earth to be buried in Christian burial at ye discretion of Executors hereafter named, nothing doubting but att the General Resurrection I shall receive the same again by the Mighty Power of God. As touching my worldly Estate and affaires wich it hath pleased God to bless me I give devise and bequeath and dispose the same in manner and forme following, viz: I give devise and bequeath unto Francis Reed and John Bevis my full and whole Executors my Guns pistols Amunition Catouch[101] Boxes all my Whearing Apparell[102] with my shears[103] of the Shipp and a Quarter part of part of

---

[101] Cartridge
[102] Clothing

what prise purchase or plunder shall be due to me from Jonathan Greene according to Contract; Item I give devise and bequeath unto Michaell Hicks one piece of Gould. Item I give devise and bequeath to Berrington Webb one piece of Gould so this being my last will and Given under my hand seal the day and year above Written.

Sighened Sealed and Delivered in presence of us,

John Watson

Michael Hicks

15. A matelotage agreement

Agreement between Francis Reed and John Beavis, 10 March, 1699. HCA 1/98, f. 193

Matelotage *was an agreement or bond between two men to share everything in common, from food and drink to money and sometimes women. It has been suggested, on virtually no evidence at all, that* matelotage *also included a homosexual element. It is, of course, not unlikely that some pirates were homosexual, but the same is true of any occupational group, and there is no reason to suppose that* matelotage *was in any way significant either of homosexual preference or situational homosexual practice. It was rare for a* matelotage *agreement to be formally drawn up as this one was, and it is interesting to note that although Francis Reed was able to write his own name, the document was actually drawn up by the witness Robert Arnott.*

---

[103] Shares

Be it knowen to all men by these preasants that Francis Reed and John Beavis are entread[104] in Consortship together, And in Caise that any sudden Axsedent[105], should happen to ye forsd Francis Reed That what gold, Silver, or any other thing whatsoever shall Lawfully become, or fall to ye forsd John Beavis

As also if that any sudden Axsedent should happen to ye above written John Beavis, That what gold, silver, or any thing ells shall Lawfully be Come, or fall to the forsd Francis Reed.

Written at Port Dolphin[106] the year of god one thousand six Hundred and nyntie nyne. March ye tenth day.

Francis Reed

IB John Beavis his marke

Sign'd and seall'd before these witness

Robert Arnott

Francis Billing

---

[104] entered
[105] accident
[106] Port Dauphin, Madagascar

16. John Brown

The Examination of John Brown, 21 October 1701. HCA 1/53, ff. 110-111

John Brown, like Samuel Burgess, had been one of Kidd's crew aboard the Blessed William *and had sailed to the Indian Ocean with Burgess, Collover et al aboard the* Jacob *before returning to America. By the time he joined Kidd's company on the* Adventure Galley *at New York he was, therefore, an experienced pirate. It is perhaps slightly surprising that Brown would want to serve under Kidd again, having already once mutinied against him, and no less surprising that Kidd allowed him to. Presumably they patched up their differences, and Kidd was probably grateful to enlist a man of Brown's experience – Brown is the only member of Kidd's crew known to have previously sailed in the Indian Ocean. It was probably men of Brown's ilk that Governor Benjamin Fletcher of New York was thinking when he described Kidd's company as 'men of desperate fortunes'.*

This Examinate saith that he was bred up to ye sea and hath used it for above thirty years that within these ten years last past he hath made sevll voyages to the Streights[107] and ye West Indies in Merchant ships: that hath been also at the East Indies that he went out from New York in ye ship *Adventure Galley* whereof Capt Wm Kidd was Comr and sailed to the Maderas from thence to Madagascar and from thence to severall Islands and places in ye East Indies, that he was with Kidd at the taking of the *Cuddy* or *Quedagh Merchant* and another ship, that the *Quedagh Mercht* was laden with bale goods that when Kidd had finished his voyage in ye East Indies he returned to Madagascar and there Kidd distributed

---

[107] Of Gibraltar

75

what he had taken just as he thought fit and gave to each man what he pleased and the Examinate had what Kidd thought fit to give him that Kid had a commission which the Examinate thought was a good Com:on and so it was looked upon at New York when ye Examinate went onbd him and the sd Kid did everywhere wear the King's Colours. That after dividing at Madagascar the Examinate got passage with Capt Shelley and went to Kayan and from thence to Surinam from which place he came to Lond abt two years ago and hath since made a voyage to ye West Indies and back again. That after he left Kid at Madagascar he the Examinate sailed abt five or six months with Capt Culliford and in that time they took off of Suratt a Moorish ship which he believes was called the *Mahomet*, that there was good quantity of gold and silver onbd the sd Moorish ship which the sd Culliford and his men took out of the sd ship and the Examinate had some share of it, then they of Culliford's ship turned the men of the Moorish ship onshore and then brought the sd Moorish ship to Madagascar and so that voyage ended and then the Examinate came from thence with Capt Shelley. That he the Examinate is an illiterate man and so cannot keepe a perfect account of the voyage. That he the Examinate hath at severall times given money to some people to wit fourteen guineas to some where John Hayles who is one of the apprehenders was present and the person who recd the sd 14 guineas said it was to be shared amongst thirty of them, that Thomas Hickman who now comes as an apprehender hath received of this Exiate's wife three guineas and they this day coming for more money wch the Exaiate had not to give they brought this Exaiate hither for piracy.

17. Robert Collover writes to a shipmate's widow

Robert Collover to Mrs Whalley, 6 April 1699. HCA 1/98, f. 171

This letter from pirate captain Robert Collover to the widow of one of his company is believed to be the only letter (though not the only document) in a pirate's own hand to have survived from the 'golden age'. Brief though it is, it speaks volumes about the concern pirates showed not only towards their families, but also towards one another.

Mrs Whalley

Beknowen[108] this is Concarninge[109] youer husbondes will which is left wholly to you and yr Children ye same. Beknown thatt he left therty hundred Pcs of eight whereof Capt. Shelley ships you ye Billes of Loading and Edward Buckmaster[110] Left in charge to be delivered the fright[111] to bee payed not mor

Madam, yours to com[mand]

Rob. Collover

April ye 6ᵗʰ 1699, from: St Maries.

---

[108] Beknown
[109] Concerning
[110] Buckmaster was a former seaman turned New York tavern keeper who signed on to Kidd's voyage, but left him at St. Mary's to join Collover.
[111] freight

18. A Pirate Reference

Certificate of James Briggs. SP 34/14/15A, f. 19

The recipient of this remarkable and unique document, James Briggs, was a fortunate man indeed. In 1700 his ship was captured by pirates commanded by Lodowick Ferdinando of the Samuel's Adventure. *Briggs was forced to join the pirate company, apparently much against his will. Later, on 30 April, the* Samuel's Adventure *took two more ships, the* John and Jane *and the* Unity, *whose captains joined Briggs aboard the pirate ship for six days. When the pirates released the prisoners they allowed Briggs to accompany them, and he returned with them to England, where he presented himself to Sir Charles Hedges, Secretary of State and judge of the Admiralty Court, and produced this certificate from the pirate captain testifying to his innocence. Ten years later Briggs was arrested for piracy in Bermuda and faced charges relating to his time as a forced member of Ferdinando's company. Briggs' defence rested on the fact that he had already been examined and discharged by Hedges. When Governor Bennett wrote to London for instructions, Briggs' original certificate was found, carefully filed away, and the Council of Trade and Plantations in consequence advised Bennett that Briggs should be released if there were no new charges against him. Bennett placed the matter before the Council of Bermuda, who voted to put Briggs on trial in order to formerly acquit him of the charges, protecting him from possible future arrest.*

I Captain Lodowick Ferdinando, do hereby solemnly protest and declare, in the presence of Capt. Benjin Joyce, Master of the John and Jane, and Wm White, Mr of the Unity, that James Briggs now aboard of Capt. Joyce, was forced by me against his will from on Board the Resolution, Captain Humphry Ware Commander, and now finding it uneasy, to carry men unwilling to my service, I have therefore both in pitty and generosity, dismissed the said James Briggs and declare him an unfaithfull servant to me but willing every way, as well as Capable, to serve any Merchant Man whatsoever, Therefore I hope these my Letters, shall never tend to his prejudice. In presence of the said Witnesses I have both signed and subscribed the same.

Lodowick Ferdinando

19. Dear British Apollo

The British Apollo, 2 June 1708

The following document may appear too remarkable to be considered genuine. Nevertheless, The British Apollo, was a newspaper of sorts specialising in providing answers to queries sent in by its readers. The first issue explained that it was a periodical 'In which we shall endeavour to answer all Questions in Divinity, Philosophy, the Mathematicks, and other Arts and Sciences, which appear fit and worthy to be answer'd', and the serious nature of the periodical was proclaimed by the editors' refusal to accept advertisements from 'Quacks'. Unlike many newspapers of the early eighteenth century, The British Apollo was not in the habit of including moralising editorials thinly disguised as genuine stories, and the queries answered in other editions of the Apollo *cover subjects as diverse as meteorology, biology, theology, etymology, history, and folklore. Queries ranged from how to calculate the odds in a game of piquet to why Welshmen wear leeks in their hat on St. David's day. Other queries in the issue of 2 June 1708, from which the following extract is taken, included why the Sunday after Easter is called 'Dominica in Albis', how to define 'jealousy', and questions about marriages performed by bogus ministers and a 99-year lease. There is therefore no reason to suppose that this document was anything other than a letter genuinely received by the editors of* The British Apollo, *and included by them in the newspaper. Whether or not it was really written by a pirate, or was a hoax, the purpose of which is unclear, is less certain.*

Q. Gentlemen, I am lately return'd from the East Indies, where I have follow'd a Course of Pyrating for upwards of 20 Years; But being under trouble of Mind, for the many Murders and Robberies I have committed; for which, it is out of my power to make Satisfaction; I desire your Advice for my future Behaviour, in order for making my Peace with God Almighty. My long Continuance in that wicked Course of Life, has given me an Opportunity of being acquainted with most of the Pyrates in the Indies, their Haunts, Force, Places of Refreshment, and Rendezvous, in all Seasons of the Year; which they are forced to observe by reason of the Monsoons; likewise their strengths; of what Nation, etc. I have be me near twenty of their and my own Sea Journal Books; some of which are the Observations of the best Artists; These give such Exact Accounts of the Winds and Currents, and such exact Draughts of most ports, Havens, Bays, and Coasts, all over the East Indies, as I never found any thing like it in an of our Common Charts and Sea Draughts; which are generally Erroneous: Likewise the Variation, Longitudes, etc. All which upon a Publication; I am sure would be acceptable both to the Merchant, honest Mariner, and Hydrographers. But how shall I make it Publick, I desire you to advice me? For as soon as ever it comes to light, I shall be found out, and am then sure to be hang'd; for there are now in England, to my certain knowledge, those whom I have Plunder'd; but they know not, neither do my Poor Relations whom I daily see, and would relieve, but dare not, for fear of Discovery. I beseech you, for God's sake! Gentlemen, to give me such Advice as may ease my troubled Mind, and enable me to make my Peace with my offended Redeemer?

20. Thomas Nichols and Francis Leslie surrender

Thomas Nichols to Benjamin Bennett, 10 January 1717/8, and *Francis Leslie to Benjamin Bennett*, 7 January 1717/8. CO 37/10, ff. 23, 25

As part of the British government's initiative to extirpate piracy from the Bahamas a general pardon was granted in September 1717 to all pirates who voluntarily surrendered themselves to any colonial governor before 5 September 1718. When news of the Proclamation of Pardon reached New York, Captain Vincent Pearse of HMS Phoenix *sailed, on his own authority, to the Bahamas to present the proclamation to the pirates there. His arrival caused a schism in the pirates' ranks between those who wanted to accept the pardon and those who refused. Many of those who decided to accept the pardon surrendered themselves to Pearse, even though he was not authorised to formally issue a pardon, as a token of their good intent* [**doc. 69**]. *Others, including Thomas Nichols and Francis Leslie, decided to sail to Bermuda to surrender to Governor Benjamin Bennett, who had also sent his son to the Bahamas with news of the pardon.*

Providence, Jany. 10th: 1717[112]

This accompanies Capt. Bennet by whom you have done us so much Honour and Service. Therefore as my Duty in the first place, return Yor Excelly my hearty and gratefull thanks, for you care and concern in dispatching his Majesties most gracious and Royal Proclamation, and that too by your only Son, who can Inform you how readily some of us as well as my self embraced the same, and should have waited on Yor Excellency by this opportunity did not some present affairs prevent me, so that I purpose to continue till I can receive advice of the arrival of Capt. Bennett, who as we Tenderly respect, wish safe to your Government, whose particular remarks of Friendship can never be forgotten by, Sir,

Yr Excellys most humble and most obedient Servt,

Tho Nichols

---

[112] Until the mid-18th century new year was celebrated on Lady Day, 25 March, but the 'new' practice of beginning the new year on 1 January began to creep in slowly from the later 17th century. Therefore, dates between 1 January and 25 March could fall in one of two years depending on who was writing. Here, Nichols and Leslie both take 25 March as new year's day, and thus refer to the year as 1717 rather than the modern calendar year of 1718. In some contemporary documents both years are written, such as 1717/8, for example.

New Providence Jany ye 7th 1717

May it please your Excelly,

Most humbly asking Pardon for my rudeness in troubling you at this present but being obligated thereto by your great Clemency in sending your son with that most welcome News of his Majties most gracious Pardon which I humbly accept of, the Gentleman your son can Inform yor Excellency of my affairs in this place which will soon be over and then I hope to partake of your Excellency's clemency, which shall be by the hearty desire of him who is,

Yor Excellys most humble and obedient Servant,

F. Leslie

21. The Whydah survivors tell their stories

The Substance of the Examinations of John Brown &c., 6 May, 1717. Printed as appendix of *The Trials of Eight Persons Indited for Piracy* (Boston, 1718), pp. 23-25

Samuel Bellamy began his piratical career in 1716 in the company commanded by Benjamin Hornigold, and was elected captain after Hornigold was deposed over his refusal to attack English shipping. The high point of Bellamy's short but very successful career came when he captured the slave-ship Whydah in early 1717, but that career was brought to an abrupt end in April 1717 when the Whydah and her consort sloop, the Mary-Anne *were wrecked in a storm off Cape Cod, Massachusetts. 144 men perished in the wreck of the* Whydah, *and only two men made it safely to shore, along with six from the* Mary-Anne. *All eight were tried and six were hanged in Boston in October 1717. When the notorious Blackbeard, who had also been a member of Hornigold's company in 1716, heard of the pirates' execution he vowed revenge on New England and burned a number of Boston ships in retaliation* [**doc. 22**].[113]

John Brown being interrogated saith, That he was born in the Island of Jamaica, is 25 Years old and Unmarried. About a Year ago he belonged to a Ship Commanded by Capt. Kingston, which in her Voyage with Logwood to Holland was taken to the Leeward of the Havana by two Piratical Sloops, one commanded by Hornygold and the other by a Frenchman call Labous,[114] each having 70 Men on Board. The Pirates kept the Ship about 8 or 10 Days and then having taken out of her what they thought proper delivered her back to some of the Men, who belonged to her. Labous kept the Examinate on board his sloop about 4 months, the English sloop under Hornygolds command keeping company with them all that time. Off Cape Corante they took two Spanish Briganteens without any resistance laden with Cocoa from Maraca. The Spaniards not coming up to the Pirates demand about the ransom were put a-shore and their Briganteens burn'd. They sailed next to the Isle of Pines, where meeting with 3 or 4 English sloops empty, they made use of them in cleaning their own, and gave them back. From thence they Sailed to Hispaniola in the latter end of May, where they

---

[113] Woodard, *Republic of Pirates*, pp. 134-135, 157-158, 196-197
[114] Oliver la Buse. [**doc. 44**]

arrived about 3 Months. The Examinate then left Labous and went on board the Sloop Commanded formerly by Hornygold, at that time by one Bellamy, who upon a difference arising amongst the English pirates because Hornygold refused to take and plunder English Vessels, was chosen by a great Majority their Captain and Hornygold departed with 26 hands in a prize Sloop, Bellamy having then on board about 90 men, most of the English. Bellamy and Labous sailed to the Virgin Islands , and took several small Fishing Boats and off St Croix a French ship laden with Flower and Fish from Canada, and having taken some of the Flower gave back the Ship. Plying to the Windward the Morning they made Saba they spy'd 2 Ships, which they chased and came up with, one was Commanded by Capt. Richards, the other by Capt Tosor both bound to the Bay. Having plundered the Ships and taken out some Young Men they dismist the rest and likewise Tosor's Ship, and made a Man of War of Richards's, which they put under the Command of Bellamy, and appointed Paul Williams Captain of their Sloop. Next Day they took a Bristol Ship, Commanded by James Williams from Ireland laden with Provisions, and having taken out what Provisions they wanted and 2 or 3 of the Crew, let he go. They parted with their French consort at the Island of Blanco and stood away with their Ship and Sloop to the Windward passage, where in the latter end of February last they met with Capt Lawrence Prince in a Ship of 300 Ton called the *Whido* with 18 Guns mounted, and 50 Men bound from Jamaica to London laden with Sugar, Indigo, Jesuits Bark[115] and some Silver and Gold, and having given chase 3 Days took him without any other

---

[115] An important source of quinine

resistance than firing his two chase Guns at their Sloop, and came to an Anchor at Long Island. Bellamy's crew and Williams's consisted then of 120 Men. They gave the Ship taken from Capt. Richards to Capt. Prince, and loaded her with as much of the best and finest goods as She could carry, and gave Capt. Prince above Twenty Pounds in Silver and Gold to bear his charges. They took 8 or 10 Men belonging to Capt. Prince, the Boatswain and two more were forced, the rest being Volunteers. Off Pettiguavis they took an English Ship hired by the French laden with Sugar and Indigo, and having taken out what they had occasion for, and some of the Men dismist her. Then they stood away for the Capes of Virginia, being 130 Men in company, and having lost sight of their Sloop the Day before they made the Land, they cruised ten Days according to agreement between Bellamy and Williams, in which time they seized 3 Ships and one Snow, two of them from Scotland, one from Bristol, and the fourth a Scotch ship from Barbadoes with a little Rum and Sugar on Board, so leaky that the Men refused to proceed farther. The Pirates sunk her. Having lost the Sloop they kept the Snow, which was taken from one Montgomery, being about 100 Ton and manned her with 18 hands, which with her own Crew made up the number of 28 Men; the other 2 Ships were discharged being first plundered. They made the best of their way for Cape Cod intending to clean their Ship at Green Island (having on Lambeth and an Indian born at Cape Cod for Pilots[116]) and on Friday the 26th of April last to the

---

[116] This reference has given rise to speculation that the Indian, or native American, may have been an officer, indicating an unusually enlightened racial tolerance by Bellamy's pirates. In fact, 'pilot' can have two meanings: one, a ship's officer responsible for navigation, the other a person of local knowledge used to guide a ship safely along a difficult stretch of coast. The context here

Eastward of Cape Cod took a Pink laden with Wine from Madera, last from Boston, bound to New York. They sent seven Men on Board called out on the Watch Bill, of whom the Examinate was one. He further saith, that there were about 50 Men forced, over whom the Pirate kept a watchful eye, and no Man was suffered to write a word, but what was Nailed up to the Mast. The names of the Forc'd Men were put in the watch Bill and fared as others, they might have had what Money they wanted from the Quarter Master, who kept a Book for that purpose, but this Examinate took only Cloaths. It was the common report in their Ship that they had about 20,000 Pounds in Gold and Silver. That Peter Hooff was once whip'd for attempting to Run-away, and that he and every one of the other Prisoners were forced to Join the Pirates.

Thomas Baker being Examined saith, That he was Born in Flushing, Aged 29 Years, by Trade a Taylor, and sometimes went to Sea, and sometimes followed his Trade ashore. That he was taken with 9 or more in a little Boat coming from Cape Francois , by Bellamy and Labous, but they were sent away being Married Men. This Examinate was never sworn as the rest were. Being on Board of Lebous he asked leave to go on Board of Bellamy, that he might have an opportunity of getting away, and accordingly he went, but found that Bellamy would not discharge him, on the contrary threatened to set him ashore on a Maroon Island if he would not be easy. When they took Richards, Tosor and Williams they spread a large black Flag, with a Death's Head and Bones a-cross, and gave chase to Captain Prince under the same Colours. They

shows clearly that the latter type of pilot is being referred to.

had on Board 20000 or 30000 Pounds, and the Quarter Master declared to the Company, that if any Man wanted Money he might have it. This Examinate came on Board the Pink which was taken off Cape Cod, Armed. The reason why he and the other Prisoners did not discover themselves to the Government when they first came ashore was because they expected to get to Boston and there Ship themselves as Sailors. In all other particulars he agrees with what is above.

Thomas Davis[117] Examined saith, He was born in Carmarthenshire in Wales, Aged Two and twenty Years, is by Trade a Ship wright, and has used used the Sea these five Years. He Sail'd from Bristol with Capt. William, and was taken on the 19th of December last, by Lebous 9 leagues to the Leeward of Blanco, and in January he joined Bellamy's company. When the company was called together for Consuls, and each Man to give his Vote, they would not allow the forced Men to have a Vote. There were One hundred and thirty forced Men in all, and Eighty of the Old company; and this Examinate being a forced Man had no opportunity to discover his Mind. From Blanco they Sail'd to the Spanish Main and water'd there, and from thence to a Maroon Island called Testegos, where they fitted up a Ship and Sloop of their own. All the New Men were Sworn to be true and not to cheat the company to the value of a piece of Eight. That when they chased the *Whido* they thought they had lost her, but came up with her the third day. Capt. Prince was treated civily. What money they got in the *Whido* was not shared. Seven or Eight of the *Whido's* Crew joined them.

---

[117] Thomas Davis, one of only two survivors from the *Whydah* herself, was genuinely forced to join the pirates, was tried separately from the others and found not guilty.

That their design in coming on this Coast was to get Provisions: That three of the Vessels they took off the Capes of Virginia, belonged to Scotland, and the fourth to Bredhampston, and when a Prize was taken the Watch-bill was called over, and Men put on board as they stood named in the Bill, and no more imposed on the forced Men than the Volunteers, they being all alike. The same day the *Whido* was lost, they took a Sloop coming from Virginia. The Ship being at an Anchor, they cut their Cables and ran a shoar, in a quarter of an hour after the Ship struck, the Main-mast was carried by the board, and in the Morning She was beat to pieces. About Sixteen Prisoners drown'd, Crumpstey Master of the Pink being one, and One hundred and forty-four in all. The riches on board were laid together in one heap.

Peter Hooff declares, That he was born in Sweden, is about 34 Years old, and left his Country 18 Years ago. He Sail'd for the most part with the Dutch on the Coast of Portobello, and has been with the Pirates fourteen Months. When he was taken by Bellamy in a Periaga[118], he belong'd to a Ship whereof Cornelson was Master: Three Weeks after he was taken they went to Portobello in a French Sloop with 60 Men on board; then stood for Havana, and from thence to Cuba, where they met with a Pink, an English-man Master, and took out some Powder and Shot, and some Men. A difference arising amongst them about taking Prisoners; Some being for one Nation and some for another; and having at that time Two Sloops and about 100 Men, Hornygold parted from them in One of the Sloops, and Bellamy and Lebous kept company together. They turned to the Windward from the

---

[118] Peragua

Isle of Pines to look out for a Ship of Force. The Money taken in the *Whido*, which was reported to Amount to 20000 or 30000 Pounds, was counted over, in the Cabin, and put up in bags, Fifty Pounds to every Man's share, there being 180 Men on Board. No Married Men were forced. Their Money was kept in Chests between Decks without any guard, but none was to take any without the Quarter Master's leave.

John Shuan declares, That he was born in Nantes, 24 Years old, a Mariner. That Two Months and a half ago he was taken by Bellamy in an English Ship, coming from Jamaica, commanded by an English-man, and a French-man bound from Pettiguavis to Rochel, with Sugar. This Examinate knows nothing of the Scotch Vessel's being sunk. When Crumpstey's Pink was taken on this Coast, He desired Bellamy to give him leave to go on board her, but could not obtain it, by reason he had not taken up Arms, yet afterwards Bellamy let him go. He further declares That he never was upon the List as the rest were: That in the Ship he belong'd to the Pirates found 5000 Livres, and on board of Bellamy's there was a great quantity of Silver and Gold.

Simon Van Vorst declares, That he was born in the City of New-York, aged 24 Years. That he went from New York to St Thomas's, and from thence to Cape Francois, where he staid three Months, and came from thence in October last in a Boat with Captain Simson's Men, who were Prisoners there, and standing over to Cape Nicholas they spy'd two Sail, which came pretty near them and firing a Gun brought them on board, three were dismist, being Married. The Examinate desired Lebous to let him go on board of Bellamy, and accordingly he went, Bellamy told him he must be easy until they could find Volunteers, or he would put him a-shoar on some Maroon Island. Nest day they took a Sloop coming from Cape Francois, and soon after a French Ship, out of which they took Claret and Provisions. They cleaned at St Croix, where 3 of their Men Ran away, and one of them being brought back was severely whipped. Plying to Windward for what they could get they took Richards, Tosor and a Bristol Ship laden with Beef. He further declares, That he saw many of Williams's, Tosor's and Richards's Men Cry and express their Grief upon their being compelled to go with Bellamy. After the Whido was taken they gave Richards's Ship to Capt. Prince and put as great a quantity of Goods on Board, as he desired. They took 10 or 12 of Prince's Men of whom the Boatswain and 2 or 3 more were forced. This Examinate went on Board Crumpsty's Pink Armed with a Gun and a Pistol, and he and the other 6, who were with him were all equal as to the commanding part, being in course according to the list or Watch Bill.

Hendrick Quintor declares, He was born in Amsterdam, Aged 25 Years, a Mariner. That he was taken in a Spanish Briganteen by Lebous Commander of the Sloop *Postillion*, and Bellamy Commander of the Sloop *Mary Anne* and being bound to [illegible] the Pirates told him he should go to the Coast of Crocus, but afterwards they compelled him to stay, and during the time he was with them they took 3 French Ships and then clean'd at the Main Land of Hispaniola. After that they took 3 English Ship, viz. Richards's, Tosor's and Williams's, and went to the Main to Water, from thence to Testegos, the Wind blowing very hard they went to St Croix, where a French Pirate was blown up. That this Examinate and the other six, who were sent on Board the Pink were Forced Men.

Thomas South[119] saith, He was born in Boston in Lincolnshire, about 30 Years of Age, a Mariner. That he came from Cork in Ireland in a Ship Commaned by Capt. Williams bound to Jamaica, and was taken by the Pirate Bellamy about four Months ago. The Pirates forced such as were Unmarried, being four in number, two of them were drown'd in the *Whido*, a Dutchman and a Welshman. This Examinate further saith, That the Pirates brought Arms to him, but he told them, He would not use any, for which he was much threatened; they staid sometime at Spanish Town; when Captain Richards's Ship was taken this Examinate did not take up Arms, he only stood by the Rigging. That they came on the Coast to meet their consort Paul Williams, whom they expected to find at Block Island. That he was One of the Seven, who were sent on board the Pink, He told the Mate that he was a forced Man, and if he could get a-shoar he would run-away. And further declares, That he has heard the other Prisoners say, They were compelled to joyn the Pirates.

22. David Herriot and Ignatius Pell on Blackbeard and Stede Bonnet

The Information of David Herriot and Ignatius Pell, 24/10/1718, published in *The Tryals of Major Stede Bonnet, and other Pirates* (London, 1719), pp. 44-48

David Herriot was the master of a trading sloop captured by the notorious Blackbeard in company with Stede Bonnet and kept

---

[119] Found not guilty at his trial

prisoner by them for several months, and was eventually apprehended along with Bonnet's company. As a forced man he stood a good chance of being acquitted, and this deposition would have virtually assured his freedom, which makes it all the more curious that on the very day he made this deposition he joined Bonnet in escaping from the Marshal's house in Charleston, South Carolina, where they were being held. They remained on the run until 8 November, when they were ambushed by a party of men led by Colonel William Rhett, who had led the capture of Bonnet's company in the first place, and during the exchange of fire Herriot was killed.[120] Ignatius Pell was a thoroughgoing pirate and boatwain of Bonnet's company, who turned King's evidence to save his own skin. He was pardoned, but in 1724 was reported to be in command of a pirate sloop of 12 guns in his old hunting grounds on the American coast.[121]

The said David Herriot and Ignatius Pell being duly sworn on the Holy Evangelists of Almighty God, depose and say as follow: And First, this Deponent, the said David Herriot, says, That about the Twenty second Day of March last he sailed out from Jamaica as Master in a sloop called the *Adventure*, of the Burden of Eighty Tons or thereabouts, whereof Matthew Taylor, of the County of Devon, Mariner; John Devine of Leyden, in the Province of Holland, Merchant; and James Robberts of Bristol, Mariner, are Owners; and was bound for the Bay of Honduras, chartered by one Major Daniel Axdell to one William Stewart, of Honduras aforesaid. Says, That about the 4th or 5th of April

---

[120] Woodard, *Republic of Pirates*, pp. 242,299-300
[121] *The Weekly Journal or Saturday's Post*, 25/4/1724

last this Deponent came into the Bay of Turneff, about ten Leagues from the Bay of Honduras, and there saw a Ship and two Sloops, which this Deponent first apprehended to be Capt. Wyar, who came out of Jamaica with four other Sloops about a Week before this Deponent, and designed to come to an Anchor there. But soon after he perceiving the said Ship did not belong to the said Wyar, this Deponent took them for Spaniards, and then tacked about, and then the Ship fired a Gun at this Deponent's Sloop; and the said sloop *Revenge*, then commanded by one Richards, a Pirate, slipped her Cable, and came up to this Deponent with a Black Flag hoisted, and ordered this Deponent to hoist out his Boat, and come on board them, which he did; and then the said Sloop *Revenge*, sent five of their Hands in this Deponent's Boat back again to this Deponent's Sloop, and brought this Deponent's Sloop to an Anchor under the Ship's stern.

Says, That the Ship which this Deponent imagined to belong to Mr Wyar, was a Ship of forty Guns mounted, named the *Queen Anne's Revenge*, commanded by one Edward Thatch, a Pirate. And says, He then was inform'd by the Pirate Crew, that the said Major Stede Bonnet was onboard the said Thatch, but out of Command, being some time before turn'd out of his Command by the said Thatch and the Pirate Crew, as he was inform'd.

And this Deponent further says, That at the time he was taken, as aforesaid, there was another Sloop in their Company, which the said Pirates called their Prize; but know not her Name, nor the Master's. And deposes, That at the time he was taken, there were on board the Sloop the *Royal James*, then called the *Revenge*, or the said Ship the *Queen Anne's Revenge*, the following Persons, viz. Edward

Robinson Gunner, Neal Paterson, John Lopez, Job Beely alias Bayly, William Scot, Thomas Nichols, Zachariah Long, Matthew King, William Livers alias Evis, Daniel Perry, Henry Virgin, William Eddy alias Nedy, James Mullet alias Millet, Thomas Price, and James Wilson;[122] but by reason of their frequently shifting from the said Ship the *Queen Anne's Revenge* to the said Sloop *Revenge*, now the *Royal James*, cannot say properly to which of them they belonged. That about the Eighth or Ninth Day of April aforesaid, the said Thatch and Richards weighed Anchor from the Key of Turnest, and came to Anchor in the Evening of the same Day at Water-Key, about a League or two from the Bay of Honduras; and the next Morning weighed Anchor, and went into Honduras-Bay, where there lay four Sloops, and a Ship named the *Protestant Casar*, Capt. Wyar Commander, from Jamaica last, but belonging to Boston, as 'twas then reported. Says, That he knows not the Sloops Names; but three of Them were commanded by Jonathan Bernard of Jamaica, Master of one of them, and Owner of three of the said four Sloops. Says, That one of the said Sloops came to descry what they were, and took said Thatch and Richards for Spaniards; but said Thatch fired a Gun, and hoisted his Black Flag. Whereupon Capt. Wyar, and all his Men took to their Boat, and went ashore; and then Thatch sent one Howard, his Quarter-Master, and eight of his Crew, on board of Wyar's Ship; but knows not what they took out of her. And says, That said Richards was employed in securing the other four Sloops.

---

[122] These men were all captured with Bonnet and Herriot and it was before their trial that Herriot made this deposition.

And this Deponent further deposes, That two or three Days after the said Thatch and Richards set fire to Capt. Wyar's Ship, because she belonged to Boston, alledging the People of Boston had hanged some of the Pirates, and so burnt her.[123] Says, The said Thatch burnt one of the four Sloops, because she belonged to Capt. James of Jamaica; which James, as 'twas alledged, had said he would not employ those Sailors in his Service that had accepted of the King's Proclamation; and the other three Sloops, Belonging to Bernard, they let go. From thence the said Richards and Thatch with this Deponent's Sloop, mann'd by some of the said Pirates, went to Turckcill, and from thence to Grand Camania, being an Island belonging to the Spaniards, lying about sixty Leagues to the Westward of Jamaica, where they took a small Turtler. From thence they sailed towards the Havana, and from thence towards the Bahama Wrecks. From the Bahama Wrecks, they came and lay of the Bar of Charles-Town in South Carolina, to wit, about the month of May last, for the space of five or six Days; where the said Thatch and Richards took a Ship commanded by one Robert Clark, bound from Charles-Town aforesaid to London. Says, He has heard by the Pirates there were both Goods and Money taken out of the said Clark's Ship, but knows not the Particulars, this Deponent being then on board his own Sloop.

Syas, That said Thatch and Richards, whilst they lay off the Bar of Charles-Town, took another Vessel coming out from Charles-Town, whose Name or Master cannot remember; and that they, the said Thatch and Richards, took two Pinks coming into Charles-Town from England; and heard them

---

[123] See **doc. 21**

say they likewise took a Brigantine with Negroes, but knows not the Names of the two Pinks or Brigantine, or the Names of the Commanders, and knows not what they took out of them; and after detaining them some few Days, they let them go again. That said Thatch and Richards set sail from the Bar of Charles-Town with this Deponent's Sloop for North Carolina; and this Deponent asked why they detained this Deponent's Sloop? They answer'd, They hoped to meet with the Laver de Cruse Fleet[124] some time or other; and that they kept her for a Fireship.

Says, That about six Days after they left the Bar at Charles-Town, they arrived at Topsail-Inlet in North Carolina, having then under their Command the said Ship *Queen Anne's Revenge*, the Sloop commanded by Richards, this Deponent's Sloop, command by one Capt. Hands, one of the said Pirate Crew, and a small empty Sloop which they found near the Havana. And this Deponent in the Voyage from South Carolina to North lost Company, but heard they took one Mason; and heard Thatch afterwards blame Richards for not burning said Mason's Vessel, because she belonged to Boston. That the next Morning after they had all got safe into Topsail-Inlet, except Thatch, the said Thatch's Ship *Queen Anne's Revenge* run a-ground off of the Bar of Topsail Inlet, and the said Thatch sent his Quarter-Master to command this Deponent's Sloop to come to his Assistance; but she run a-ground likewise about Gun-shot from the said Thatch, before his said Sloop could come to their Assistance, and both the said Thatch's Ship and this Deponent's Sloop were wreck'd; and the said Thatch and all the other Sloop's Companies went

---

[124] Vera Cruz Fleet, a squadron of Spanish vessels employed in carrying the treasures of Asia and South America from Vera Cruz to Spain.

on board the *Revenge*, afterwards called the *Royal James*, and on board the other Sloop they found empty off the Havana.

Says, 'Twas generally believed the said Thatch run his Vessel a-ground on purpose to break up the Companies, and to secure what moneys and Effects he had got for himself and such other of them as he had most Value for.[125] That after the said Ship and this Deponent's Sloop were so cast away, this Deponent requested the said Thatch to let him have a Boat, and a few Hands, to got o some inhabited Place in North Carolina, or to Virginia, there being very few poor inhabitants in Topsail-Inlet, where they were; and desired the said Thatch to make this Deponent some Satisfaction for his said Sloop; Both which said Thatch promised to do. But instead thereof, ordered this Deponent, with about sixteen more, to be put on shore on a small Sandy Hill or Bank, a League distant from the Main; on which Place there was no Inhabitant, nor Provisions. Where this Deponent and the rest remained two Nights and one Day, and expected to perish; for that said Thatch took away their Boat.

That said Thatch having taken what Number of Men he thought fit along with him, he set sail from Topsail-Inlet in the small Spanish Sloop, about eight Guns mounted, forty White Men, and sixty Negroes, and left the *Revenge* belonging to Bonnet there, who sent for this Deponent and Company from the said Sandy Bank. And then said Major Stede Bonnet reassumed the Command of his Vessel. And said Bonnet informed this Deponent, that his Intentions was to go to St. Thomas's, and there take a Commission against

---

[125] The debate about whether the wrecking of the *Queen Anne's Revenge* was deliberate or not still rages in 2014.

the Spaniards, hearing there was a War between the Emperor and Spain; and that he would give this Deponent his Passage thither, but could not pay him any Wages: Which this Deponent gladly accepted of.

That the said Major Bonnet being inform'd by a Bomb-Boat[126] that brought Apples and Cyder, that Thatch lay at Ocricock-Inlet[127] with only eighteen or twenty Hands, he resolved to pursue him, and cruised after him for four Days: But missing him, made to Virginia; and standing in with the Land, they met a pink about ten Leagues to the Southward of Cape Henry about July last, whose Name or Master he knows not. And said Bonnet ordered the Pink to send their Boat, and come on board them. And the said Bonnet took out of her about ten or twelve Barrels of Pork, and about four hundred Weight of Bread.

Says, That several of the said Bonnet's Crew went aboard the said Pink: Knows not their particular Names who went on board the Pink; but says, That at the time when they took the said Pink, there belonged to the said Bonnet the Mariners following, viz. Robert Tucker, Edward Robinson, Job Beely alias Bayly, William Scot, Neal Paterson, John Lopez, William Livers alias Evis, James Mullet alias Millet, James Wilson, John-William Smith, Thomas Nichols, John Ridge, William Eddy alias Nedy, William Hewet, Daniel Perry, Alexander Annand, John Thomas, Matthew King, Zachariah Long, Henry Virgin, Samuel Booth, Thomas Price, and John Robinson, and eight others, who afterwards run away: All which bore Arms, and all assisted to take the said Pink. But

---

[126] Bumboat
[127] Ocracoke

they gave instead of what they took eight or ten Cask of Rice, and one old Cable.

That about the Month of July aforesaid, the said Bonnet, and Crew last aforesaid, gave Chace to a Sloop, about two Leagues off of Cape Henry aforesaid, of about sixty Tons, Master unknown, and Sloop's name unknown to this Deponent; and fitted out a Dory after her with five Men, who took her, and brought her to the said Bonnet. And the said five Men took out of her two Hogsheads of Rum, one or more Hogsheads of Molosses, and two Negroes, and brought them on board said Bonnet.

Says, That said Bonnet, and all the Mariners last abovesaid, to wit, Robert Tucker, Edward Robinson, Job Beely alias Bayly, William Scot, Neal Paterson, John Lopez, William Livers alias Evis, James Mullet alias Millet, James Wilson, John-William Smith, Thomas Nichols, John Ridge, William Eddy alias Nedy, William Hewet, Daniel Perry, Alexander Annand, John Thomas, Matthew King, Zachariah Long, Henry Virgin, Samuel Booth, Thomas Price, and John Robinson, were all helping and assisting to take the Sloop last abovesaid; and that eight Men of the said Crew were put on board her, and afterwards run away with her.

Says, That one William Morrison was taken out of the Sloop last abovesaid, and continued a Prisoner about four or five Days, and then took on with Bonnet, and began to take Arms with the rest at the taking of the two Snows hereafter mentioned, and not before, for that he assisted at the taking of the two Snows. Says, That about the same Month of July, as they lay off Cape Henry, the said Bonnet and Crew took two Ships bound from Virginia for Glascow, whose Names or

100

Masters can't remember, and took about one hundred Weight of Tobacco out of each, and then discharged them.

That about the same Month of July, the said Bonnet and Crew took a Sloop bound from Virginia to Bermudas, about fifty Tons, Master's Name, Sloop's, or Owners, can't remember. And the said Bonnet and Crew took out of her twenty Barrels of Pork, some small Quantity of loose Bacon, and gave him again two Barrels of Rice, and a Hogshead of Molosses, and sent her away. That , Robert Tucker, Edward Robinson, Job Bayly alias Beely, William Scot, Neal Paterson, John Lopez, William Livers alias Evis, James Mullet alias Millet, James Wilson, John-William Smith, Thomas Nichols, John Ridge, William Eddy alias Nedy, William Hewet, Daniel Perry, Alexander Annand, John Thomas, Matthew King, Zachariah Long, Henry Virgin, Samuel Booth, Thomas Price, and John Robinson, were then on board the said Bonnet, and bore Arms, and helped and assisted to take the last mentioned Sloop; and that two Mariners, named Thomas Carman and George Ross, came out of the said last mention'd Bermudas Sloop voluntarily, and that they took on with Bonnet, and bore Arms afterwards among the rest. That sometime in the month of July the said Bonnet and Crew took another Ship, bound from Virginia to Glascow, can't remember her Name, or the Masters, and took nothing of Value, save only a few Combs, Pins, and Needles; and gave her instead thereof a Barrel of Pork, and two Barrels of Bread.

That about the same Month of July, the said Bonnet and Crew, that is to say, Robert Tucker, Edward Robinson, Job Beely alias Bayly, William Scot, Neal Paterson, John Lopez, William Livers alias Evis, James Mullet alias Millet, James

Wilson, John-William Smith, Thomas Nichols, John Ridge, William Eddy alias Nedy, William Hewet, Daniel Perry, Alexander Annand, John Thomas, Matthew King, Zachariah Long, Henry Virgin, Samuel Booth, Thomas Price, John Robinson, Thomas Carman and George Ross, took a Scooner as they sailed from Virginia to Philadelphia, in the Latitude of Thirty eight North, coming from North Carolina, bound to Boston, about thirty or forty Tons, Name of the Vessel or Master unknown to this Deponent, and took out of her about two dozen Calf-Skins to make covers for Guns, and kept her about three Days; and that the said William Wallis and John Levit came out of the said Scooner voluntarily, and took on with said Bonnet and Crew, and bore Arms with the rest.

That during the said three Days the said Bonnet and Crew, that is to say, Robert Tucker, Edward Robinson, Job Beely alias Bayly, William Scot, Neal Paterson, John Lopez, William Livers alias Evis, James Mullet alias Millet, James Wilson, John-William Smith, Thomas Nichols, John Ridge, William Eddy alias Nedy, William Hewet, Daniel Perry, Alexander Annand, John Thomas, Matthew King, Zachariah Long, Henry Virgin, Samuel Booth, Thomas Price, John Robinson, Thomas Carman, George Ross, William Wallis, and Joseph Levit, took two Snows off Dellaware Bay, thirty nine Degrees North Latitude, near Philadelphia, of the Burden of about ninety Tons, each bound from Philadelphia to Bristol, Snows Names and Masters knows not. Believes there was Money and Goods taken out of the said Snows, but knows nothing of the Particulars. Detain'd them about a Day, and dismissed them. That at the same time the said Bonnet and Crew took a Sloop of the Burden of sixty Tons, bound from Philadelphia to Barbadoes, Names of Vessel or Master unknown. Knows not whether they took Goods out of her, or not; dismiss'd her with the Snows. But says, That George Dunkin, came out of said last mentioned Sloop voluntarily, at the same time when Read was taken, as hereafter mentioned, and took on with said Bonnet, and bore Arms among the rest at the taking of Manwareing and Dalton, hereafter mention'd. That during those three Days in the Month of July aforesaid, to wit, about the 28th, 29th, or 30th of the same Month, the said Bonnet and Crew took a Sloop, Burden on fifty or sixty Tons, commanded by Capt. Thomas Read, as they lay off Delaware-Bay, about six or seven Leagues, bound from Philadelphia to Barbadoes, loaden with Provisions, and put four or five Hands of the said Bonnet's Crew on board her. That about the last Day of July, the said Bonnet and Crew, as they lay at the Hore-Kills in Delaware-Bay aforesaid, off Cape Inlopen, took a Sloop about the Burden of sixty Tons, commanded by Peter Manwareing, bound from Antegoa to Philadelphia, loaden chiefly with Rum, Molosses, and Sugar: The said Bonnet and Crew took Molosses out of her, and put in on board the said Scooner; but knows not the Particulars, because he lay at a distance.

That the next Day the said Bonnet and Crew sailed out of Delaware-Bay, and carried said Read's and Manwareing's Sloops along with them; and about the 12th Day of August they came into Cape Fear River, in order to repair their Sloop the *Revenge* alias *Royal James*, which was very leaky, and stayed there till about the 29th of September following, waiting till the time of the Hurrican Weather was over, being bound for St. Thomas's next.

That at the time of the taking the said Sloops, belonging to Read and Manwareing, there were on board the Sloop

Revenge alias *Royal James*, or on board the said Scooner, the said Major Stede Bonnet, Robert Tucker Quarter-Master, Edward Robinson Gunner, Thomas Carman, John-William Smith, Neal Paterson, John Lopez, William Hewet, John Levit, Job Beely alias Bayley, William Scot, Thomas Nichols, John Ridge, Zachariah Long, Matthew King, James Robbins, Samuel Booth, William Livers alias Evis, William Wallis, Daniel Perry, Henry Virgin, George Ross, Alexander Annand, William Eddy alias Nedy, William Morrison, John Thomas, James Mullet alias Millet, Thomas Price, James Wilson; but that George Dunkin was only at the taking of Manwareing and Dalton.

That all the said Crew bore Arms freely and voluntarily, and were all consenting and assisting in taking the said two Sloops belonging to the said Read and Manewaring, except the said George Dunkin, who was only at the taking of Manwareing and Dalton, and then bore arms likewise amongst the rest. And as the said last mentioned Sloops lay in Cape Fear, said Bonnet, and all or the greatest part of his Crew, were on board said Read and Manwareing's Sloops; and said Read and Manwareing were detain'd by the said Bonnet and his Crew in Cape Fear River aforesaid, for the space of six or eight Weeks. That there were several Parcels of goods taken by the said Bonnet and his Crew both out of Read and Manwareing's Sloops, but cannot tell the Particulars. That whilst the said Bonnet and Crew lay in Cape Fear River, the said Bonnet and Crew took a little Shallop of about six Tons, belonging to one Dalton, and ripped her up to mend the *Revenge* alias the *Royal James*.

That about the 27th Day of September last, the said Bonnet and Crew, as they lay in Cape Fear River, were attacked by two Sloops, under the Command of Colonel William Rhett, who were fitted out by the Government of South Carolina to take Pirates, as he has heard; and after a Fight of six Hours, the said Bonnet and Crew surrendered themselves under certain Terms, which are now in the Pirate Prisoners Custody, to which he refers himself.

Says, That at the time of the Engagement with the Sloops under the Command of Colonel William Rhett, there were belonging to the said Sloop the Royal James, the said Major Stede Bonnet Commander, Robert Tucker, Edward Robinson, Thomas Carman, John-William Smith, Neal Paterson, John Lopez, William Hewet, John Levit, Job Beely alias Bayley, William Scot, John Ridge, Zachariah Long, Matthew King, James Robbins, Samuel Booth, William Livers alias Evis, William Wallis, Daniel Perry, Henry Virgin, George Ross, George Dunkin, Alexander Annand, William Eddy alias Nedy, William Morrison, John Thomas, James Mullet alias Millet, Thomas Price, and James Wilson; but says, That Thomas Nichols would not bear Arms at the time of the said Engagement, but went down in the Hole all the time, and was very uneasy about two Months before, and wanted to quit the *Revenge*.

And this Deponent further says, That at the time of the Engagement there were likewise on board the said *Revenge* alias *Royal James*, those five several other Persons which were not concerned in the taking any of the Vessels before mentioned, viz. Thomas Gerrat a Molatto, which was one of the said Manwareing's Mariners; Rowland Sharp, which came from North Carolina in a Perriager; John Brierly, which came in a Boat from North Carolina, Robert Boyd, who came with Brierly from North Carolina, and Jonathan Clarke, which came out of Mr Dalton's Sloops; which said five Persons, viz. Garrat, Sharp, Brierly, Boyd, and Clarke, all bore Arms voluntarily at the time of the said Engagement. Says, The last five mentioned Persons were taken at first, but bore Arms freely afterwards in the said Engagement. And says, That John Dalton never bore Arms at the time of the Engagement, nor no other time; nor was the said Dalton concerned in any Act of Piracy whatsoever, to this Deponent's knowledge.

And this Deponent Ignatius Pell deposes, That all and singular the Matters and Things herein before deposed by the said David Herriot are true, in such manner and sort as the same are above declared to be done and transacted from the 4th or 5th of April last; with these additional Circumstance, That the said Bonnet and Crew took out of the Pink they met as they came from Topsail-Inlet an Anchor and Cable; and that said Thatch took out of the Brigantine he took off the Bar of Charles-town fourteen Negroes; and that he heard Thatch tell the Commander of the said Brigantine, That he had got a Baker's Dozen.

That there were a Cable and about twenty one Hogsheads of Molosses taken by said Bonnet and Crew out of said Manwareing's Sloop while they in Delaware-Bay, and some Rum and other Provisions, as the said Bonnet and Crew wanted them. Says, The said Bonnet and Crew took out of the said Read's Sloop, while she lay in Cape Fear River, several Barrels of Pork and Flower, and other Provisions, but knows not the Particulars; as also said Read's Square-Sail, and Topsail, and his Chain-Plates.

Says, The said Bonnet's Crew, about three Days before they came to Cape Fear, shared about ten or eleven Pounds Sterling each Man, which is all the Money they shared.

Says, He heard by the Pirate Crew aboard Thatch, that Thatch took out of the Vessels that were taken off of the Bar of South Carolina, in Gold and Silver, to the Value of one thousand Pounds Sterling Money; and by others of them, to the Value of fifteen hundred Pound Sterling Money: But that when Thatch broke up the Company, and before they came to any Share of what was taken by Thatch, Thatch took all away with him.

23. Bartholomew Roberts writes

Bartholomew Roberts to Lt. General Mathew, 27 September 1720. CO 152/13, f. 34

Bartholomew Roberts is often described as the most successful pirte of the 'golden age', with around 400 captured ships to his credit in a career lasting over three years. His raid on the harbour of Basseterre, St. Christopher's, has been overshadowed in popular pirate studies by Blackbeard's raid on Charlestown [doc. 22] but was, if anything, more spectacular. General Mathew, governor of St. Christopher's had advanced warning of Roberts approach, but the guns of the forts defending the harbour were neglected and lacked ammunition. Roberts sailed into the harbour, urned three ships, left one alone whose captain had agreed to negotiate on behalf of the pirates for fresh meat, and towed the fifth out of the harbour. In the course of the following evening Roberts wrote the letter below to General Mathew, and the following morning attacked a second time. By this time more guns had been moved into the forts and gunpowder had been acquired, and after seven shots hit Roberts' ship, he decided to retire. Roberts had sailed to St. Christopher's to meet a smuggler named Dunn who was selling some of Roberts' spoil on the island, but who was captured before Roberts arrived and, while in prison, warned the authorities of Roberts' imminent arrival.[128]

Royall Fortune, Sept. 27th, 1720.

---

[128] Aubrey Burl, *Black Barty, the Real Pirate of the Caribbean* (Stroud, 2006), pp. 152-158

This comes expressly from me to lett you know that had you come off as you ought to a done and drank a Glass of wine with me and my Company I should not harmed the least vessell in your harbour. Farther it is not your Gunns you fired yt affrighted me or hindred our coming on shore but the wind not proving to our expectation that hindred it.[129] The *Royall Rover*[130] you have already burnt and barbarously used some of our men but we have now a ship as good as her and for revenge you may assure yourselves here and hereafter not to expect anything from our hands but what belongs to a pirate as farther Gentlemen that poor fellow you now have in prison[131] at Sandy point is entirely ignorant and what he hath was gave him and so pray make conscience for once let me begg you and use that man as an honest man and not as a C[132] if we hear any otherwise you may expect not to have quarters to any of your Island, yours,

Bathll. Roberts.

---

[129] While this sounds like bravado, it is probably true. When Roberts arrived in the harbour only two of the forts' guns were capable of firing.

[130] Roberts' first pirate command, the *Royal Rover* was stolen by his lieutenant, Walter Kennedy. Kennedy then left his crew and sailed for England with a group of deserters [**docs 24, 25**]. The remaining crew sailed her to St. Thomas, where she was captured and subsequently taken to Basseterre as a prize and burned there.

[131] Dunn

[132] In the surviving copy of this letter, a transcript of the original made by one of General Mathews' secretaries and sent to the Lords of Trade and Plantations, the rest of the word beginning with C has been omitted deliberately by the copyist, presumably to protect their Lordships' sensibilities. It is doubtful whether Roberts would have been so prurient, but the original has been lost. In any case, the missing word was undoubtedly obscene.

24. Walter Kennedy's deposition

The Examination of Walter Cannady, 28 April, 1721. HCA 1/54, ff. 121-122

*Walter Kennedy's career is fairly well told in the following two documents, especially the second [**doc. 25**]. Briefly, he sailed to New Providence on Woodes Rogers' expedition, joined in a mutiny led by Howell Davis, and served in Davis' crew until he was killed and replaced by Roberts. He continued to serve under Roberts for a while until he stole the Royal Rover, continued piracy on his own account for a time, and eventually returned to England where he was recognised and captured.*

This Examinate saith that about three years since he the Examinate shipped himself as a foremastman on board the *Buck* sloop then lying at Spithead and bound for Providence Island and proceeded in her thither where she delivered part of her outward Cargo and supplied the same with Beef and flower and proceeded from thence to Hispaniola and as soon as she was upon the Coast the Men (whom Capt Brook the Comander of the said sloop had taken in at Providence Island) rebelled and subdued the said Captain and the rest of her Company and confined them, except 2 or 3 who joyned with them and then cut her away from her Anchor and carried her to sea and one Howell Davis took comand of her and took two sloops, the one of which was an English sloop from Filadelphia and the other belonging to the French and the next Day they took another French Vessel and then went

110

and watered at St. Nicholas Island and from thence to the Isle of May and there anchored where all ye men except he the Examinate and another man were set at Liberty. and then (to wit) in the beginning of Febry 1718 a vessel which proved to be the *Robert and Jane* (whereof John Bennet was Comander) appeared in sight and thereupon the Company of the sd sloop split their Cable and gave Chase to her and took her and he the Examinate then had his Liberty. and they afterwards took the *Loyal Merchant*, and then went to Ceralone[133] and there the Examinate quitted the said sloop and entered into the service of another pirate ship called the *Royal Rover* under the Command of Bartholomew Roberts[134] and therein took the *Experiment* (whereof Captain Grant was Comander) and then went to Brazil and there took two Portugal Vessels and afterwards came to Kyan belonging to the French where the said Captain Grant was turned on Shoar, and he the Examinate desired that he might there go on Shoar with him but the Ships Company would not let him go and then they proceeded to an Island about three Leagues from Kyan and there anchored in order to clean the ship and there he the Examinate John Haswell and Thomas Jones[135] cut away the Boat and went to the French upon the Main and there he the Examinate shipt himself on board of an English Vessel called the *Joseph* whereof Captain James was Comr, belonging to Jamaica and bound thither and he proceeded thither in her and from thence came as a Passenger to Ireland in the *Arklin Gally* belonging to Belfast and from thence

---

[133] Sierra Leone
[134] This is not accurate: Davis commanded the *Royal Rover* after the *Buck*, and Roberts succeeded to command on Davis' death. The reason for this lie is unclear.
[135] See **doc. 32**

111

came as a Passenger to England. And saith that the Persons named in the underwritten Schedule were on board of the *Buck* and the *Royal Rover* and were present and aiding and assisting in the taking of the Ships and Vessels beforementioned (to wit).

Thomas Lambun whose father and mother live in Robin Hood's Ally in Suffolk Street in the Mint.

James Bradshaw living at the Cork, a publick house in Cork Lane in Spittlefields and keeps the said house.[136]

John Cherry lodging at the White Lyon, a publick house in Wheeler Street Spittlefields.

Thomas Jenkins (whose true name is Francis Channock) to be heard of at the Sign of the Yorkshire Grey or Golden Bull a little above the wet Dock in Rotherhith.

Charles Radford a Lodger at Mr Hitchcock's, a musician near the Watch house in Brook Street in Ratcliffe

Thomas Haydon, gon to Sea, but when at home lodges at Mrs Prices in Elephant Lane Rotherhith.

Thomas Burnaby – not to be found.

William Callifax at Dublin near Cable Street

John Williams – not to be found

Richard Blanford – not to be found

Nicholas Symonds – not to be found

William Gray – not to be found

---

[136] Of all the people whose names Kennedy gave to the authorities, Bradshaw [doc. 26] was the only one arrested and tried. He as found guilty but pardoned.

George Carlisle – not to be found.

25. Walter Kennedy's views on the pirate life

The Weekly Journal: or British Gazetteer, 29 July, 1721

Walter Kennedy was condemn'd at the Sessions of Admiralty; for that he with other Pirates, had robb'd and plunder'd the Ship, call'd the *Loyal Rover*, andc.

He said he was not 26 Years of Age; born at Pelican-Stairs in Wapping; where he had an Opportunity of learning his Father's Business of an Anchor-Smith. He said he served Her Majesty Queen Anne in the Wars against France; but being told what Lords the Pirates in America were, and that they had gotten several whole Islands under their own Command, he coveted to be one of those petty Princes: That he harboured these aspiring Thoughts, for soon after, he said, he was one of the Sailors sent with Captain Rogers, to recover, if possible, the island of Providence from the Possession of the Pirates; that as soon as they landed on the Shore, the Captain read the Act of Grace, or General Pardon, to evey Pirate that would enter into Her Majesty's Service; whereupon most of the Islanders submitted, and the rest dispers'd and fled, refusing an honest Life. That this Capt. Rogers being confirmed Governor, fitted out two Sloops, and directed them where to sail; that Kennedy was in one of them, they had not gone many Leagues before they held Consultations together, to turn their Vessel into a Pyrate-sloop, and all who refused were to be kill'd, they empty'd the other Vessel of every Thing of Value, then turn'd it afloat; after which they made themselves Masters of two large Ships, and grew strong for an Engagement.

He also said, it was a most unhappy as well as wicked Life; that they were always in dread, and forced to fly from, or fight with every Ship they met. That they were twice obliged to fight in the Night Time, besides their frequent Skirmishes in the Day Time; but they were never taken, it being their Maxim, to overcome, or to escape, or to die.

But once he said, they were in most especial Danger; for having resolv'd to make their Fortunes at once, or to be all Kill'd, they fell in with the whole Portuguese Fleet of 20 and odd sail; finding one Ship separated from the rest they took her without firing a Gun, by bidding a Portuguese among them to call the Captain aboard their Ship, and sending Men to take possession of his Ship. After which he said, they compell'd the Captain to discover which Ship carried the Gold; and attacking it at a time when separated from the rest, they had almost overcome it at once, nor forsook their Violence upon it till they were well nigh surrounded by the whole Portuguese Fleet; and that 'twas owing to their own Swiftness, and to the Cowardice of the Portuguese, that they at all disengag'd themselves.[137]

On the Coast of Brazil, several of them going on Shore, the Governor of the next Port discover'd they were Pyrates; but being unable to cope with such a Number as was then on Land, he invited the Captain, this Kennedy, and 10 others on Shore the next Day, to partake of a Collation at his Seat or

---

[137] Roberts' capture of the *Sagrada Familia* occurred in November 1719 near Bahia in Brazil. See **doc. 27**.

Castle; but they going accordingly, were attack'd by several Negroes, who lay in wait for them by the Sea-side; Davis and all were kill'd but this Kennedy and another, who escaped up a Mountain, and leap'd thence into the Sea, while they expected him below; and was accidentally taken out of the Water alive, by the Boat that carried them to the Shore.[138]

In the whole he appear'd altogether sensible, that Men are widely mistaken who enter into such a vicious Course of Life for worldly Benefit and Advantage.

He said, as for himself, tho' he had receiv'd very great Shares of Booty, it had so ill prosper'd, that he believed he should want a Coffin to cover his Carcass in; That he lost most of his Gold in the Highlands of Scotland, whither their Ships were driven by a Storm, while the captain an Irishman intended for Ireland, but they leaving their Vessel, and separating, and the Captain also there Dying, he himself went for Ireland, but meeting with no Encouragement; nor finding a Maintenance, came for England, and after sometime, was observ'd,[139] apprehended, try'd and convicted.

He was also saying, that he knew Captain Roberts, so known for his Piracies; That he was once First Mate of his Ship; but separated from them on the Coast of Africa, in a stolen Vessel, of which he was chosen Captain, but afterwards got two Ships of above 30 Guns each; That he us'd to say, nothing from the King of England should content him, but the Government of the Leeward Islands; and if he could not

---

[138] Kennedy's chronology and geography are both confused here. The event described took place at Principe, and before the capture of the *Sagrada Familia*.
[139] Kennedy was recognised in London and denounced to the authorities by Thomas Grant, who had been captured by Roberts' company on the coast of Africa [**doc. 53**]

peaceably obtain them, he would e're long hold them by force.

He also said, That he would not be in the high Condition of this Roberts for all his Wealth and his Ships, being assur'd he can have no Peace of Mind, if 'twas only for having murther'd the French Governor of an American Island and hang'd the First Mate for some Minutes, because the said Governor executed one of his best Men whom he catch'd on Shore for robbing him on the Sea with Roberts.

He was very easy he said, to die, and hoped he had fully made his Peace with God; and knew not when he could be better prepar'd to leave this World. Adding that as he had only a Wife, and no Children to provide for, his Thoughts were not at all on this Life.

The Morning of his Execution, he receiv'd the Sacrament with much Attention and Devotion; but appear'd extreamly terrfy'd and concern'd at the near approach of Death. When he was on the Scaffold erected for him, he apprehended he should faint, and call'd for some Water to drink, he requested that the People present might be caused to attend to some few Words he had to say, viz. I am brought to this Place of Shame and Disgrace, for Crimes which fully deserve so vile a Death; and I freely confess my self guilty of the crimes I was convicted of, as well as many other Faults of the like Nature, for which I beg the Pardon of God, and of you my Countrymen; and I hope all here will be warn'd by my dismal Example, and not fancy Happiness can arise from Robbery and Cruelty; and I believe all my former Companions are, or will be, as wretched as I am. I declare that I think my Wife a pious and virtuous Woman, and she

116

was always against my Vices. I die in Charity towards all the World, and hope all will pray for my poor Soul. I pray God preserve my Country.

26. James Bradshaw

The Examination of James Bradshaw, 17 May 1721, HCA 1/54, f. 125

Bradshaw was denounced by Walter Kennedy [doc. 24] and tried alongside him. At his trial he claimed that he had been forced and another pirate, John Eastwell, who had been tried and acquitted previously in Scotland [doc. 27], came to his defence and testified that he really had joined the pirates under duress. The evidence against him however was overwhelming and he was condemned to death, but managed successfully to plead for a pardon.

This Examinate saith that in Janry last was two years he the Dept in the Downs shipped himself as a foremastman on the ship the *Princess* (whereof Captain Abraham Plumb was then Comander)[140] bound to Guinea and Jamaica and from thence to the Port of London, And saith that on the 6th Day of June following as she was trading upon the Coast of Guinea she was taken by a Pirate Ship called the *King James* (whereof Captain Davis was Comr) And saith that the Pirates belonging to her took the Examinate and 9 or 10 thereof the Company of the *Princess* and carried them on board the *King James*[141] and the next Day discharged the *Princess* and he the

---

[140] Bartholomew Roberts was third mate of the *Princess*.

Examinate was obliged to act as a Mariner on board the *King James* for about four Months within which time she took two Ships (to wit) an English ship belonging to the Port of London upon the Coast of Guinea whereof one Grant[142] the mate was Comander, (the master being dead) and another large Vessel upon the Coast of Brazile manned with Portuguese,[143] and also a new England sloop. And then about forty of the Company of the *King James* manned the said sloop in order to come to England and Walter Cannady now a Prisoner in the Marshalseas was then Comander of her. And they sailed to the high Lands in Scotland and there left her and all of them then went on shore there and dispersed in order to go to their respective homes. And he the Examinate travelled from thence by Land on foot to London.

27. Richard Luntly

The Last Speech and Dying Words of Richard Luntly (Edinburgh, 1721)

Richard Luntly was one of Roberts' company who sailed to Scotland with Walter Kennedy and others [**docs 24-26**]. *Along with six of his comrades he was hanged in Edinburgh in January 1721, despite his claims that he had been forced to join the pirates. This was a common defence plea in pirate trials, and only occasionally successful. Luntly was a carpenter, a man whose skills were in*

---

[141] Including Bradshaw's defence witness, John Eastwell.
[142] See **doc. 53**
[143] See **doc. 25**

great need aboard a wooden ship, so it is quite likely that he was
telling the truth, and maintained his innocence until the end.

The great End that all of us purpose to our selves, is
Happiness though our Mistaken Notions, lead us to wrong
Objects to obtain it, no Sublunary Enjoyment is capable of
producing it, for after all the Experiments that have been
made that Way, even by the wisest of Mortals, yet this was
the Result, Vanity and Vexation of Spirit, as for my part I
have Sufficient Reason to Subscribe my Assent to this Truth,
for I could not be contented with staying in the Island of
Barbadoes, and Use the Home Trade; but I must Ship my self
for Guiney, belonging to a Sloop, called, the *Guiney*, then
bound for Gambo[144], and other Places upon the Coast,
Captain William Slade Commander, who Parted or Sailed
from the Island of Barbadoes, in order to proceed his lawful
Trade, for his intended Voyage, upon the 23d Day of
December 1718, and arrived upon the Coast of Guiney, in the
said River of Gambo, upon the eight of February following,
and was taken by the Pirate Davis, who commanded then the
Ship, called, the *King James*, with another Sloop, in
Company, which they called, the *Buck*, and parted with the
Buck in the said River of Gambo, which in a very short Time
after I was taken at the same Place, there happened to come
another Pirate Vessel commanded by one Captain L'Bouse,
which joined in Consort with the Pirate Davis, and Sailed
from the River of Gambo, unto another Place, called,
Seralone[145], where happened to be another Pyrate lying there,[146]

---

[144] Gambia
[145] Sierra Leone
[146] Jeremiah Cocklyn

with several other small Merchant Ships, which said Pirate had taken, some Time before this Pirate had a Ship of thirty Guns, called, the *Murrune galley*, but she being old and not fit for his Purpose, there happened to come in to the Place, in a very short Time afterwards, a Galley belonging to London,[147] which they soon took, and thought her much better than the *Murrune*, so they quite then with their old Ship which they had before, and took to this *Galley* which they had taken belonging to London, and made a Pirate of her, and afterwards the three Pirates joined together in Consort, and Sailed from thence, naming of the other two Ships, the one the *Duke of Ormond*, the other the *Windum*,[148] and in some Time afterwards Sailed down along the Coast, they happened to have some Debate about a Ship which they had taken, and so parted, the other two went together, and left the *King James* by her self, which was Davis great Desire, and the very next Day the *King James*, Lite of[149] a Ship belonging to Ostend, being bound for Guiney and the East Indies, and when Davis came to where she was, not thinking that she was of the Force of Guns, as she was thought, that they would stand no Resistance against them, but the Ostender

---

[147] The *Bird*, commanded by William Snelgrave, whose account of his time as a prisoner of the pirates is one of the most detailed and fascinating of contemporary first-hand accounts of pirates. Regrettably, it is far too long for inclusion here.

[148] Several pirate vessels such as Davis' *King James* bore names which proclaimed their support for the Jacobite cause of the exiled James Stuart. These two ship names also fall into that category: the Duke of Ormond and Sir William Windham were two leading Jacobite figures, and the use of their names by pirates speaks volumes about the breadth of their commitment. For a much deeper analysis of pirates' engagement with Jacobite politics see my article 'Jacobitism and the "Golden Age" of Piracy, 1715-1725', *International Journal of Maritime History*, XXII (2010)

[149] Lighted on, came across.

made such Resistance against them; that it was the next Day at four in the Afternoon before the Ostender did Strike to Davis, and afterwards Davis finding that his Ship was better for his Purpose than the King James was, he took some other Vessels in a short Time afterwards, belonging to London and the Island of Barbadoes, which he obliged then most part of their Men to go along with him upon the Peril of immediat Death, which some of them came with me, and has suffered the same Death as I am now going to do, I shall Name their Names, John Stewart with some others were taken out of the Ship Ostender, which made the Resistance as I have laid down; another poor Man that has suffered, whose Name was William Fenten, which the Pirate Davis gave his Vessel to those Ostenders, that they might go away, and forced the said William Fenton and all their Crew to go along with them, and at last parted with Captain Fenton, and put him on Board of a Ship belonging to London and would not part with any if his Crew by no Means, which you knowing very well that all Pirates carry their own Commission, and will not part with any Man whom they think is any ways Servicable for them. So Gentlemen I shall go away upon my Discourse of the Rest of the Voyage, which my short Time will not me allow to lay down every particular saying of their whole Actions of the Voyage in my Time, I cannot pretend to say it, what was done before, you would think, or at last I should Count my self unwise, to lay down any of the Passages that was before, but to the Truth as I shall say, and so parting with those other two Pirates Ships, after having gone down the Coast with this Ostend Ship whom I have given you an Account of before, and Davis thought her more fit for his Design, Sailing with her in Company along the Coast, until he came to a Place, called, the Bite or Old-cally bar[150] upon the Coast of Guiney, where they came to an Anchor, and consulted whether they should keep both Ships, and after having passed their Approbation they consented for to quit with the *King James*, and take to the other Ship Ostender, thinking she was better for their Design then the *King James* was, and so Davis consented to quite the Ship, the *King James*, and Davis and his Crew with all the forced Men to put them on Board of the Ostender, which they after named the *Royal-Rover*,[151] which is as I believe remaining upon the Sea to this Time, which is the Man that we ever came to got clear of, but having made the hard Attempt as we have done, in taking one of their Prizes away from them, and made our Escape from them, taking all their Treasure away from them, that some of them had got for several Years in that Practice, and after having, Davis parted with the Ship *King James*, in the Bite of Old-cally bar, upon the Coast of Guiney, and left her riding at an Anchor in this Place, forced with the rest of Davis Crew, compelled us that were forced Men to go on Board of the *Rover*, or suffer immediat Death, while they were on Board of the *Rover*, they concluded for to Sail for an Island, called, Princess, belonging to the part of the King of Portugale, and whose Inhabitants dwell there, it is an Island which lyes upon, or were the Latitude of those as I shall Mention, the Island Saint Thome, which lies in or upon the Equinoctial, or upon the Meridian Line, which is the Place that parts the North from the South, and after Sailed and came to this Island Princess, Captain Davis would go on Shore,

---

[150] Calabar, Nigeria, near the Bight of Benin.
[151] See **docs 23, 25, 26**. *Royal Rover* also has Jacobite overtones, the phrase being one of many used to refer to James Stuart.

acquainting the Governour of the said Island that he was a Kings Ship belonging to England, which for some Time was entertained accordingly, till some Passages happened between Davis and the Governour, about some Reasoning why a Kings Ship should not be supplied there, as well in the Wants as in Britain, the Governour taking some Resentment at his Discourse, made it his Business to prepare from him the next Morning, in Order to Receive him with all Friendship; but to his Misfortune they received him and those that were with him in a very Barbarous Manner, which was about the Number of Twelve People, and he and eight more they killed in a very Barbarous Manner, and afterward Davis was killed,[152] they parted from thence, and Sailed away to another Island in the Latitude two Degrees South, who was inhabited by Negroes, where there is good Eatables, such as, Caberitto, or Goat in abundance, and likewise Hog in Abundance, Yams and Putato, in which they made those Natives supply them with as much fresh Stock as supplied us to the Coast of Brazile, and after being supplied at this Island, Sailed away from this Place for an other Island, near the Coast of Brazile, called, Ferdenando, which lyes in the Latitude five Degrees South, which not inhabited, by any Creature, there is several Islands of them which lyes all in a Cluster, but all Barron and Destitute, they thought to got Water there, which at length they found a small Place that yielded some Water, but it being the dry Time, that Way they made a Shift for to fill about nine Buts of Water, and carrined the Ship and departed that Island, and then ranged along the Coast Brazile, as low as the Place, called, Bayhia, or the Bay of all Saints, went as near as they could see their

---

[152] See **doc. 25**

Forts and Shiping, lying in that Place, there cruised for about a Fortnight or there away, of and one in that Bay, but they could not get any Things there, but two Indians that was Fishing for their Father, and gave Captain Roberts an Account that the Fleet was Sailed two Days before he came to Cruise there, which made him very Mad, but they told him there was another Fleet to Sail in a very short Time, so he concluded with his Crew to strike away in Latitude of about 23 Deg. 35 Min. South, and then for to Taik and stand away for the Northward as they did, and met with the Portuguese Fleet, that those two Indians had given Captain Roberts an Account of, they Lite of this fleet of a Place, called, Pernabocko[153], which lyeth to Northward of Cape Augustine in the Latitude of about 7 Deg. 25 Min. South, where Captain Roberts finding them to be all great Ships, excepting three, which he made it his business to take one of the small Ships without firing of a Gun; and afterwards made the Captain of the Ship tell him, which was the best Ship, which proved to be the Vice Admiral of the Fleet, which Roberts came along side off immediatly, and the other thinking he was a French Gollone-haile, and asked him where he was Bound, and Roberts told him on Board of him, and him to come, which immediatly Roberts clapped his four Top-sails a back, and fell on Board of him, and lashed fast along side of his Ship, and then he entered his Men, and in Half an Hour carried her, puting all the Men of the great Ship into the small one, and turned the small Ship away, and kept the great Ship to himself, their Fleet consisting in Number 48 Sail, then all about when they found their Vice Admiral was taken, some of them Run away till the other Men of War came up, and

---

[153] Pernambuco

then they joined and gave Chase, which they had as good sent a Cow after an Hare, and so Captain Roberts and his Quarter-Master with the rest of his Crew concluded to go to a Place, called, Ciana[154] in the West Indies, where they were, and fitting of their two Ships, with a Sloop in Company, which they had taken some Days before belonging to Road-Island,[155] which they fitted upon Speed and Mounted 10 Guns, besides several other small Swivile Guns, so lying in this Place, and fitting both their Ships for to go, and lye in Latitude of Barbadoes, and Cruise there all Winter, and take as many Ships with Provision and Men as they should have Occasion for to proceed for the East Indies; and we that were forced Men, were compelled by the force of Arms to do Things that our Conscience thought to be Unlawful; we were one Night consulting to Run away with the Sloop, and make the best of our Way to the West Indies; there happened one of the Pirates to over-hear us, and went and told Captain Roberts of it, and his Quarter-Master,[156] and immediatly all Hands were called up to know what they should do with us, some of them was for shooting of us, other some not, and so they consented to put us away upon a Desolate Island, Esphealy,[157] we that was first, which was Richard Jones and my self, and William Fenton, they happened to see a Sail, which upon Captain Roberts and about 40 more of his Crew went away, in Order to take the said Vessel, but returned not that Night, next Day his Quarter-Master went and fitted both

---

[154] Cayenne
[155] Rhode Island
[156] Walter Kennedy
[157] Unknown. Probably one of the Iles du Salut, of which Devil's Island is the third largest, and was where Roberts' company were based at the time of the incident.

Ships, and Sailed in Order to Lite of Captain Roberts, but could not find him, so they gave the Portuguese Ship unto him that was Captain of the Sloop, and told him where Roberts was, and bid him to follow them to the Latitude of Barbadoes, and there they should find them there, and after in a short Time afterwards took this Vessel in which we came to Britain in, and in hopes to get Justice, knowing very well that if we had found any Justice, you could not have brought us to an untimely End. But God forgive you all, and I shall indeed, for I think I have made an happy Exchange. I shall say no more upon this Respect, but shall Praise my God for all Thing, and shall conclude with this saying, Lord be Merciful to me a poor Sinner.

Richard Luntly.

Written with my own Hand the 9th Day of January 1721.

28. The petition of John Massey and George Lowther

EXT 1/261, ff.197-199

John Massey, the author and co-signatory of this petition, was a military officer in the service of the Royal African Company, who arrived at Fort James in the mouth of the Gambia River aboard the Bumper Galley, *of which ship George Lowther was second mate. Massey found that the victualling of his garrison was in the hands of the local merchants and far from adequate, while a dispute between Lowther and the captain of the* Bumper Galley *simmered into an outright rift. Eventually the rift turned to mutiny and*

Lowther's suggestion of sailing home to England met with approval from Massey and his soldiers. At this point Massey almost certainly believed that the plan was to return to England, but once at sea Lowther suggested a course of piracy. Massey and some of his supporters took an opportunity to leave the pirates and sailed for Jamaica in a schooner they had captured. There he surrendered himself to the governor and obtained permission to go to sea to hunt down his erstwhile colleague, Lowther. Unsuccessful, he returned to England and wrote to the directors of the Royal African Company with a full account of the mutiny and subsequent piracies. He then went to the Lord Chief Justice's chambers to let the authorities know where he could be found if an arrest warrant was issued for him.When he was arrested there were no witnesses available to testify against him, but he insisted that he had written the letter and was sent for trial. At his trial he once more admitted writing the letter and gave a long speech expanding on its contents. Some witnesses had been found and he invited them to offer corrections if he erred in his version of events. His friends claimed that 'they never knew him do a Rational Action, and that he was a poor crazy rattle-brain'd Fellow', and his inevitable death-sentence came with a plea for mercy to be extended to him on the grounds of his apparent insanity. Nevertheless, he was hanged on 26 July 1723.[158] *The first few pages of Captain Johnson's chapter on Lowther in the* General History of the Pyrates *follows the content of the petition so closely that it is almost certain that Johnson met and interviewed Massey while the latter was in London, probably during the time of his incarceration.What Johnson wrote about Massey's activites after the mutiny described in the petition paints him as keen to be free of*

---

[158] *The British Journal*, 13/7/1723; *Weekly Journal or Saturday's Post*, 27/7/1723

the pirates,[159] and was presumably retailed to Johnson by Massey himself, but the testimony of Alexander Thompson [doc. 30] tells a very different story.

To His Most Sacred Majesty George, by the Grace of God King of Great Britain, France and Ireland, Defender of the Faith andc.

May it Please Your Majesty,

Your Majesty's clemency having given liberty to ye African Company of England to enrol artificers and soldiers and transport them to Africa where the said Company had a settlement in the River Gambia on ye North Coast of Africa w[hi]ch was reduced by ye French in the late War and amongst many of Your Majesty's dutiful (but miserable) subjects happened to be one who went in ye Quality of Capt Lieut Engineer the next Commanding Officer to Col[one]l Whitney who is the Company's appointed Governor there, he is a man of honour and integrity and hath served the African Company as far as ye merch[an]ts in Africa did permit him they having ye prerogative in Africa, the Governor being very old and hath not had one hours health since his landing which caused the aforesaid merchants to usurp and tyrannize over him and the artificers and soldiers under his command with such barbarity being an evident proof of their clandestine designe making it their chief study to enrich themselves in a small time by bringing their scant money to a head without having any regard to ye Company's interest and entirely without thought of supporting a settlement.

---

[159] Johnson, *General History*, pp. 304-311

Two of Your Majesty's ships (vizt) the *Swallow*[160] and *Weymouth* w[i]th the transports designed for Africa rendezvouzd at Portsmouth where Coll Whitney the appointed Governor went on board the *Swallow* as passenger.

All the fleet saild but the ship Your Majesty's dutifull subject was in with sixty five artificers and soldiers provd so leaky that the commander was obliged to leave the fleet and return to Portsmouth from thence we saild to Plymouth where the African Company sent to us another ship called ye *Bumper* which took in our cargo together wth ye artificers and soldiers before mentioned and accordingly pursued our voyage.

When arrived at Gambia we had ye melancholly news that ye soldiers and artificers that were undr ye command of Lieut Shott to the number of between fifty and sixty were ye most part of them dead and ye rest allmost perishing for want of necessaries.

This unfortunate lieut wth Ensign Sooly, and ye chief chyrurgeon[161] amongst ye rest dyed for want of due care.

Coll Whitney at the arrival of our ship told me he wanted bread. The place where these unfortunate wretches met their deaths is called Jollifree[162], a heathenish village not producing any thing to drink but water yt the Negro's daily wash themselves in.

---

[160] HMS *Swallow*, commanded by Chaloner Ogle, was the ship that finally brought down Bartholomew Roberts' gang [**doc. 75**]
[161] surgeon
[162] Jufureh, Gambia

All our men was in perfect health when arrived. I was orderd to land them upon James Island a sterile place not affording any thing that was necessary for ye use of man.

The Merchants promised they would performe every thing that was mentioned in the Company's printed proposalls and signed by their sec[re]t[ar]y, they being ye only persons appointed by the Company to supply us, the Gov[eno]r being excluded from every thing but martial discipline and fortifye a place for Trade, but they acting quite reverse to ye Company's proposalls much augmented ye misery of Your Majesty's distressed subjects upon ye island and ye Govr coming there but a few days before we left ye place, he wth the merchants finding the country so destructive that they continually reside on board the ships.

A further rehearsall of Your Majesty's dutifull subjects miserys while upon James Island in a few days after ye men was landed they were in Generall seas'd[163] with a flux w[hi]ch proceeded from eating salt Provisions without any sort of Bread and having nothing to Drink but bad Water. The Men under my Command besides thirty black slaves have been without Water twenty four hours and when supply hath come it hath been half salt Water.

Some of the Weakly men that had Money due to them desired of ye M[er]chants to support them upon Acc[oun]t of their Wages, They Answered them there was no allowance granted from the Company neither would they supply them wth what was Necessary upon any Terms, but proposed the[164] have shot three or four Men for an Example to prevent the

---

[163] seized
[164] to

rest makeing their just Complaints upon which sundry of the Men gave Warning it being Expressly said in ye Company Proposals (Vizt)

That each Man after six Months Notice given should have his passage home at the Company's Charge, But the Merchants look upon this warning as nothing and told ye Men They should stay till they Rotted There being none of the Drs alive but one who lay at ye Point of Death, the sick lyeing in a languishing Condition Vizitted Once in three of four days by the ships Dr and had no other prospect but to Dye there neither being due Care, Provision, nor Lodging suitable for any Christian.

The Commander of ye *Bumper* aforementioned Contracted with his Men in England that they should not stay in Africa but make a Voyage to America and from thence to England but ye Merchants order'd that ye said ship should stay in ye Country as Guard ship wch would have Rend[e]red her for ever incapable of performing a Voyage.

The last Guard ship yt lay there was Man[ne]d three sev[era]ll times, the Country being so Destructive and hath not left above three Men alive, which is all ye Men that this dismall Country spar'd since the settlem[en]t in the Duke of York's time, and we humbly presume that from time to time there hath been sevll Hundreds of Men Transported to their destruction in this part of Affrica.

These frightful Omens with other sundry substantiale reasons the seamen found of Bondage, Barbarous, and Unhumane Usage from their Commander Charles Russell induc'd them to a Resolution to return home. And I finding ye Major part of the Passengers brought over in two ships Dead, and the

131

rest at ye point of Death the Men under my Command on James Island were afflicted with sickness to a very high degree.

These Inevitable Proofes of Destruction forced me to Use my utmost Endeavour to preserve the Lives of Yr Majesty's Dutifull subjects whose distressed Condition renders them Incapable of future service.

Therefore with humble submissions, I on Acct of they[165] Destressed Artificers and soldiers, and Mr Lowther, second Mate of the said *Bumper* upon acct of ye sailors, We Yr Majesty's Dutifull subjects thought ourselves bound in Duty to Relieve those poor wretches from a Visable and Tyranicall Calamity.

Wherefore we seas'd ye sd *Bumper* for ye use of ye Distressed without doing this neither We nor any of our Miserable Country Men would ever had opportunity to return home Priviledge to have sent Intelligence to England of Our Miserable state.

When we had seas'd ye sd ship We sent to the Merchts in Order to have treated wth them for ye sustenance of Life and sent sundry Times to the Govr but instead of anyone Coming to doe us Justice thereof, of ye ships that lay in the Harbour fired at us likewise fired from ye fort, wch Obliged us to put ye ship we are now in a posture of Defence and get Ready for ye sea with a small quantity of Water and Provisions, there being Eighty Men on Board besides Officers

---

[165] the

We Brought away all the sick men that were upon ye Island but could not have an Opportunity to bring they small Number wch Remained on ye Main

We Brought from the Island Eight Pipes of Wine wch was for ye use of all ye white Men that was upon the Island but the Merchants would not allow any thing that was necessary, Notwithstanding ye Company Ordered yt Each Officer should have an Equall Allowance of Wine and yt Each Artificer and Soldier should have a pint every Day. The country being so Unhealthy that it is impossible for White Men to Live in w[i]thout some Liquor to support nature, Note the Company gave Orders for such allowance to be made to ye artificers and soldiers upon Acct. of their pay they men being in a weak Condition would have Comply'd wth these proprosalls, if they might have had the same granted but ye Merchts would not allow any thing sufficient for their sustenance.

We delivered [to] the Merchts what they required of ye ship's Cargo wch was ye Major part of the Cargo yt Remained in ye sd *Bumper*, we also returned them one Pipe of Wine, When they Desisted sending for ye rest of the Cargo wth a full Resolution to make ye best of our Way for England but coming to a second consideration supposing the African Company will be ready to Charge us wth Fellony although our Designes was only to fly from ye apparent Death of Perrishing as they rest of our Country Men did for Want of Necessary sustenance.

We therefore humbly implore Your Majesty's Gracious Pardon for the Reliefe of Yr Majesty's miserable subjects who are now Tossing upon ye seas Depending on Yr

Majesty's Unpar[al]elled Goodness and Clemency not daring to come near any Christian port.

But soe long as our small store will support us we shall live in Hopes that Yr Majesty's Royall Pardon will be Extend to e Enlargement of Yr Majesty's miserable subjects who if not relieved before our small stores be Expended Necessity will oblige us to take some Irregular method we never designed.

The unexpressible miserys of Yr Majesties Dutifull subjects who now hopes to Receive Yr Majesty's mercifull Pardon is intolerable not haveing any Conversation nor hopes of any but what we have aversion to. But so soon as Yr Majtys Great Goodness shall grant yr Royall Permission for our return we will not only bring home ye aforesd ship and ye remaining part of her Cargo wth our Dutifull acknowldegmts of Your Majy's Gracious favour but will use our utmost Endeavours to perswead all ships we meet wth yt use any Irregular practice to return wth us and as providence hath been pleased to Release us from Imminent death wee humbly hope yr Majty will take our Miserable Case into Consideration and Defend us from all other.

The Burthen of the ship we are in is about Two hundred and fifty Tunn Carry's Twenty two Gunns and hath on board one hundred men besides Officers, all wch humbly beg leave to subscribe ourselves yr Majesty's Dutifull subjects who always did and ever will vindicate Yr Majesty's succession and the Posterity of Yr Majesty's Royall Issue whilst we have Life, and shall in Duty Bound for Yr Majesty and Yr Illustrious Progeny ever pray andc.

We humbly beg Yr Majesty will be pleased to order this Declaration to be Printed for the satisfaction of our friends and Relations.

On board the *Delivery*[166] al[ia]s *Bumper* in the Latitude of Barbados Distance seven Leagues, July 22nd 1721.

John Massey, George Lowther.

29. William Ingram

The Examination of William Ingram, 17 September, 1724. HCA 1/55, ff. 75-76

William Ingram was a member of Thomas Anstis' company, and the only one to be executed in England for his crimes. Anstis began his piratical career in the summer of 1718 when, in company with Howell Davis, Walter Kennedy, and a handful of others, he took part in a mutiny aboard the Buck. *Anstis was a prominent member of Davis' company and was probably one of the 'Lords' of the pirate council, the select group of elite pirates who ran the ship and company. After Davis was killed, Anstis continued to serve under Roberts for two years in a variety of roles, sometimes as an officer, sometimes as boatswain, and sometimes a foremastman. In 1721 Anstis was placed in command of Roberts' consort vessel, the* Good Fortune, *and after falling out with Roberts decided to slip away with his ship and begin an independent career. Within a short time Anstis commanded two ships, the* Good Fortune *and a newly acquired 32-gun ship, the* Morning Star, *which he placed under the command of gunner John Fenn. At the end of 1721 Anstis and his company wrote to the British government begging for a pardon, and ceased their piracy while they waited for a response. Eventually hearing that no response was forthcoming,*

---

[166] The *Bumper* was renamed after the mutiny which, despite the protestations of innocence contained in the petition, was a damning sign of piracy to follow.

they resumed their piracy, but while anchored in the Cayman Islands were attacked by HMS Hector *and HMS* Adventure, *only narrowly escaping by using oars when the wind died down. Anstis' poor success as a commander led his men to depose him and place Fenn in command, but while the pirates were cleaning their ships at Tobago in May 1723 they were attacked by HMS* Winchelsea. *Many of the pirates fled into the hinterland of the island, where Fenn and eight others were rounded up by the Royal Navy, taken to Antigua, and there seven of them were executed. Anstis and several of his supporters managed to escape in the* Good Fortune, *but most of the company, many of whom were unwilling conscripts forced to join the pirates, were tired of piracy. One night, shortly after their escape from Tobago, the unwilling members of the crew murdered Anstis and his key supporters in their sleep, and took the ship to Curacao, where they handed over those pirates whom they had not killed, and were granted a pardon by the Dutch authorities there.* [see also **docs 32, 42-43, 46, 61**]

This Examinate saith that about six years since he this Examinate went as a passenger on board the ship *Sarah Galley* (whereof one James Atkinson was then mr) lying in the Downes bound upon a voyage to Jamaica, where they arrived about two months afterwards which was (as he believes) about the month of May 1718 and in about ten days afterwards he this Examinate entred himself as a foremastman onboard the ship called the *Bennet* sloop then at Jamaica bound on a voyage to a fort called the Royal de Hatch[167] in the Spanish West Indies, but in her passage thither, the said sloop was taken by a Spanish man of war called (as this Informant thinks according to his best remembrance) the *Don Francisco*, and by her carried into

---

[167] Rio de la Hacha

Carthagena where this Examinate and some others of the Crew were kept prisoners onboard the said man of war for about 11 months at which time the Spanish war with England[168] broke out whereupon this Examinate and the other prisoners were released and put onboard his Maties man of war called the *Happy Snow*, which was then riding at anchor in the Road of Carthagena, and carried him the Examinate and others to Jamaica again, where he the Examinate continued about a fortnight, and he then entred himself as a foremastman onboard the sloop called the *George* (whereof Capt Latherdale was Mr) bound on a voyage to the Island of Hispaniola in the Spanish West Indies with several negroes on board, under convoy of the *Dudley Castle* man of war, but by the stress of Weather was drove back to Port Royall in Jamaica and in about a Weeks Time set sail again from Jamaica to Hispaniola where they arrived in the year 1719 and the Negroes were there disposed of and the said sloop *George* was there laden with Indigo and Clarett with which they sailed back to Jamaica where she arrived about the latter End of the Year 1719 and soon afterwards this Examinate entred himself as a Foremastman on the the sloop called the *Ruby*, Captain Fernando, bound on a Voyage to a Place call the Grout[169] near Portobello in the Spanish West Indies with negroes and Bale Goods on Board which were then disposed of, and further this Exmainate saith he made two other Voyages with the said Captain Ferdinando of the like Nature, and he afterwards made several other such trading Voyages in the West Indies on Board other sloops till about the middle

---

[168] The War of the Quadruple Alliance
[169] More commonly known in English as Monkey Key, a small island lying off the coast of Portobelo, Panama.

of the Year 1721 about which Time he and several others were hired by one Captain John Lewis of Kings Town in Jamaica to go to Cape Caterhe[170] in the Spanish West Indies to cut Logwood and they were accordingly sent thither on Board a sloop provided for that purpose where they arrived, and after they had so been there about two Months a pirate Brigantine called the *Fortune* whereof one Thomas Anstice was Commander of about 18 Guns and near one hundred men came and lay at anchor near the said Cape to careen, soon after which several of the said Brigantines Men armed with small Arms came in a Boat on Shore and forced and compelled this Examinate and seven or eight others (that were employed in cutting of Logwood there as aforesaid) to go with them into the said Boat and so on Board the said Pirate Brigantine which they coulnd not resist they having no arms to defend themselves and they being come on Board the said Brigantine's Crew forced and obliged the Examinate and the others with him so taken to sign their Articles of Piracy, and also to swear to be true to that Crew threatening them with death in case of Refusal, and in about a Week afterwards the said Brigantine sailed away towards Campechy Bay with this Examinate and others aforesaid on Board, and arrived at Campechy Bay where there being a Spanish Ship at anchor laden with Logwood the said pirate Crew fired at the said Spanish ship which obliged her company to quit the same and go off in the Long boat, and then several of the said Pirate Crew went on Board and plundered and rifled the said Spanish ship of some small arms of little Value, and then burnt the said ship but this Examinate was not one of them that went so on Board, after

---

which the said Pirate Brigantine went a Cruising about Jamaica for about two or three Months during which Time the said Pirate Crew came up with the Ship called *Don Carlos* (of which one Lott Nickens was Master) then at Sea near Cape St. Anthony and several of the said Pirate Crew (but not this Examinate) went on Board the said *Don Carlos* and plundered and rifled her of Gold and Silver of the Value of one thousand Pounds and upwards (as this Examinate believes) which was by the Captain and the Quartermaster of the said pirate Brigantine shared among the said pirate Crew and this Examinate was obliged to take his share thereof which he believes might amount in Value to about ten or twelve pounds, and the said pirate also came up with several small Vessels but took little or Nothing from any of them after which the said pirate Brigantine went and lay at anchor near the Island called Ratan towards the Island of Cuba to careen, and then went again a Cruising about Jamaica for about three Months according to this Examinate's best Remembrance as to the Time and afterwards went towards the Island of Pines near Jamaica[171] and lay at anchor near the said Isle to careen but there being no Convenience for cleaning they there cut a Main Mast and then went again to Ratan, after which they went through the Gulph to the Windward of Barbadoes where they arrived in or about the month of January in the Year of Our Lord 1722/3 and that in their Way to Tobago they came up with a Dutch Merchant ship called the Morning Starr loaden with sugar and tooke her as prize near Surinam and some of the said pirate Crew of which this Examinate was one were obliged to go on

---

[171] Presumably Isla de la Juventud, though it is much closer to Cuba than Jamaica.

Board her, and after they had sent away the master and several of the men belonging to the said Dutch Ship they were obliged to dispose of the Sugars on Board her by giving some away and by throwing some over Board, and then they were also obliged to carry her to the Island called Chymarnees[172] near Jamaica and to make her a pirate ship also, but that soon after their arrival at Chymarnees she was lost by Stormy Weather and the said pirate Brigantine proceeded to Tobago. And further this Examinate saith that about 14 Days after their said arrival at Tobago this Examinate and about sixteen others left the said pirate Brigantine and came away in a sloop (which had been before taken by the said pirate Brigantine) from thence to a Sandy Bay near Bristol[173] in England where he left the said sloop and came away to London and arrived there about April 1723 from which Time he hath used the Fishing Trade upon the English Coast till he was apprehended by Virtue of a Warrant from the Right Honble the Lords Commissioners of the Admiralty.

30. Alexander Thompson

The Information of Alexander Thompson, 2 March 1722. HCA 1/55, ff. 23-24

Thompson was one of the crew of the Bumper *(which he confusingly refers to as the* Gamboa Castle *throughout) who took part in the mutiny led by George Lowther and John Massey* [doc. **28**]. *He left the pirates at the same time as Massey, and his version*

---

[172] Cayman Islands
[173] Possibly Sandy Bay near Weston-Super-Mare, though other related sources suggest that the pirates came ashore nearer Minehead.

of events differs somewhat from that described by Charles Johnson in his General History of the Pyrates, *which was probably told to him by Massey himself. Of the two sources, Thompson's testimony is probably the more reliable, particularly as he made no attempt to exculpate himself.*

This Informant saith that on or about the 12th Day of June 1720 he this Informant being one of the Boats Crew belonging to the ship the *Gamboa Castle* (whereof Charles Russell was Comander) in the service of the Royal African Company of England and being then in the River of Gamboa he the Informant and the rest of the Boats Crew were ordered by George Lowther the 2d mate in the Absence of the said Comander to go on Shoar to a Castle upon a small Island and to bring off from thence on board the said ship Captain John Massey and between 30 and 40 soldiers who were under his the sd Massey's Comand at which time Mr Dudley the chief mate was confined to his Cabin by the sd 2d mate and thereupon he the Informant and the sd Boats Crew went on Shoar and brought off the said Massey and his soldiers. And then they the sd Massey and Lowther took upon themselves the Comand of the sd ship and sent the Boat on Shoar again to fetch off the Wine and Provisions form the sd Castle and the same were brought on board. And then they sent the sd chief mate on Shoar, sailed away with the sd Ship and named her the *Delivery*. And as soon as they were got out at Sea they the sd Massey and Lowther and the sd Soldiers and the sd Ships Company agreed to go a pirating And took oaths and entered into Articles in Writing for that purpose and prepared black Colours. And about 5 or 6 weeks afterward in the Latitude of Barbados they took a Brigantine belonging to

141

Boston (whereof one Douglass was Comander) and took out of her 3 or 4 Casks of Mackerel and Sturgeon or thereabouts and a Cask of Beer and gave the sd Douglass some Arms, Iron and other Goods belonging to the sd Royal African Company. And they kept company with the sd Brigantine about two Days and then discharged her. And saith that they took her in the night time and as soon as it was Day light they hoisted their black Jack, but before they saw her they made a clear ship that they might be ready to fight if there should be Occasion and the sd Massey put the sd souldiers into a fighting posture and about 5 or 6 Days afterwards they were watering at the Island of Dominico[174] under English Colours and a French sloop coming into the Bay they hailed her and desired yt some of her Company would come on board and thereupon about 6 or 7 of their hands in their boat came on board the sd *Gamboa Castle* and were imediately bound and confined and he ye Informant and nine others of the Company with one McDonnell a sergeant of the Soldiers by the Order of ye sd Massey and Lowther went on board the sd Sloop double armed and brought her to an Anchor by the side of the said Ship *Gamboa Castle* and then took out of her and put on board the *Gamboa Castle* two or three and thirty Anchors[175] of Brandy, about six hogsheads of Clarrett and about seventy pounds in Money and plundered the Master and men having first broad open the Cabin and the Chests and hatches. And they the sd Massey and Lowther locked up the sd Money in an iron bound Chest which was called the Companys Chest to the lock of which Chest there were two keys and the sd Massey kept one and the sd Lowther kept the

---

[174] Dominica in the Lesser Antilles
[175] Anker: a small cask containing around 35 litres

142

other and the said Massey had a pair of gold Buttons which were found in a Bag amongst some of the Money, and there were ten of the Company of the sd Sloop carried on board ye *Gamboa Castle* where their hands were tyed behind them and they were confined in the Roundhouse by Order of the sd Massey and Lowther and the next Day they were set at Liberty and sent on board ye sd Sloop and they hoysted the black flag and wore the same all the time they were at Dominico and they then proceeded to St Cruz and there hoisted English Colours and afterwards the black flag and there was a new boat lying there and the men belonging to her left her and ran away into the woods and thereupon they manned her and brought her off and from thence they sailed to Hispaniola where they wore the black flag and chased a Scooner on Shoar and her men leaving her they manned her and brought her off. And then the sd Massey and Lowther having quarrelled he the sd Massey with the Informant and 12 Soldiers left the *Gamboa Castle* and went on board ye sd Scooner and he the sd Massey then declared that he would take the first ship that they should meet, but there not being any sailor on board besides him the Informant they were obliged to put into Jamaica where they surrendered themselves to Sr Nicholas Laws the Governor who thereupon sent out a small Man of War to seek for the sd *Gamboa Castle*. And saith that when the sd Massey left her he took out of the aforesd Chest about twenty pounds in Money, the aforesd gold Buttons and some Cloth and Silk to make Cloaths which were taken from the Ma[ste]r of the aforesd French sloop. And further saith that when they came from the River Gamboa the time aforesd they brought from thence some Perukes[176] which were then on board the sd ship and which belonged to Coll Whitney ye Gov:r of the aforesd Castle and which were taken from the rest of his things by the sd Massey when the rest were sent on Shoar to the said Collonel.

31. Philip Roche

The Examination of Philip Roche, 11 April, 1723. HCA 1/55, ff. 36-41

Philip Roche and his comrades barely count as pirates of the 'golden age' and would probably remain unheard of today had Captain Johnson not included an account of their misdeeds,[177] which included murder and theft at sea (technically piracy) but no seizure of other ships, in his General History of the Pyrates. *Johnson's account was largely drawn from the dying confession of Richard Neal, printed in* The Weekly Journal: or British Gazetteer, *8 December 1722. Roche's own account differs from Neal's, largely by denying his own leading part in their crimes. Since Neal's account was given at a time when he was coughing and urinating blood and begging for a priest to hear him confess his sins, and since he made no attempt to conceal his own involvement, we may assume that his, and subsequently Johnson's, version is the closer to the truth. Roche, Neal, Wise and Pierce Cullen [doc. 76] were all arrested and taken to London: Neal and Cullen both died in prison; Wise was never brought to trial and so presumably was set free as a result of Neal's assertion that he was an unwilling*

---

[176] wigs
[177] Johnson, *General History*, pp. 372-376

accomplice; only Roche was brought to trial, on the same day as John Massey [**doc. 28**], *and was executed some months after his capture. Andrew Cullen was never caught.*

This Examinate saith that he was bred to the Sea Service and hath been Master of several Ships. And in the Month of September 1721 he being at Cork wrote and sent a Letter to Peirce Cullen at Shillbaggen in the County of Wexford informing him that he the Examinate was going Master of a Vessel belonging to James Roch of Kingsale and James Galway of Cork and that if he thought it worth his while to come to Cork he might have a better Prospect of Busyness there than at Waterford and that there were several Ships lying there. And about a Fortnight afterwards the sd Cullen arrived at Cork and came to the Examinate. And he the Examinate recommended him to several Persons as a Master of a Ship. And then he the Examinate being disappointed of going Master of the sd Ship resolved to go as a Passenger to Nants (where he was well known) in order to get an Employment there. And he the Examinate informed the said Cullen thereof, and some time afterwards Richard Neal and Andrew Cullen the Brother of the sd Peirce Cullen came to Cork. And he the sd Peirce Cullen told the Examinate that he had sent for Richard Neal and Andrew Cullen thither. And they being all four of them out of Busyness and he the Examinate having some Days before (to wit) in the said Month of September agreed with Peter Tartoue Master of the *St. Peter* about 40 Tonns then lying at Cork bound for Nants, to go as a Passenger thither he the sd Peirce Cullen agreed to go as a Passenger to Nants with him, he the sd Peirce saying that he saw no Likelyhood of getting an Employment at

Cork. And he the Examinate went with the sd Peirce Cullen
to the sd Peter Tartoue to ask him if he would carry the sd
Peirce Cullen as a passenger to Nants and he agreed to carry
the said Peirce Cullen as a Passenger thither for a moydore.[178]
And some time afterwards they the sd Peter Tartoue and the
said Peirce Cullen drinking several times together and
becoming well acquainted with each other he the said Peirce
prevailed upon the said Peter Tartoue to carry the said
Andrew Cullen and Richard Neal as Passengers to Nants.
And about 3 or 4 Days afterwards the sd Vessel fell down the
River to ye Passage. And he the Examinate fearing that she
was gon to sea he hyred a horse and went down by Land and
finding that she was not gon and the Master informing him
that he should not go away that Night he returned to Cork.
And the same Night or the next Day about the Dusk of the
Evening he the Examinate and ye sd Peirce Cullen went
down to the Passage in a boat with the Tide, at which time
his the Examinate's Chest had been on board the Vessel a
Day or two. And he does not know what ship or Person the
sd Boat belonged to and they met the sd Richard Neal and
Andrew Cullen at Passage where they all lay on Shoar that
Night. And the next Day he the Examinate went on board the
sd Vessel to help to carry her to Cove where he went on
Shoar and there he met the sd Peirce and Andrew Cullen and
Richard Neal. And they all lay a Night or two on Shoar there.
And then he the Examinate went on board in the Ships boat
and the sd Cullens and Richard Neal soon afterwards came
on board in a hired Boat at which time the Customs house
Boat was gon off from the Vessel, and they sailed away for
Nants being laden with Beef, and when they had been a Sea a

---

[178] Moidore: a Portuguese gold coin.

few Days, being about 20 Leagues to ye W:S:W of Scilly the sd Richard Neal (as the Examinate was informed) quarrelled or pretended to quarrel with one of the French mariners of the sd Ship, and threw him over board, at which time he the Examinate was between Decks and he was also informed that the sd Richard Neal went upon Deck to help two of the French mariners who were handing the foresail, at which time there was a storm and the vessel lay by under her Reef Mainsail. And he was likewise informed that the sd Neal quarrelled or pretended to quarrel with them concerning their handing the Sail and that as soon as he had thrown one of them over board the other cryed out 'Au Moy'. And he the Examinate the sd Cullens and the rest of the French Men (to wit) 4 or 5 Men and a boy hearing the sd mariner cry out 'Au Moy', they all went upon deck. And the said French Men took up handspikes or other things which fist came to hand, and struck at the sd Neal, and the said Cullens assisted the sd Neal. And they the said Neal and the said Cullens knocked down all the sd French mariners and the Boy as they came athwart them and threw them over board and afterwards, the sd Peirce Cullen took the boat hook from the Master and beat and wounded him very much and in a very cruel and barbarous manner and knocked him down. And he the said Master then begged for mercy and that they would not throw him over board, nothwithstanding which they threw him over board.[179] And the next Morning they the sd Neal and Cullens consulted where to go to get more hands. And he the Examinate asking them what they designed to doe and telling

---

[179] Roche's account of the murder of the Frenchmen tallies more or less with other accounts, though other accounts, particularly Charles Johnson's, suggest that Roche rather than Neal was the ringleader, and that the murder of the Frenchmen was pre-planned rather than the result of an argument.

them that wherever they went they would be discovered by the Papers they told him that they could not be discovered by any but themselves. And that when they came to any Port or Place they would report that two of their Men fell over board and that if he the Examinate would not consent to say and doe as they did they would serve him as they had served the French Men that he might not discover them or to that effect. And then they talked of making for some part of Spain and the Wind not being fair they agreed to beat the sea and to wait for a fair Wind. And accordingly they crossed the Channel and made the Land of Ireland and then wore the Vessel and stood over again and a few Days afterwards (to wit) in or about the latter end of October or the beginning of November they hailed a Vessel from Lisbon belonging to Hamburgh or bound thither. And he the Examine or the sd Peirce Cullen told them that two of their men were dropped over board and that they were bound for Spain. And saith that the Company of the said Hamburgh Vessel advised them to bear up Channel and to get to the first harbour that they could and to get more hands and they kept company with them till night and then lost sight of them. And the next Days made in for the Land and made the Start[180] and there a Pilot came on board and carryed them to Dartmouth, and before they got in there the said Cullens and Neal agreed that he ye Examte should declare himself to be Master of the Vessel and should act as such. And that the sd Peirce Cullen should pass for the Merchant or Super Cargoe. And he the Examinate telling the sd Peirce Cullen that the Papers would discover them he ye sd Cullen told the Examinate that he would alter them, and accordingly did alter them by striking

---

[180] Start Point, Devon

out the Name (Tartoue) and inserting the Name (Roch). And when they came to Dartmouth the sd Peirce Cullen ordered the Examinate to procure a Carpenter and to agree with him to run a spare Deck upon the Vessel and to alter her to a Snow by taking down the Misen Mast, and he the sd Cullen pro[c]ured one Taylor a Carpenter to doe the same; And he the sd Cullen and the aforesd Neal before she came to Dartmouth took off the Figure that was in her Head and painted her. And at Dartmouth the sd Carpenter run a spare Deck[181] upon her and took down the Mizen Mast and put up a Lyon in her Head. And then by the Permission of the Officers of the Customes part of her Cargoe was sold to defray the Charges thereof. And he the Examinate there shipped John Rossiter, Robert Connor, John Dent, and John Fitzgerald for Ostend and the Name of the Vessel was changed to the Mary. And after they were gon from Dartmouth the sd Peirce Cullen told the Examinate that there was a Master of a Pink there bound for Nants who knew the *St. Peter* and that he the sd Master had put a Letter into ye Post to be sent to Cork and that he ye sd Cullen had got the sd Letter from the Post Office, and he the Examinate then told the sd Cullen that if he the Examinate had known the same at Dartmouth he would not have come from thence. And farther saith that they proceeded from Dartmouth to Dover and there took in a Pilot for Ostend and the next Day they arrived there and applied to Patrick Sarsfield by a Recommendation which they received from Capt Saunders at

---

[181] Spar deck: normally a light deck running the length of a vessel and built above the main deck, but sometimes used to refer to the quarterdeck at the stern. In this case it is difficult to discern which meaning is intended and although the first definition was the most common, the removal of the mizzen mast may point to the second definition.

Dartmouth. And at Ostend at the request of the sd Sarsfield they sold two Barrels of Beef to a Master of a Ship and from Ostend by the Recomendation of the said Sarsfield they sailed to Rotterdam where they arrived in January following and there called the Vessel by the Name of ye *Mary* and delivered their Lading to one Mr Archdeacon who disposed of the same and sent on board four Vatts of Mather[182] and about 5 or 6 Tons of Iron, part of which was the Produce of the sd Lading of Beef and they there took in upon freight from Patrick Campbell a hundred Hogsheads of Hemp seed and from the Widow Harper and her sons two Hhds of Geneva[183] and 6 or 7 pieces of Holland Cloath and the said Hemp seed was consigned to be delivered to one Captain Eastwick of Waterford and the sd Geneva and Holland were to be delivered to Patrick Shae of Kilkenny. And also saith that at Rotterdam they took on board as a Passenger one Henry Owsley of Topsham who brought on board with him nine Boxes or Cases of Wood about three Foot long and about a Foot and half square containing Silks, Tea and other India Goods, and they were to put him and his Goods on Shoar at Topsham or Dartmouth or any other place thereabouts. And at Rotterdam they turned on Shoar the aforesd John Fitzgerald because he was not an expert Sailor and the aforesd Richard Neal and John Rossiter left the Ship there and they then sailed from Rotterdam and designed to proceed to Waterford and arrived at Dover on or about the third of March and were obliged to lye there for about 10 or 12 Days by contrary winds and then followed their Voyage, and on the 17th Day of ye sd Month they came to an Anchor

---

[182] Madder, a source of red dye
[183] Hogsheads of gin

in Dartmouth Range and whilst they lay there a small fishing boat came to them and informed them that if they went in there they would be seized and that orders were brought thither a few Days after they went from thence to have seized them. And (to his best Rememberance and as he believes) Andrew Norton a sailmaker of Dartmouth was then in ye sd boat and at the same time another fishing Boat coming on board of them he the said Henry Owsley knew some of the Persons in her and called to them and they came on board and the sd Henry Owsley agreed with them to come on board in the night and to carry him and his Goods on Shoar. And as soon as the sd Boat was gon from the Ship they weighed Anchor and stood off from the Shoar. And it being St Patrick's Day and the sd Henry Owsley being to go on Shoar that night they drank very hard and he the sd Henry Owsley gave his Liquor to the Company and told them that he would not carry any Liquor on Shoar and he the sd Owsley was very drunk and went upon the Deck to make Water (he and the Examinate and Peirce Cullen having been drinking together in the Cabin) and the sd Cullen was very drunk but he the Examinate saw the sd Owsley upon the Deck between the Companion Door and the Rails on the Quarter Deck standing against the sd Rails making Water. And the aforesaid Slade, Dent and Wise were then upon the Deck and Andrew Cullen and Robert Connor were then sick in their Cabins. And saith that he the Examinate then saw the sd Slade and Dent throw the sd Henry Owsley over board and he was drowned. And the sd Wise as then at the helm and as they were throwing him over board the sd Wise left the helm and came to the sd Slade and Dent and looking over the Rail said 'Damn him Let him goe'. And some or one of them sayd

'Damn em if we had Roch or Cullen here wee'd serve them the same sauce'. And soon afterwards he ye Examinate called to the sd Dent and he came down and then the Examinate saying 'where's Owsley?' he ye sd Dent replyed 'He went forward'. And then the Examinate bad him take a Candle and Lanthorn and look for him and he the sd Dent then went upon Dek with a Candle and Lanthorn and pretended to look for him and sayd that he could not find him. And he the Examinate then went upon Deck and pretending Ignorance of what had happened he asked the sd Slade and Dent what was become of Owsley and they then told the Examinate that he went forward and they did not see him come back nor know what was become of him and that they believed he was fallen over board.[184] And then there was a Discourse amongst the sd Slade, Wise, Dent, the Examinate and Peirce Cullen what they should doe with ye sd Owsley's Goods (vizt.) if they should carry them to Waterford he the Examinate and the sd Peirce Cullen considered it might be the meanes of a Forfeiture of the Ship and Goods and they resolved not to deliver them to the said Boat. And the sd Slade, Wise and Dent refused to ~~carry things~~ out of the Channel and thereupon they bore away for Weymouth and not being able to get in there by reason of contrary Winds they bore away to Cows. And the next Day the said Dent, Wise, and Slade demanded the sd Owsley's Goods of the Examinate and threatened him that if he refused it they would swear that he the Examinate and the sd Cullen murdered ye sd Owsley and saith that he gave them the key of the Hatches, but before they had the said Key they went

---

[184] Roche's part in the drowing of Owsley may not have been as innocent as he claimed.

down by the Scuttle and broak open all or the greatest number of the sd Owsley's Boxes and carryed away such of his Goods as they thought fit, and Peirce Cullen asking them if he must not have a snack with them, they told him that there were 2 or 3 Boxes left and that he might have them and that they were as much as came to his share and the sd Cullen took the same, and afterwards run them on Shoar upon the main near Gosport. And they ye sd Slade, Wise and Dent run such part of the rest of ye sd Goods as they thought fit at the Isle of Wight, and then left the Ship. And he the Examinate, at the Desire of the sd Cullen went to Portsmouth in order to ship three men, and there took upon him the name of Rossiter and at Gosport shipped David Stretch, Alexander Lyn and Jasper Butler and they went on board the ship at Cows at which time she was called ye *George* of Bristol. And at Cows he ye sd Cullen shipt Jacob Mason who there came on board and lay in the Cabin and acted as Master but under the Comand of the sd Cullen and in or about the latter end of the sd Month of March the sd ship with the Examinate the sd Peirce and Andrew Cullen, Robert Conner, and the sd Stretch, Lyn, Butler and Mason set sail from Cows with the aforesaid Iron, Hemp, Lead, Matthe[185] and Linnen on board bound for Havre de Grace and in her way thither they lost their foremast in a Storm and were forced to put into La Hogue Bay where they put up a Jury Mast. And there he the Examinate left the Ship and went by Land to Honfleur and there crossed over to Havre de Grace and met the said Cullen and went on board the ship. And saith that whilst the ship lay at la Hogue Bay he the Examinate informing the sd Cullen that he would leave the ship and that it was hard upon him

---

[185] Madder

153

that he should have no money and yet be answerable to the aforesd Mr Archdeacon for the Bills which he the Examinate had given him upon the Account of the Ship and Lading, and thereupon he told the Examinate yt ye sd Archdeacon might pay himself out of the Insurance Money. And he the Examinate saying 'How can that be when the ship is not lost?' to hich he replyed 'Never fear that for we shall manage that well enough, I'le put you into a way how to doe it. And some time afterwards he the sd Cullen desired him to copy two Draughts of Certificates of the Ships being run down by an English Gally in the Channel and of the mens being taken up by one Capt Jones and put on board of a Lugger. And saith that the sd Draughts were of the sd Cullen's handwriting and he the Examinate at his request copyed the same. And the sd Cullen desired the Examinate to read them and see how he liked them. And he the sd Cullen and the Examinate (at the sd Cullen's Request) wrote several Draughts of a Letter to be sent with the sd Certificates to the aforesaid Mr Archdeacon at Rotterdam. And they perused the said Draughts and consulted together which was most proper to be sent. And he the Examinate wrote and sent the Letter dated ye 17th of April 1722 and ye Certificates dated the 29th of Mar and 13th of Apr: 1722 now shewn to him to the said Mr Archdeacon at Rotterdam from Honfleur. And he the Examinate, Andrew Cullen and Robert Conner at Honfleur made the Protest now shewn to him dated the 27th of April 1722 (new style). And the said Peirce Cullen was very angry with the Examinate for appearing at Havre de Grace and he believes that the mariners were there ordered by the said Cullen not to take any notice that they knew the Examinate. And he the Examinate there rece'd of the sd

154

Peirce Cullen ten Guineas or thereabouts, to carry him home to Ireland, and then got his Passage in a ship (whereof his Cosen Thomas Edwards was Mar bound for Waterford and arrived there in the sd Month of April (Old style) and from thence went to Ross and Dublin and at Dublin he the Examinate (pursuant to the Desire of ye sd Cullen) wrote to him at Havre de Grace advising him that the matter was discovered at home and that one Barden a Master of a Ship was to be hanged for carrying Wild Geese meaning Persons that were carryed to France contrary to the Law of the Country. And soon afterwards he made the best of his way to London and came from Park Gate by Land and arrived at London in the Month of May 1722 and quartered at the Ax in Aldermanbury by the name of John Eustace and went by the sd name from the time of his coming from Dublin and at the Ax in Aldermanbury he was arrested by Wm Rous and Daniell Fox at the Suit of the aforesd Mr Archdeacon at which time he had in his pocket the letter now shewn to him signed Mary R and dated the 11th of May 1722 which was wrote and sent to him by his wife Mary Roch.

32. Thomas Lawrence Jones

The Examination of Thomas Lawrence Jones, 13 February 1724. HCA 1/55, ff. 50-52

Thomas Jones joined Howell Davis' company at the same time as Bartholomew Roberts, but never rose to Roberts' heady position. Jones joined Anstis' company and was one of those who returned to England, where he was arrested in incarcerated in the Marshalsea prison. While there, it is highly probable that he met and was interviewed by Charles Johnson, and that his testimony informed some of the major changes incorporated into the second edition of the General History of the Pyrates. *Johnson's account of Roberts' piracies included the tale of an argument between Roberts and Jones which escalated into physical violence and the wounding of Roberts by Jones. For his part in the affair, Jones was punished with two lashes from each member of the company which, if true (and there is little reason to doubt it), may explain his willingness to desert Roberts and join Anstis' company.*[186] *Jones died in the Marshalsea in May 1724 before he could be brought to trial.*

This Examinate saith that in the Month of July 1720[187] the Ship or Vessel call the *Morris* Sloop (whereof one Fenn of Bridge Town in Barbados was Commander and to which Vessel he the Examinate belonged as a foremast man) and two other vessels (to wit) the *Hind* of London (Capt Hall Commander) and the *Primrose* (Capt Plumb Commandr) being at an Anchor at Animaboo[188] upon the Coast of Guinea they were all taken by two piratical Vessels (to wit) the *Rover* of 32 Guns (whereof one Davis and afterwards one Roberts was Commander) and the *King James* of about 26 Gunns. And he the Examinate and 14 others of the Company of the sd Sloop were by force taken out of her and put on board the sd Ship the *Rover* and therein carryed to Princess Island[189] where she lay about 15 or 16 Days within which time the Company of the *Rover* would not suffer the Examinate or any of the Company of the sd Sloop to go on

---

[186] Johnson, *General History*, pp. 224-225
[187] 1719
[188] Anomabu, Ghana
[189] Principe

Shoar. That in their passage to the sd Island, the sd Ship took a Dutch Gally and the Quartermaster and others of the Pirates went on board of her and there was one of her Men came voluntarily on board the *Rover* and joyned with the Pirates and a few hours afterwards the sd Gally parted from the *Rover*. That from Princess Island they went to the Ferdinando[190] upon the Coast of Brazile and there took two Portuguese vessels and afterwards discharged one of them and carryed the other to the Coast of Surinam in the West Indias and there took a Rhode Island Sloop (whereof one Captain Cane was Commander) and named her the *Good Fortune* and manned her with about 40 or 50 Men whereof he the Examinate, Thomas Grimes and Michael Ashburne (who had belonged to the sd *Morris* Sloop) were three and the aforesd Capt Roberts was made Commander of her and carryed her to Tobago where she took several Vessels but he the Examinate was then sick. And from thence they proceeded to another Island in the Spanish West Indias called Curmaroo[191] where she was cleaned and he the Examinate was sick all the time she lay there (to wit) for about a week. And then she went upon a Cruize and afterwards to Black Star at the Island of St. Christophers and there burnt one Vessel (whereof one Wilcox was ma[ste]r) and took several others. And Bridstock Weaver (who was the chief mate of the sd Vessel that was burnt) was then forced by the sd Roberts and the sd Roberts and the rest of the Pirates in the sd Vessel the *New Providence* to go aft and two Negroes with loaded Pistols were presently afterwards called into ye Cabin. And the Examinate then apprehended and believes that the sd Pirates

---

[190] Fernando de Noronha
[191] Possibly Camanoe

forced the said Bridstock Weaver[192] to sign their Articles and to go into their Service and that if he had refused the same they would have killed him.[193] And then they stood to the Northward and took several English and French Vessel, and particularly a Brigantine of Rhode Island (whereof Capt Norton was Commander). And the sd Roberts sent the Examinate and the sd Bridstock Weaver and about 40 others out of the New Providence to man the sd Brigantine and one Bradly[194] by the sd Roberts's Order had ye Charge of her. And she was then named the *Good Fortune* and was ordered to keep Company with the *New Providence* and the 4th or 5th Night afterwards they being almost all of them forced Men they agreed to run away with her to the West Indias and to live a marooning Life till they could have an Answer to a Petition to his Majestie for a Pardon[195] and they accordingly

---

[192] **Docs 42, 61**

[193] For a similar account of the article-signing process, see **doc. 61**

[194] George Bradly was a member of Anstis' company [**doc. 43**], but it is unclear why Jones, who must have known otherwise, pretended that he was given command of the *Good Fortune* by Roberts.

[195] The petition reached London in November 1722 and was brought to the attention of the Lords of Trade and Plantations, who declined to respond to it. The text read:

To His Most Gracious Majesty, by the Grace of God, Of Great Britain France and Ireland Defender of the Faith.

The Humble Petition of the Company, now belonging to the Ship *Morning Star* and Brigatine *Good Fortune*, lying under the ignominious Name and Denomination of Pyrates, Humbly Sheweth:

That we your Majesty's most loyal Subjects have, at sundry Times, been taken by Bartholomew Roberts, the the Captain of the aforesaid Vessels ad Company, together with another Ship, in which we left him, and have been forced y him and his wicked Accomplices, to enter into, and serve, in the said Company, as Pyrates, much contrary to our Wills and Inclinatios: and we, your loyal Subjects utterly abhorring and detesting that impious Way of Living, did, with unanimous Consent, and contrary to the Knowledge of the said Roberts or his Accomplices, on, or about, the eighteenth Day of April, 1721, leave, and ran away with the aforesaid ship *Morning Star* and Brigantine *Good Fortune* with no other Intent

run away with her in the Night time and about 3 Days afterwards they took a small West Country English Vessel of about 90 Tons coming from the Western Islands with Wine bound for Newfoundland and some of her Men came on board the sd Brigantine and joyned with her Company. And then she was discharged and about 3 Weeks afterwards to the Westward of Jamaica they took the *Hambleton* of Bristol (whereof on Joseph Smith was Master) and carryed her to a maroon key and took out Henry Treehill[196] and about 12 or 13 others of her hands and also some Liquors and kept her about 11 Weeks and then discharged her and afterwards took several other French, Spanish and English Vessels whose Names or the Names of the Commanders he knows not. And there were Provisions and other things taken out of them and then they were all discharged except a Spanish Ship of 36 Guns which they burnt as she lay at an Anchor at Campechy. And almost two Years since they being to the Northward met with an English Vessel bound from Virginia to London by which Ship the Examinate and the rest of the Company of the said Brigantine sent a Petition to his Majtie for a Pardon and then proceeded to the Marvane Keys and there lived a marooning Life upon the Island of Rattan and other Islands in the Spanish West Indias for about 8 Months. And then believeing it to be a proper season to meet with Ships bound from London to Barbados they proceeded and beat to

---

and Meaning than the Hopes of obtaining your Maty's most gracious Pardon. And, that we, your Majesty's most loyal Subjects, may with more Safety return to our native Country and serve the Natio, unto which we belong, in our respective Capacities, without fear of being prosecuted by the Injured, whose Estates have suffered by the said Roberts and his Accomplices, during our forcible Detainment, by the said Company. We most humbly implore your Majesty's most royal Assent, to this our humble Petition.
[196] **Doc. 43**

Windward and got through ye Windward Passage and in the Latitude of Barbados they spake with two English Ships bound to Barbados and enquired if they had brought any Answer to the aforesd Petition and were told by them that they had not any such Answer. And thereupon the Examinate and the aforesd Henry Treehill and 17 others told the rest of the Company of the sd Brigantine that they would not follow that wicked Course of Life any longer but would go home and trust to the King's Mercy. And then they all went on board of a Sloop which had been taken by the said Brigantine and therein came into a small Bay near Minehead in the West of England and there left the sd Sloop afloat and travelled from thence by land to Bristol and he the Examinate lived there and thereabouts in Shoar about 8 Months. And then (to wit) about three Months since he the Examinate with the aforesd Bridstock Weaver (who had left the aforesd Brigantine when they were at Rattan the time before mentioned) and the said Henry Treehill were taken and imprisoned at Bristol.

33. James Williams

The Examination of James Williams, 27 March, 1725. HCA 1/55, ff. 103-104

The careers of John Gow, alias Smith ('Smith' is a literal translation of the Gaelic 'Gow'), and his company are well told in the following three documents. Like Roche and his companions,

160

Gow's company were unsual amongst pirates of the 'golden age', firstly because they operated mostly in European waters rather than the broader Atlantic or Indian Oceans, and secondly because they had no contact with other pirates active at the same time. Like Roche, Gow's company were captured, tried and executed in Britain – in Gow's home region of the Orkney Islands, and like Roche they were the subject of intense interest for a while because of their essentially local nature and their perceived level of barbarity. James Williams was Gow's lieutenant until the two men fell out, and Williams became the victim of a unique pirate punishment when his own company handed him over to the authorities. By the time Williams was returned to England the rest of the company had already been captured and they were reunited to stand trial together.

This Examinate saith that in or about the Month of July last past he the Examinate was shipped at Amsterdam to serve as a foremastman on board of a ship called the *George* Gally then lying there (whereof one Oliver Fourneau a French man was then Master). And saith that on the first Day of August following the sd ship came from the Texell in ballast bound for Sta Cruz in South Barbary[197] in order to purchase a Cargoe there. And accordingly proceeded thither and there purchased a Lading of Bees Wax and Copper and few Bales of fine Matting and Turky Leather bound to the Streights[198], and about four Months since the sd Ship with her sd Lading on board came from Sta Cruz in an Evening about 5 or 6 of the Clock and about ten of the Clock the same Evening five

---

[197] Santa Cruz de Tenerife
[198] Of Gibraltar

of her company (to wit) John Winter, John Peterson and Peter Rowlandson (who was a Dutch man) together with an Irish Man called Michael and a Scotch Man called Daniel went down in the steerage and they or some of them cut the Throats of the Mate the Doctor and Super Cargoe as they lay in their hammocks, and the Doctor after his Throat was cut came upon Deck and fell down by the Man at the helm and the sd John Winter threw him over board and at the same time one John Smith the old mate shot the said Oliver Fourneau with a Pistol and threw him over board. And the sd Mate and Super Cargoe were also thrown over board. And then the sd six persons and another Scotch man named (William) drove the Examinate and all the rest of her Company (to wit) eleven other Persons into the great Cabin and there confined them till the next Day and then made a pirate Ship of her and named her the *Revenge*. And the sd. John Smith (who had before been 2nd Mate and Gunner of her and who was the only Person on board of her who understood Navigation) was made Comander of her and Peter Rowlandson the Cook was made Gunner of her and he the Examinate and the other eleven who were foremast men were obliged to continue on board of her in the same capacity. And about ten Days afterwards about 18 or 20 Leagues from Cadiz they took a Sloop laden with fish from Newfoundland belonging to Pool called the *Delight* (whereof Thomas Wise was master) bound to Cadiz and took out all her Company and Provisions with 2 or 3 Casks of Rum and a Cask of Wine and then sunk her, and about a fortnight or three weeks afterwards they took a Scotch Snow laden with Sammon and herrings bound for the Streights and took out all her Men and part of her Cargoe and sunk her. And on or about the 13th of December last past about 20 Leagues Westward from the Port of Lisbon they took a Ship called the *Bachellor* (whereof Benjamin Cross was Master) laden with Timber from New England bound for Lisbon and took out all her Company and some of her Timber and Provision and put them on board of the sd. Pirate Ship and gave the sd. Ship *Batcher* to the aforesd. Thomas Wise and his Company of Mariners and a few Days afterwards about 12 Leagues from Cape Finister they took a French Vessel laden with Wine, Almonds, Reasons, Oranges and Lemons from Cadiz bound to France and took out all her Men and part of her Cargoe and put them on board the sd. Pirate Ship, and then he the Informt. happening to quarrell with the aforesd. John Winter was confined for about two Days and three Nights and was then put on board of a small Bristol Vessel (whereof one Davis was Master) laden with fish bound for Lisbon, which had been taken whilst he the Examinate was under Confinement. And saith that one Ditty the mate and John Brown and John Bembrick two of the Company of the sd ship the *Bachellor* and ten of the Company of the sd. French vessel were also put with the Examinate on board the sd. Bristol Vessel and therein carryed to Lisbon where the Examinte and the sd, Ditty, Brown and Bembrick were carryed on board of the *Argile* Man of War. And saith that the Mate of the aforesd. French Ship, one of the Company of the aforesd. Scotch ship and John Harris and two others of ye Company of the sd. Ship the *Bachellor* had their Liberty and voluntarily acted with the Pirates. And he the Examinate never had any share of the Money, Goods or Plunder that were taken within the time aforesd. saving that he gave an old Coat to Michael the Irish Man for the Surgeons scarlet

Cloath Jacket and Breeches which he the Examinate now wears.

34. John Smith, alias John Gow

The Examination of John Smith, 2 April, 1725. HCA 1/55, ff. 105-106

This Examinate saith the in the beginning of June last past this Examinate was shipped at Amsterdam by Oliver Fourneau the Master of a Ship called the *George* Gally of the burthen of about 200 Tonns carrying 14 Gunns belonging to Mr Bougar a French Merchant living at Amsterdam to serve as 2d Mate and Gunner of the sd Ship from thence to Sta. Cruz in South Barbary in ballast to purchase a Cargoe and she accordingly proceeded thither and there purchased her sd Cargoe (to wit) about 200 frails of Bees Wax, a small quantity (to wit) about 2 or 3 hundred wt. of old Copper and some Morocco Pins and was to have proceeded from thence to the Streights and on or about the 2d Day of November about 6 or 7 of the Clock in the Evening the sd Ship with her sd. Lading came from Sta. Cruz and about ten of the Clock the same Evening some of the Ships Company but which of them in particular he knows not killed Bonadventure Jolfs the Mate, John Guy the Surgeon and also one Hedger the Masters Clark as they were in their hammocks in the steerage and they then flocked about the sd Mar who was walking upon the Deck and killed him and threw him over board. And he the Examinate was then walking upon the Deck but the night was so dark that he could not discover which of them did the fact saving that he saw John Winter and John Peterson come out of ye steerage with a Light and their knifes in their hands immediately after the fact was committed. And the sd Mate, Surgeon and Master's Clark were also thrown over board. And then James Williams one of the Company proposed to the rest of the Company that he the Examte should be the Comander of her by reason that there was not any Person on board who understood Navigation but him the Examinate and ye sd Williams gave him the Examinate the Master's Watch and Sword and then all ye Company in general (to wit) the sd. Williams, Winter and Peterson and also Peter Rolandson, James Belbin, Timothy Murphey, Wm. Booth, Wm. Melvin, Daniel McCanley, Michael Moor, George Dobson, John Phinnis and Robert Reed and five others who left her at the Orkneys (to wit) John Mills, Henry Jemmison, Joseph Wheatley, James Newport and Peter Janson a boy , imposed the Comand of the sd ship upon the Examinate in order to proceed with her as a Pirate. And on or about the 12th of November aforesd about 8 or 10 Leagues from Cape St. Vincent they took a Sloop called the *Delight* of Pool whereof Thomas Wise was Mar laden with fish from Newfoundland bound for Cadiz. And they took out all her Company and Provisions and sunk her and about 3 weeks afterwards about 20 Leagues West from the Port of Lisbon they took a Scotch Snow whereof John Sommervile was Mar. laden with herrings, sammon, lead and logwood from Glasgow bound for Alicant and took out all her Men and Provisions and sunk her and on or about the 18th of December about the same Distance West from the Port of Lisbon they took the *Batchellor* (Benjamin Cross Mar.) laden with Timber from New England bound for

Lisbon and took out all her Company and some of her Provisions, Timber and stores and then put the aforesd. Thomas Wise and his Company of Mariners on board of her with Liberty to carry her where they would and on or about the 27th Day of the same Month they took a French Vessel laden with Wine, Oyl and Fruit from Cadiz bound to France and took out all her Company and about a third part of the Cargoe. And then put the sd. John Sommervile and his Company and the sd. Benjamin Cross on board of her to carry her where they would and 2 or 3 Days afterwards about thirty Leagues from Vigo they took a Bristol Ship (whereof one Davis was Mar.) laden with Fish from Newfound Land bound for Vigo and took out some of her Provisions and let her goe having first put some of the French Prisoners and the 2d and others of the *Bachellors* Men (to wit) Francis Ditty, John Brown and John Bembrick on board of her. And saith that Alexander Robb one of the Company of the aforesd. Scotch Snow, Robert Teague and the Cook and one Harris, three of the Company of the *Bachellor* and also one of the Company of the said French Ship voluntarily joined with the Pirates. And then they went to the Orkneys to clean and there the Examinate voluntarily surrendered himself to James Fea of Clasteron and caused all the rest of the Ships Company to be seized and confined till they were put on board the *Greyhound* Man of War.

35. Robert Reid

The Examination of Robert Read, 3 April, 1725. HCA 1/55, ff. 132-133

This Examinate saith that he was a foremast man of the *George* Galley (Olliver Fourneau Mr) at the time when she came from Amsterdam and saith that about three hours after she was come from Sta Cruz (to wit) about 9 or 10 of the Clock at Night being about 5 or 6 Leagues from the Shoar the sd Master was sitting abaft upon the hencoop and ordered the Boatsn James Belbin to send up a hand to reeve the flag Line and he the Examte by ye order of the sd Boatswaine went up and reeved the same and then the weather being good he sat down upon the Cat Harpin[199] and when he had sat there a few minutes he hears the sd Boatswain call out saying there's a man over board and then hearing a great noyse abaft upon the quarter Deck and ye Master crying out O mon Dieu mon Dieu, and then heard a Pistol discharged upon Deck and being then in a great Consternation he came down and went between Decks and there saw James Williams, John Winter, Daniel McCauley, John Smith, Wm Melvin, John Peterson, Peter Rollson and Michael Moor all armed with Pistols and he the Examte not knowing the Occasion thereof and believing that they were armed to defend their own Lives he called out to them saying for Gods Sake give me a Pistol and some of them sayd to him (Get out of the way you Dog or else you'l be shot). And thereupon he stept upon Deck and went forward and then heard the sd Wm. Melvin between Decks say Damn you you Doggs I'le hang you when you are Dead and then came upon Deck and took the end of the Whip[200] fall and went down again and put

---

[199] Catharpin: a short rope used to pull the top of the shrouds in towards the mast.

[200] A line reeved through a block on the yard for the purpose of lifting

it about the chief Mates Neck who then lay dead between Decks and hoysted him upon Deck and then put the same upon the Super Cargo's Neck who then also lay dead between Decks and hoysted him upon Deck and then they were thrown over board. And then the sd Boatswain with Timothy Murphey the Carpenter John Phinnis and one other of the Company were put into the Cabin and there confined for several hours and he the Examte continued upon Deck and then saw ye sd Williams come up with a silver hilted Sword and a silver watch and he gave the said Watch and Sword to ye sd Smith saying welcome Capt Smith the Doggs are gone I wish you good Luck and Prosperity in your Comand and Peter Rollson the Cook was made Gunner and the sd Williams made himself Leiftenant and the sd James Belbin was ye same Night continued to be Boatswain and the sd Smith declared that if any of ye Company except ye sd Williams, Winter, Peterson, Rollson, Belbin McCauley, Melvin and Moor went between Decks or abaft the mainmast they were dead men. And they afterwards took a Pool sloop a Scotch Snow, a New England Ship, a French Vessel and a Bristol Ship, and saith that Alexander Robb one of the Company of the sd Snow and a little black French man (who is one of the Prisoners and was chiefe mate of the sd French Vessel) took some of the Cloaths which had been plundered and taken from the Prisoners, and the sd Smith made the sd French man his 2d Mate and he and the sd Alexnder Robb appeared to joyn and act freely and voluntarily with the sd Pirates. And when the Master and Company of ye sd Snow went away in the sd French Vessel he the Examte was present and knows that the Carpenter of her wept very much and begged that he might go with them but ye sd. Smith

168

would not suffer him to go saying Damn you you Dog you was willing to stay at first and you shant go. And then the sd Ship proceeded to the Orkneys and there ten of ye men (to wit) John Phinnis, George Dobson, John Mills, John Harris, James Newport, John Mings, Joseph Wheatley, James Ballis, John Read and one of the Bristol Men went away in the long boat. And he the Examte went on Shoar with Robert Teague and Wm. Booth who were sent on Shoar in the yawle upon the Island of Carsten and he the Examte there made his Escape and went to the Customs house and gave an Information to the effect before set forth and was then examed by the Custom house Officers who delivered him the Schedule now left by him and marked at ye top with the Letter A: and was afterwards examined by Mr Thomas Bell Admiral substitute of ye Orkneys and after that by Mr Henry Graham a magistrate of Kerston and about 10 or 12 Days afterwards he voluntarily entered himself on board of his Majesty's ship the *Greyhound* where the Schedules marked with the Letters B and C were sent to him. And saith that he the Examinate was under force and Restraint during all the respective times of the Murthers and Robberys beforementioned and was wholly and entirely innocent and in no manner guilty thereof and had not any part of the Plunder taken in either of the Vessels beforementioned.

2. FORCED MEN

Forced men, innocent sailors conscripted through fear of violence or death, were present in most pirate companies, sometimes in greater numbers than volunteers. When volunteers were plentiful, pirates usually confined themselves to forcing skilled specialists, particularly surgeons [**doc. 44**], carpenters and coopers, but also navigators [**docs 40, 42, 46, 48**], riggers and musicians, but when voluntary recruits were scarce pirates conscripted anyone who could haul a line or load a cannon.

The testimony of forced men can be extremely valuable, they having often spent prolonged periods aboard pirate ships, living amongst the pirates and taking part in all the pirates' actions, without necessarily being implicated themselves in the pirates' crimes. Nevertheless, a forced man still had to be careful not to incriminate himself, so although the level of self-exoneration is often less in the testimony of forced men than that of volunteer pirates, it was still an important feature in their accounts. In many cases this led forced men to include fairly vivid accounts of pirate torture and brutality which, while surely based on real experiences, may well have been exaggerated or their importance overstated.

36. Philip Middleton

Narrative of Philip Middleton, 4 August, 1696. *Calendar of State Papers, Colonial: America and the West Indies*, 1696-1697, item. 517iii.

Philip Middleton, a boy member of Henry Every's company [**docs 2-5**], *surrendered himself to the authorities as soon as he reached Ireland, and became one of the government's most prolific witnesses. He gave at least five different depositions, one of which is printed below, and was a witness at the trial of John Sparks and others. His depositions are among the most detailed and precise, and although his age might lead us to conclude that they contain some fanciful elements he seems, on the whole, to have been a sensible lad and a very reliable witness.*

The ship *Charles Henry*[201] first plundered three English vessels at the Isle of May of provisions only. Nine of their men joined her, mostly West-Country-men. Thence she went to the coast of Guinea, where she took two Danes, from which they took a quantity of elephants' teeth, and divided eight or nine ounces of gold per man. Fourteen of the Danish crew joined them. Thence they sailed to Madagascar and Johanna,[202] where twelve French pirates came on board, and afterwards took a French pirating junk with about forty men, who had good booty with them. These also joined them, and made them up to 170, viz., 14 Danes, 52 French, 104 English.

---

[201] Middleton is the only person to use the name *Charles Henry* to describe Every's vessel, which began life as the *Charles II* and was renamed *Fancy*. Possibly it is a seventeenth-century transcription error.
[202] Anjouan.

From Johanna they sailed to the Red Sea, and heard of two rich ships from Mocha bound to Surat, but passed them in the night, as they learned from a small junk which they took next day. They came up with the smaller vessel, which made little or no resistance, but the great ship fought for two hours, having about 1,300 persons on board. The other had 700. They kept possession of both ships, and all the crew except one man boarded her by turns, taking only provisions, necessaries and treasure, which was very great, but little in comparison with what was on board; for though they put several to the torture they would not confess where the rest of their treasure lay. They took great quantities of jewels, and a saddle and bridle set with rubies designed as a present for the Great Mogul. Several of the Indian women on board were, by their habits and jewels, of better quality than the rest.[203] Having taken these prizes the pirates went to Rajapere[204] for water, and then to Mascarenas, where all the Danes and French were set ashore with their share of booty, amounting to £970 per man in value. Thence they sailed to Ascension, where they turned fifty turtle,[205] and found letters of two English ships having been there. This was in March last; and at the latter end of April they arrived at Providence,[206] having

[203] Legends of the atrocities committed by Every's men against high-born Indian ladies were rife in England following the capture of the Gang-i-Sawai, but were vigorously denied by captured or surrendered pirates. Here Middleton admits the quality of the women aboard; in another deposition he claimed that many of the pirates 'lay with' them. He himself may not have been involved in the rape because of his age.

[204] Rajpur

[205] Turtles provided meat popular with seafarers in the seventeenth century. Because of their slow movement they could easily be caught and turned onto their back, preventing their escape, and could be kept alive in this state for some time to provide fresh meat

[206] New Providence, Bahamas.

but two days' provisions left. They gave Governor Trott a present of twenty pieces-of-eight per man besides two chequeenes[207] of gold, on which he allowed them to come on shore, and gave them a treat at his house, at which one of the men broke a drinking glass, and was made to pay eight checqueenes for it. The men also presented the Governor with the ship and all on board her, including some elephants' teeth. The Deputy-Governor, Richard Tallia, shared with Trott in the booty. Here the Captain changed his name from Every to Bridgeman, and went ashore with about eighty men, who dispersed to several ports and bought sloops there.[208] Every and nineteen men embarked in one of them called the *Seaflower*, and landed about two months since twenty miles north of Lough Swilly by Londonderry, and thence came by land to Dublin. Every went on to London, another of the leaders stayed at Londonderry. Another sloop commanded by Hollingsworth was chased into Dublin by a French privateer. She had sixteen more of the crew of the *Charles Henry* aboard. Several of the crew went to New England, one to Pennsylvania, two went to Jamaica and returned to Providence, another remained with his booty at Providence, another was killed by a shark, another was seen in Dublin. Trott took several guns out of the ship (which mounted forty-eight) and planted them on a platform for defence against the French.[209]

---

[207] Chaquins, or sequins, an Arabian coin.

[208] See **doc. 2**

[209] Trott was investigated and censured for his apparent collusion with the pirates. It is unlikely that he was completely innocent, and he certainly made a handsome profit from the encounter, but it must be noted that the pirates told him they were traders interloping the monopoly of the Royal African Company, and in any case the defences of New Providence were in no condition to resist Every's powerful ship and company.

37. Henry Watson

Narrative of Mr. Henry Watson, who was taken prisoner by the pirates, 15 August, 1696.

Calendar of State Papers Colonial: America and West Indies, 1697-1698

Henry Watson's account of his time on board the John and Rebecca, *commanded by John Hoar is included here because of the wealth of interesting detail it offers. After the capture of the* Ruparrel *and* Calicut *rumours began to circulate that one of the captains, named Sawbridge, had had his lips sewn together by the pirates to prevent him railing against their way of life. The fact that Watson does not mention the incident, in what is otherwise a fairly detailed account, suggests that in reality the atrocity did not occur.*

On 14 August, 1696, I embarked on board the ship *Ruparrel*, bound to Bombay, having freighted on her thirty-five bales of coffee, etc., and other goods on the *Calicut*, merchant, which was to sail in her company. On 15 August both ships were taken by a pirate which came out of the Babs. It was proposed to the Captain of the *Ruparrel* that she should be redeemed at Aden for 35,000 pieces of eight, and it was so agreed upon, though I advised to the contrary, because neither he nor his owners had ever been or had any correspondents at Aden; hence they could not expect the money to be provided and the Governor would be greatly to blame if he permitted it to come on board, this being the best way to spoil the trade of the port, encourage pirates to use these seas, and so to ruin the traffic of Mocha, Aden, etc. However, the ship was brought to Aden, when a native merchant and another young merchant-freighter (upon whose credit the money was apparently to be procured) were sent ashore, but after staying two days there was no sign of their getting the money or of their coming off themselves. On the third day the Captain was sent ashore with some lascars to hasten off the money, lest the pirates should burn the ships, as they threatened to do. That night two fires were seen ashore, which were supposed to be the two boats, and next morning a shot was fired as a signal that the ship would not be redeemed. Thereupon they fell again to plundering the ship, which I thought had been effectually done before. On 22 August about eleven o'clock the ships were set on fire in sight of the people of Aden, first the *Calicut*, then the *Ruparrel* with the English ensign flying. The lascars were sent away on floats, and the mate, gunner and myself were carried on board the pirate-ship, which was a prize taken from the French, formerly called the *St. Paul*, but now the *John and Rebecca*.[210] The master of the *Calicut* proposed to them to plunder Congo in Persia,[211] and they accordingly proceeded on the voyage. On the 22nd September we arrived at Tompo, called by the pirates Antelope Island from the great number of antelopes there, from whence they sent their boats to view Congo; but learning from two fishing-boats, captured in the night, that six Portuguese men-of-war were lying there, they resolved to stay a while in the hope that these might depart shortly. They careened their ship and

---

[210] Commanded by John Hoar, a New England privateer turned pirate.
[211] Gombroon, now Bandar Abbas

killed great quantities of antelopes, until being weary of that kind of flesh and having nothing but stinking beef and doughboys (that is dough made into a lump and boiled) they weighed anchor on 16 October and came down again to Cape Mussington. There they plundered a small fishing town and got good store of dates and salt fish, but returning on the 20th they saw four Dutch ships and fled for fear of them into Cape Mussington, turning up next day towards the Island aforesaid. Off Hisnies they took a Frank, that told them of two great ships, supposed to be English from Europe, at Gambroon, which scared them not a little. On the 22nd they arrived again at Tompo and on the 25th sent boats to view another island up the Gulf. These had not been long gone before a boat was seen to come and view the ship, which they suspected to be a spy from Congo, as she in reality was. That night the mates and gunners of the *Calicut* and *Ruparrel* contrived to escape in a small boat, which made them think their designs frustrated. Thereupon they called for me and threatened to make me fast and beat me, and afterwards turn me on shore naked on a bare rock, or maroon-key as they called it, without food, wood or water. I told them that they knew my daily solicitation to them to be put on shore, that I knew nothing of these men's going or I should certainly have escaped with them. This abated their rigour and villainous design against me. They would have weighed and gone away that night but for their unwillingness to leave behind them their boats and men, which came not back till the 30th. During my residence with them they were very kind to me in giving me my clothes again, with leave to sell them. Afterwards they put it to the vote whether I should bring the money or not, and at about one o'clock they gave me a boat and ten Arabs, whom, knowing something of their language, I persuaded to carry me to Gomron, where the East India Company has a factory. I landed there at sunrise on 2 November, and found the four escaped men already there. During my residence with the pirates, whose chief rendezvous is at an island called St. Mary's near Madagascar, I understood they were supplied with ammunition and all sorts of necessaries by one Captain Baldridge[212] and Lawrence Johnston, two old pirates that are settled in the above islands, and are factors for one Frederick Phillips, who under pretence of trading to Madagascar for negro slaves, supplies these rogues with all sorts of stores, consigning them to Baldridge and Johnston. These two are both of them married to country women, and many of the others are married at Madagascar. They have a kind of fortification of seven or eight guns upon St. Mary's. Their design in marrying the country women is to ingratiate themselves with the inhabitants, with whom they go into war against other petty kings. If one Englishman goes with the Prince with whom he lives to war, he has half the slaves that are taken for his pains. I have often heard the commander and many of his men say that he took the ship from the French near the river of Canada, and that they had a commission from the Governor of New York to take the French. They fitted their ship from Rhode Island, and the then Governor of New York knew their designs as also the Governor of Rhode Island. Another pirate-ship of equal burden was fitted out there at the same time with this, which Hore commands. The Captain of the other ship is Richard Glover, brother-in-law to Hore. He also was in the Gulf of Mocha to leeward of us when I was

---

[212] **Doc. 63**

taken by Hore, and came on board to see us prisoners and to filch what they could from our ships, knowing from us that no more ships would come from Mocha. Glover would have persuaded Hore to return to Mocha, burn the ships in the port and plunder the town, to which Hore complied not; so she remained in the Gulf, and what is become of her since I know not.[213]

38. John Ireland

The Examination of John Ireland, 26 May, 1701. HCA 1/53, ff. 88-90

John Ireland's tale, like many others, illustrates well the transient and frequently unpredictable life of an early-modern seafarer. Embarked on a simple two-week voyage from New York to Boston, he sailed half-way around the world before ending up in prison in London some years later. Ireland was never brought to trial, probably because there were no suitable witnesses available, but his circumstances before he got involved with pirates suggest very strongly that he really was forced to join them and thus emphasise the probable truth and accuracy of his testimony. As a ship's master, he belonged to a group statistically unlikely to embark voluntarily on a course of piracy, but as a navigator his skill would have been much in demand by pirates who had no scruples about forcibly conscripting him. His companion and commander, Thomas Tew, is one of the most interesting and enigmatic characters of the great wave of Indian Ocean piracy, and it is to be

---

[213] In fact, Glover was deposed from his command and replaced by Richard Sievers [**doc. 6**], and the ship was renamed *Soldado*.

regretted that we cannot know more about him. Ireland's assertion that Tew himself was forced is particularly interesting: Tew would not have been the only forced commander of a pirate ship in the 'golden age'. By the time Ireland gave his deposition Tew was long dead and so in no need of Ireland's defence, which does not add materially to Ireland's own defence, so there is little reason to doubt the basic truth of Ireland's assertion.

This Exaiate saith that in the year 1694 he was mr and part owner of a Brigantine called the *Dolphin* and came with her from Providence laden with Brasiletto wood to New York and there sold his wood and laid up his Vessel intending to go to Boston by Land but taking leave of his Friends at New York one Capt Tew Comr of a sloope called the *Amity* came and asked for the Exaiate and said he understood that the Exaiate was going for Boston and he the sd Tew was going with his sloop to that place and wanted a Pilote but the Exaiate at first was unwilling to go by sea for feare of the French who were very brief[214] in those parts but at last by the perswasion of his Friends and the faire promises of Capt. Tew who said he had Governr Fletchers[215] Commission against the French and promised the Exaiate not to be above a fourtnight he the Exaiate consented to go and did go onbd the said sloope with ye sd Capt Tew and sailed from thence to Rhode Island and from thence they sailed to for Boston, but in the course of the voyage the Company of the sloope or the greatest part of them rose up against the Capt and told him they came for money and money they would have before

---

[214] active
[215] Benjamin Fletcher. Governor of New York

they went home again, to which Tew replyed and desired that he and also this Exaiate might be sett onshore and then they might take the sloope to themselves and go where they would, but the men would not agree to let this Exaiate go ashore saying they had no body else to carry them to their designed port so the Exaiate was kept onbd and had with him then onbd abt £300 of his owne money,[216] that the men having made themselves masters of the sloop they bore away to sea and threatned the Exaiate if he would not pilot them to Madagascar he should be starved so after some time the Exaiate was forced to doe it and arrived at Madagascar where they fitted the sloop, and from there they sailed to ye Red Sea and meeting with a small boate were told the Mocha Fleet were gone so from thence they sailed away to ye Coast of Surat and off of Persia they met with a Moorish ship which they went onbd of and finding nothing onbd her but ballast they let her go, but took out of her a Moorish Pilot and so sailed away for St. Maries neare Madagascar where they went onshore and there the Exaiate got his things onshore, but the men going to one Baldridge[217] he informed them there was an English ship at Marytam upon ye Island of Madagascar so ye men returned again onbd the sloope and then sent five of their men onshore to find out the Exaiate who forced this Exaiate to go againe onbd ye sloop and came to Marritam and theer they made themselves master of the ship wch was called the *Charming Mary*[218] whereof one Robt

---

[216] This fact would have been important if Ireland had any money in his possession when he was arrested.

[217] **Doc. 63**

[218] This incident is significant because it marks probably the first time that Anglo-American pirates operating in the Indian Ocean took another Anglo-American vessel, which was considered a far worse crime than stealing from the

Glover[219] was Comr and going onbd that ship they gave Glover the sloope and the Exaiate continued onbd the sloope to have gone home with ye sd Glover but the men came afterwards onbd ye sloope and tooke this Exaiate by force out of her onbd the ship and tooke also along with them seaven or eight men whereof Thomas Hitchman was one and so the said ship and sloope sailed to Augustine bay where they fitted the sloop and gave her to Glover and some of his men to carry them home, but would not suffer the Exaiate to go along with them, they setting a watch over him for feare he should make his escape, then the men fitted out the said ship and sailed away to the Coast of Mallaber and from thence to the Niccambar Islands neare the Streights of Molacco where they met with the *Moco* Frigot whereof one Stout was Comr which two ships for some time consorted together and neare the straights they met with a Moorish ship which they afterwards sunck and then afterwards met with a ship whereof one Willocks was Comr wch they also sunck takeing first out of her some sugar and afterwards met with a fought and tooke a Portuguese ship which they afterwards let go and then met with a Moorish pinke which they fought and tooke and carryed with them to ye Maldivia Islands where the two companies quarrelled and so they parted leaving the *Mocho* Frigot and ye pinke together and standing over for ye Niccambar Islands they met with a Moorish ship out of wch they tooke out some provisions and ye Moorish pilot and so sailed to ye Niccambar Island where they watered and form thence went through the Streights of Molucca and came to an Island called Pullycondore where they arrived in Aprill 1697

---

non-Christian 'moors'.
[219] Probably unrelated to Richard Glover [**doc. 37**]

and continued there till September following and then on ye 7th of that month by a storme they lost their ship and continuing upon that Island abt three months after a Portugueze ship came thither and abt twenty of ye men that had belonged to ye *Charming Mary* went down and surprised the ship, as also ye Master and some Merchants that were come onshore, and from thence they sailed to ye Coast of Mallays where ye Portugueze Mr went onshore and bought a Vessell of abt 50 tons and afterwards at the desire of this Exaiate Thomas Hitchman and three others the Portugueze Mr went again onshore and bought another vessel of abt eighteen tons and so they all sailed again to Pullycondore where they fitted the said small Vessell telling this Exaiate and the other four persons who were minded to leave them, that there was a Vessell to carry them home and so the Exaiate ye sd Hitchman and ye three others went onbd the sd small Vessel as did also four Portugueze and four Spaniards who desired to go with this Exaiate but ye day before they sailed a quarrel happening amongst the men of the Greater Vessell three more of the Company to wit Daniell Kenny or Kenedy, Roger Keene and a Frenchman came onbd the sd small Vessell and so they set saile designing for Madras or Bengall but in their passage for ye Streights of Molacco they fell in with a small Island called Surasan where they wooded and watered intending to saile ye next morning but in the night abt 10 or 11 Clo[ck] the sd Kenny or Kenedy agreed with ye Portugueze and Spaniards and sett upon and killed four of the men whilst a sleepe and so sett this Exaiate and also Thos Hitchman and George Morse onshore amongst the Molays and then ye said Kennedy sailed away with ye Vessell, that the Exaiate and also ye sd Hitchman and Morse

183

continued abt three months upon that Island and finding an opportunity they seized upon a small boate in the night time and put out with her to sea and after two days and three nights they made an Island uninhabited where they went on shore and there the boate staved and having mended the boate as well as they could they put out again to sea and after some time they met with a Molay boate but could not come up with her wch said boate going afterwards into a Creek some of their men came by Land and their boate being driven onshoare they carried this Exaiate and ye other two persons to their Molay boate where they gave them Victualls and being bound to Jehore they carried the Exaiate the sd Hitchman and Morse along with them and being come to Jehore, where Morse dyed, they tarried there abt eight weeks and then got passage in a Moorish ship bound to Acheen[220] but happening to touch at Malacca they met with ye beforenamed Daniell Kennedy that had killed ye men, and tarrying there abt five or six weekes there came in one Papte Goff who happening to Quarrell with ye sd Kennedy went to the Governr to tell him what a Rogue the sd Kenney was and desired the Governr to send for this Exaiate and ye sd Hitchman onshore and they being come before the Governr declared that Kennedy was and thereupon ye sd Kennedy was kept at one end of the fort and this Exaiate and ye sd Hitchman was kept at ye other end of the Fort till Goff sailed away and ye next day Kennedy was sett at liberty and ye morning after ye Exaiate and ye sd Hitchman were also set at liberty ye Capt of ye Fort declaring they were Free men of Molacco and might go where they pleased, that tarrying afterwards at that place for a passage abt three months there

---

[220] Achin, now Bandar Aoh

came in to that place one Capt Loggitt Comr of an English ship with whom they shipt themselves bound for Madras or Bengall and the Exaiate one morning happening to meet with Kennedy in ye street ye said Kennedy said to ye Exaiate, what, I hear you are going for Madras, to wch the Exaiate replyed yes and hoped ere long there to see him ye sd Kennedy so the sd Kennedy swore a greate oath, that if it cost him five hundred pieces of eight he would send this Exaiate thither in Irons, and so Kennedy who was married at that place and had greater interest agreed with ye Fiscall or head sheriff and for a small matter of money got this Exaiate and the sd Hitchman put onbd of Capt McFarden in irons and from thence they were carryed to Acheen and were there putt onbd of a Danish ship and carryed to for St. Davids where they continued abt six months and a halfe and from thence were sent home to England by the *Howland*. That when Kennedy killed the men ye Exaiate was run through the shoulder and Hitchman shott into ye head between ye Eyes by the sd Kannedy.

39. Richard Appleton and others

Minutes of the Provincial Council of Pennsylvania, vol. III (Philadelphia, 1852), pp. 50-52

There is little to add to Richard Appleton's account of his time with the minor pirate Captain Greenway. Like so many of the less notorious pirates, even the final fate of Greenway and his company is obscure. A full inventory of all of the equipment left on board the sloop was made by the Philadelphia authorities and is reprinted below [**doc. 71**]

At a Council held at Philada[lphia], the 22d July, 1718.

The Governour acquainted the Board that several mariners, who had lately been taken by pirates, having made their Escape in a Sloop to which some of them formerly belonged in the merchant service, were Come hither for protection, & had Voluntarily delivered themselves & the Sloop into the Governrs. hands, and the sd. mariners attending, they were ordered to be Called in and answered to their names, as follows, Vizt.: Richard appleton, John Robeson, William Williams, John Ford, Benjamin Hodges, John Barfield, James Mathews, Samuel Barrow, Gregory Margoveram, Renold Glorence, Walter Vincent & Timothy Harding, Richard Appleton for himself, and in the name of all the others present, being desir'd to give the Governr. and the Board as Particular an account as he Could of himself & his Fellow Companions. The Following narrative was taken from his mouth, to which they all agreed, Vizt.:

That he had sailed from Jamaica about five months ago on board this very Sloop, under the Comand of Capt. Pinkethman.[221] in Order to Go upon the Wrecks:[222] That the Captain Dying Outward bound, one Tempest, who was

[221] Pinkethman, for reasons unknown, was deliberately sought out, in vain, by Blackbeard
[222] The wrecks of a Spanish treasure fleet, suk by a storm near Florida in 1715. The prospect of recovering treasure from the wrecks drew mariners to the Caribbean from all over the Atlantic, and has often been cited as one of the principal factors that kick-started the wave of piracy in the region from 1716 onwards.

master, had the Comand after him: That they Called in at
Providence at the same time that his majesties ship *Phoenix*
was there,[223] and sail'd out from thence with the man of war
and proceeded to Walkers Key, where in Company with
another Sloop, Capt Greenway, they workt upon a wreck
almost three weeks, but not with any Success; So that both
Sloops went to the Bimmenys other Keys, where they found
another wreck, but nothing Left upon it. This bad Fortune so
Discouraged the people, that by Greenways Instigacon, upon
the Twenty Fourth of May Last they mutiny'd, took
possession of this Sloop & all the arms, & threatened to shoot
Captain Tempest & all that wou'd not Go along with Them,
under Greenways Comand, to Death Immediately; but in a
Day or two they put Capt. Tempest and ten or twelve men
along with him in the other Sloop, and then they departed on
pretence to Go upon the Florida Wrecks, where they arrived
& Came too under one of the Spanish Batteries; But the
people from shoar firing upon them they went from thence a
Little to the Southward of Charles Town, in South Carolina,
and Came on shore in Order to fit the Sloop with a new mast,
which accordingly they did in about three Weeks time;
Coming out from thence they met with a small Sloop from
Providence, bound for Carolina, Daniel Stillwell,[224] master,
but Took nothing from him Except what they paid for,
afterwards they Concluded to Go into the Latitude of
Bermuda, and in their Way met with a French Ship, about
twenty four Guns, they Fired a shot at the French man, who
Returned another & Slung his yards Ready to Engage them,

---

[223] See **doc. 69**
[224] Stillwell was himself a former pirate, who had surrendered under the terms of
a general pardon in the winter of 1717/18

187

but they Chose to Leave her, knowing the ship to be the same which Jennings[225] had formerly taken and sent to Jamaica ; Upon which account he was First Declared Pirate, two Days after this they saw Eleven sail which they supposed to be the Spanish Fleet and gave them Chace, but observing one Large Ship Lie by untill the other Got a head, they Left the Pursuit and kept on the same Latitude, about thirty Leagues distant from the Island of Bermuda, where they met with a small Sloop from Maryland, bound to Bermuda and Barbados, took some Tobacco and hoggs from her, and Forced two of their men, vizt.: John Ford & Gregory Margoveram, both present, next Day they Came up with a Bermudas Sloop, put Five and Twenty men on board of her and kept her for a Consort; One of the men belonging to the Bermudas Sloop is here, vizt.: Benjamin Hodges, then they stretched to the Eastward for three Days, with Intent for Mona or some part of the West Indies. On the third about two o'clock, being Sunday, the Sixth Day of this month, in the morning, they Gave Chace to a Ship, and when they Came up with her fir'd a Shot with a Volley of small arms, upon which she struck; she belonged to Liverpool, about one hundred and thirty tons, homeward Bound from St. [Chris]tophers, with sugar, Richardson, master. The Pirate, Capt. Greenway, the Gunner, Doctor and other officers went Immediately on board the Ship, but the Sloop being to Leward of the Ship the Ship took the wind from their sails, by which means they accidentally fell on board the Ship and broke a Set of Oars upon the Sloops Quarter, this Gave Occasion for most of the men in the

---

[225] Henry Jenning, who had also surrendered in early 1718, was a former privateer from Jamaica who had at one time been styled 'commodore' of the New Providence pirates.

Sloop, being eager for plunder to Jump on board the Ship, and when the Sloop sheer'd off these men here whisper'd one another, that now was their Best Opportunity to Escape, Whereupon Richard Appleton being armed, seized the Helm, sent John Robinson down to Secure the Stores & order'd the Negroes to hoist the sails, upon which one of the Pyrates took up a musket & snapt it twice at the sd. Richard, then fired but missing, he Club'd the peice[226] and wounded Richard on the head, upon which One of the Negoes shot the Pirate with a Pistol through the belly, and another wounded him in the Thigh ; then they bound this Fellow & Seven morre of his Companions, being half Drunk, put them in the Canew and Set them adrift, the Ship and Sloop Gave us Chace, and we saw them take up the men in the Canoe, but this Sloop sailed so well that we soon Lost them; We saw several Sail in our way hither, but avoided Speaking with any, being all Resolutely Determined to Blow our selves up before we shou'd be taken by any Pirate; that we were unanimous in Coming into this Place to Deliver the Sloop and ourselves up to the Governr, and to Implore his Countenance and protection, not as Pirates, but as honest men Imploy'd in the mercht. service, and who never had been accessary or in the Least Concern'd in the Villainous Designs and practices of those from whom we have now made Our Escape with the utmost Risqe of our Lives, and all of them with one Voice submitted themselves in this manner, affirming the same thing.

The above narrative being taken into Consideracon with all the Circumstances, it was the unanimous opinion of this

---

[226] ie. turned it round to use the heavy butt as a club

Board, That it did not appear that these men bad been Guilty of any piracy whereby to subject them to any punishment or other Legal process, but rather that they ought to be well used and Civilly Intreated for the Service they had Done in order to Encourage others to Do the Like, That the Present most Dangerous and too frequent Practice of Piracy in these parts may at Last be subdued.

40. Henry Hunt

The Examination of Henry Hunt, 27 September, 1720. HCA 1/54, ff. 115-116

Henry Hunt was captured by one of the most powerful pirate consortia of the 'golden age', and pressed into their service as a pilot, or navigator. After he was freed by them he sailed first for America and then to London, where he was recognised by Thomas Creed, one of the pirates' victims, and arrested. Hunt, along with Captain Oldson of the Charlotte, *was tried on 31 October, 1720, but the ships' owners appeared on behalf of the defendants and 'gave them very good Characters', and they were both acquitted.[227]*

This Examinate saith that on or about the first Day of March 1718/19 he arrived in the River of Gamboa in the *Sarah Gally* (whereof he the Examinate was then Mar) laden with Goods from the Port of London proper for the Trade of that River and there took in 133 Slaves. And on or about the 27th of May following a pirate Vessel called the *Royal James*

---

[227] London Journal, 5/11/1720

(whereof Edward England was then Comander and which had been formerly called the *Pearl* and belonged to the Port of London and commanded by one Tizard) came into the said River with two other English Ships which had been taken by the sd Edward England and by him manned with Pirates. And the sd Ship *Royal James* and a ship called the *Charlot* fired at the Examinate's said Vessel with 5 Shot and took her and commanded the Examinate on board of one of the sd Ships. And he the Examinate slipped his Cable and endeavoured to have escaped from them but could not effect the same, and when the Examinate was on board of them they beat him with their Cutlaces and threatened to kill him for endeavouring to escape from them and also threatened to burn his said Ship, and soon afterwards they forced the Examinate to go on board of the *Buck* sloop[228] and ordered him to take Charge of her as Pilote of her and threatened to blow out his Brains if he suffered her to touch the Ground. And he the Examinate was very unwilling and refused to go on board of her and told them that he was unacquainted with the River, but they threatened to shoot him if he would not take Charge of her and thereupon he was forced to pilot her up the River Gamboa where they took the *Mercury* (whereof Captain Market was Comander) and a Snow (whereof Captain Lynch was Comander). And then they permitted the Examinate to go on board the sd *Sarah* Gally which was then in the possession of the sd Pirates, and where he the Examinate then lay every night upon the Hen Coop on the Quarter Deck but in the Day time they forced him into their

---

[228] This suggests that England and Davis at some time worked in consort off the African coast, which is not particularly surprising. Both were Jacobites, and according to Charles Johnson, England had once captured Davis, before the latter turned to piracy.

Service on board the sd Sloop and compelled him to pilot her down the sd River where they took the *Coward* Gally (whereof Thomas Creed was Comander) and brought her to the other Ships which they had taken. And the sd Pirates took the Lading out of the aforesd Ships and put part thereof on board the sd Ship *Royal James* and threw the rest over board. And on or about the 5th of July 1719 they delivered to the Examinate his aforesd Gally and Negroes and permitted him to sail away with them and he the Examinate proceed to Maryland and there took in a Lading of Tobacco and brought the same to the Port of London. And he the Examinate denys that he had any part of the Goods which were taken out of any of the aforesaid Vessels. And saith that he was wholly ignorant of the Design of burning the *Coward* Gally and did not know any thing thereof till he saw the same on Fire.

41. John Matthews

The Examination of John Matthews, 12 October, 1722. HCA 1/55, ff. 20-21

*Oliver la Buse had one of the longest careers of any 'golden age' era pirate, beginning as early as 1716 and continuing until at least 1722. However, much of the middle part of his career, particularly that time between his cruising on the West African coast with Cocklyn and Davis and his later Indian Ocean consortship with John Taylor, is obscure. This document, along with **doc. 44**, shows that la Buse continued in consortship with Cocklyn for some time after the noted memorialist William Snelgrave met them at the*

Sierra Leone river, and that by the time they parted company they had already been joined by John Taylor, with whom la Buse would later resume his consortship. See also docs 21, 44, 55, 56, 57 and 73.

This Examinate saith that he was born at Chilham in the County of Kent where he lived with his parents til he was about thirteen years of age and was then put an apprentice to a Fisherman at Faversham for seven years which he served, afterwards he entred himself on board several Merchant ships and served in them as a Foremast Man for several voyages. That in the year 1719 he enterd himself as a Foremast Man onboard the ship *Heroine* whereof Richard Bleurow was Mr then in the River of Thams and bound on a voyage to Guinea. That the said ship proceeded accordingly to the said Place and safely arrived in Widaw Road on the Coast of Guinea where the said ship trafficked for slaves. That during the said ship's stay there and before she had taken in her whole quantity of Slaves vizt. In the year 1720 Three pirate Ships vizt. the *Speakwell* Capt Taylor Comd, the *Duke of Ormond*, Oliver de la Bouche Comd and the *Courade*,[229] Jeremiah Cocklin Comd;[230] came down the Coast of Guinea to Widaw Road aforesaid and took the aforesaid ship *Heroine* as she lay at anchor there and carried her to the Island of Coreno a desolate Island upon the said Coast where the pirate ships usually harbour and refit. That before the said ships arrival there the said Jeremiah Cocklin commanded this Examinate and sixteen others of the said ship *Heroine's*

---

[229] In other sources this ship is referred to both as the Comrade and the Courage
[230] Cocklyn is usually called 'Thomas' by modern authors, but this is one of several sources to suggest his given name was Jeremiah

Crew on board the sd Pirate ship ye *Courade* about four of whom went upon their own accord. That afterwards some of them were carried on board the said pirate ships *Speakwell* and *Duke of Ormond* and this Examinate and seven more were forced to continue on board the said ship *Courade*. That the Examinate desired the said Capt de la Bouche (who had exchanged his ship with Capt Cocklin for the sd ship *Courade*) sev times to set him on shore that he might come home again to England but the said De la Bouche refused to let him go telling him that he wanted hands and must go with him otherwise he would shoot him which he offer'd to do sevl times upon the Exaiates refusing to work onboard the said ships which the Examinate was forc'd afterwards to do for preservation of his life seeing no possibility then to get off. That after the said ship *Courade* left the Coast of Guinea the said Capt de la Bouche proceeded with her towards the East Indies and in her passage thither met with an English Merchant ship called the *Indian Queen* laden with slaves which he took and afterwards went onboard the same with all his crew and gave his own ship the *Courade* to the Comd of the sd ship *Indian Queen* and put all the men of the said ship *Indian Queen* onboard the *Courade* with him except seaven whom he detained onboard his new ship the greatest part of whom were unwilling to stay with him but the sd de la Bouche forced them. That they proceed afterwards to the Island of Mayotte upon the Coast of India to careen their ship. That upon their arrival there this Examinate and four others found an opportunity in the night to get away from thence in a small Canoe belonging to the Blacks who inhabited the Island to the Island of Johanna upon the same Coast where they stay'd abt two months before they had an

194

opportunity to get off after which a Mercht ship call'd the *Greenwich*[231] bound to the East Indies arrived there whereupon the Examinate and the four Marrs aforemention'd went to Capt. Richard Kirby Comd of the sd ship and told him of the treatment they had met with and desir'd to be entred as foremast Men onboard his ship which the said Capt agreed to and hired them at five and twenty shillings a Month for the rest of his Voyage. That the Examinate continued aboard the said ship *Greenwich* for and twenty Months and returned wth her into the River of Thames and work'd onboard her for about a Month in the sd River and then was taken from onboard by a Warrant from the Lds of the Admy[232] and carried to the Marshalsea prison where he has continued ever since. That he had no share of the ship *Indian Queen* or her Lading taken as aforesaid nor was any ways assisting in the taking her being then between decks. That he knows of none of the sd de la Bouches Crew being in England but believed they are still with him and further saith not.

42. Bridstock Weaver

The Examination of Bridstock Weaver, 13 February, 1724. HCA 1/55, f. 53

---

[231] See **docs. 55 and 56**
[232] Lords of the Admiralty

Bridstock Weaver's status as a forced man rather than a volunteer is somewhat fragile. A good, though not entirely adequate, indicator of an indivdual's forced status is the acceptance by an Admiralty Court that he was genuinely conscripted against his will, as courts tended to be reluctant to accept that a defendent was forced unless presented with overwhelming evidence. Probably many more innocent forced men were sent to the gallows than guilty volunteers escaped justice by a plea of forcing. However, in Weaver's case the court that tried him [doc. 61] was not convinced by either his own testimony or that of his witnesses, but he escaped execution and received a pardon while his co-defendent, William Ingram [doc. 29] did not, suggesting that there may have been some doubt in Weaver's case. Weaver himself maintained that he had been forced into piracy, and most significantly, other pirates acknowledged Weaver's forced status [docs 32 and 61].

This Examinate saith that in the Month of September 1720 this Examinate being then chief Mate of the *Mary and Martha* of Bristol (whereof Thomas Wilcox was Mr) which then lay at Anchor at the Island of St Christophers went out in the boat with the Boatswain to see what Ships were coming to the sd Island and they then saw a Ship and a Sloop coming under English Colours and they proved to be Pirate and the sd Ship was called the *Royal Fortune* and one Roberts was Comander of her and the Sloop was called the *Good Fortune* and one Montanie a French Man was Comander of her and some of her Men held up their Pieces[233] at the Examinate and the Boatswain as they were lying upon

---

[233] guns

their Oars and threatened to fire at them if they refused to go on board of her and thereupon they were obliged to go on board of her where they put Pistols to the Breasts of the Examinate and ye sd Boatswain and threatned to shoot them if they refused to sign their Articles whereupon they to prevent their being killed signed the same. And then the sd Pirates burnt the sd ship *Mary and Martha* and took a New England Man from her Anchor and left her adrift and then the sd Pirate Vessels went to St. Bartholomew one of the Leward Islands and in their way thither they took several Sloops and other Vessels and particularly a Brigantine of New England (whereof one Norton was Comander). And ye sd Roberts ordered the Examinate and the rest of the Company of the sd Sloop to leave her and to go on board the sd Brigantine wch they accordingly did and the rest of the Vessels were discharged and one Anstis was made Mar of ye sd Brigantine and she was named ye *Fortune* and she took several Vessels and particularly the *Hambleton* (whereof one Joseph Smith was Mar) and Henry Treehill[234] and about13 others of her Company was taken out of her and put on board the sd Brigantine and when he the Examinate had been on board of her about 3 Months she run away from the sd Roberts and then went a cruising amongst the Islands in the West Indias and took more Vessels and discharged them and then went to Rattan where she was cleaned and he the Examinate there made his Escape and went on board of a sloop (whereof John Kent was Comander) which came there for Logwood and was bound to Holland and she put into Falmouth for a Pilot and he the Examinate there went on Shoar and travelled by Land to Bristol in May last and begged for Sustenance in his

---

[234] See **doc. 43**

way thither and from thence went to Hereford and lived on Shoar from that time and in or about the Month of September last he the Examinate together with Henry Treehill (who was taken out of the sd Ship Hambleton) and Thomas Lawrence Jones[235] (who had belonged to ye sd Roberts) were taken up at Bristol and there imprisoned. And he the Examinate was twice confined in irons at Sea (to wit) at the first time about five Days and the other time about 2 Days for endeavouring to run away wth the aforesd Brigantine. And he the Examinate always gave away what Share belonged to him out of what was taken by the aforesd Pirates. And as soon as he came to Bristol he surrendered himself up to the Major who discharged him.[236]

43. Henry Treehill

The Information of Henry Treehill, 21 March, 1724. HCA 1/55, ff. 64-68

The recollections of Henry Treehill, who appeared as a witness at the trial of Bridstock Weaver and Willliam Ingram [doc. 61], are of general value for their length and detail, and also for the number of pirates' names they contain. One name in particular, though, sands out in importance: John Philips. Charles Johnson, in his General History of the Pyrates, *claimed that the pirate captain*

---

[235] See **doc. 32**

[236] These last three points are almost formulaic, answering in advance the three key questions that could be used to prove his guilt: was he willing? Did he profit by it? Did he attempt to evade justice?

John Philips had earlier served as carpenter to Thomas Anstis, but there is little to explain where Johnson's knowledge of Philips' early career might have come from or how reliable it might have been. This document, if it does not enlighten us as to the nature of Johnson's source, does at least corroborate Johnson's statement and to some exent validates his research.

This Informant saith that on or about the 22d Day of June in the year of our Lord 1721 the Ship *Hamilton* of Bristol (whereof Joseph Smith was then Master and he the Informant a foremast man) in her passage for the Island of Jamaica, between 20 and 30 Leagues to the Leeward of the said Island was taken by a pirate Brigantine called the *Good Fortune* (whereof Thomas Anstis was Comander) an he the Informant and twelve others of the Company of the sd Ship the *Hamilton* (to wit) Wm Wilks[237] ye 2d Mate, Henry Chaplin, Rt. Gibson, Wm. Wayman, Wm. Stibbs, Wm. Amos, Rowland Hughs, John Ford, John Cadwell, John Smith, William Simms als Cook and Thomas James were taken out of the sd Ship the *Hamilton* and put on board the said pirate Brigantine. And the said Pirates took several Goods out of the *Hamilton*. And saith yt Thomas Lawrence Jones[238] a foremast man, Claus White a Quartermaster, Thomas Wiltshire a foremast man, John Phillips[239] ye Carpenter, George Weedon and Wm. Hall a foremast man, a person called Old South who was an Officer, Cary Crossman als Crosswell a foremast man and Samuel Davis a Carpenter and also a Negro and a Malotta all belonging to the sd pirate

---

[237] See **doc. 46**
[238] See **doc. 32**
[239] See **doc. 47**

Vessel first came on board the *Hamilton*. That they were all of them acting in the plundering of her and more particularly the sd Jones and White the Quarter Ma[ster] who gave Orders for the delivering and sending several goods out of her on board the sd pirate Vessel as also the sd Hall, Old South and Davis (who the Informant particularly remembers took away the Carpenters Chest of Tools) and that Bridstock Weaver,[240] John Fenn, John Morris, Nathaniel Bird, Jacob Mansel a Carpenter, Thomas Ward, John Holladay, Roger Jackson, John Taverner, Michael Ashburnham als South, Martin Kendall, George Bradly, John Orma, Peter le Motte, John Reynolds, Nicholas Mappin, one Watkins a Gunner, one Montanie and Daniel Gladden were then belonging to the said pirate Vessel. That after the said Pirates had plundered the sd Ship ye *Hamilton* they carried her to Key Mohair where they lay about two or three Months, within which time one George Blackater a Wood Cutter at Cape Catarh and John Hodges and 2 or 3 others voluntarily entered themselvs on board ye sd pirate Vessel. And then the sd Pirates gave the said Smith the possession of the *Hamilton* with thirteen of his Men, but he the Informt and the 12 Persons beforenamed were continued on board the sd pirate Vessel. And then she sailed to the Bay of Campechy and there took and burnt a Spanish Vessel and obliged one other to run on shoar. That they took out of the sd Spanish Vessel that was burnt about ten pounds in Money and some silver buckells and buttons and cups and the same was divided amongst the Company of the sd Brigantine and amounted to about three pounds for each Mans Share. That the aforesd Jones, Hall, Taverner, Jackson, Old South, Watkins, Pillips,

[240] See **doc. 42**

200

Crossman and Davis were chiefly acting in the plundering of the sd Vessel. That they stayed but one night in the Bay of Campechy and the next Day beating to Windward they met the sd Ship the *Hamilton* in company of a Spanish Privateer who had the possession of hre. And then the sd pirate Vessel retook the *Hamilton* from the sd Spanish Vessel and drove the said Spanish Vessel on Shoar, and that one George Hooper who was left on board the *Hamiton* by the sd Spanyards declared that ye Spanyards had put the aforesd Capt Smith and his Men into his ye sd Captain Smith's Boat and turned them adrift. And farther saith that it being proposed to turn ye *Hamilton* to Windward in order to seeke for ye sd Smith and his Men, but the aforesd Thomas Lawrence Jones opposed the same and then it being debated what they should doe with the *Hamilton* the sd Jones advised that she should be burnt adding these or the like words 'what Occasion had he (meaning ye sd Capt Smith) to stay behind to pick up empty Bottles'. And then the sd Ship *Hamilton* was accordingly burnt and then ye sd pirate Vessel proceeded to Key Mohair to take in Water and from there proceeded for Cap St. Antonio and took an English Vessel called the *Don Carlos* belonging to the Port of London (whereof Lot Nickins was Master) and plundered her of money, Rum, Sugar and other Goods. And the sd Plunder was divided amongst all the sd Pirates and amounted to forty pounds sterling to each man. That the aforesd Jones and Phillips were two of the Persons that went on board and were very active in the plundering of her, yt John White, Peter Miller and John Foster three of the Company and also John Macklin one other of her Company voluntarily entered themselves on board the sd pirate Vessel. That on the same

201

Day the sd pirate Vessel off of Cape Antonio took a Ship and a Sloop belonging to New England and took some Goods out of them. That at Cape Antonio they took two small Spanish Vessels and plundered them of some small fire Arms, Beef, Bread and other Provisions, and there Richard Knowls, Edmund Tiley, Old Anthony a Greek and a French man voluntarily entered themselves with the pirates, and from thence they plyed to Windward and about two Days afterwards off of Hispaniola they took an English Ship which (as her Company declared) had been at Guinea and Jamaica and was bound for England that they took out of her some Rum and Sugar and about 2 or 3 hundred pounds in Money which was shared amongst the sd Pirates. And then Captain Anstice asked his Men if any of them was desirous to go home to England and thereupon the aforesaid George Blackater getting into the Boat in order to go on board ye sd English Ship the aforesd Wm. Hall jumped into the sd Boat after him and with a Gun Rammer struck him under the Eye and swore at him and sayd these or the like words 'you came on board voluntarily and now you are leaving us.' That about 2 or 3 Days afterwards between Cape Nichola[241] and the Hanavassa Island they took a French Ship bound to Cuba and took out of her several hogsheads of Wine and (as he believes) some Money, and Wm. Patroon one of her Company was taken out of her by force, and about 2 or 3 Days afterwards they arrived at the Isle of Pynes and there took a Vessel called a Turtler belonging to Jamaica (as appeared by her Clearings) the Company having left her. That at the sd Island they went on Shoar and cut several Trees for a Mainmast foremast and Boom and put them on

---

[241] Cape St. Nicholas, Haiti

board the sd Turtler and therein carryed the same to an uninhabited Island called Rattan and from thence proceeded through the Gulph to the windward of Antegoa and there took an English Ship and also a French Vessel and took out of them some Rum and Sugar. And the aforesd Jones advised the taking out of the said English Ship two of her Men saying 'Wee want Men and Wee'l have em.' And thereupon two of her company were taken out of her and from thence they proceeded to the Eastwards of the Island of Desiada and there a Bristol snow whereof one Jones was Mar and took out of her some Ale, Syder and other Provisions and they there also took four other English Vessels and plundered them and then stretched to the Northward and took a Dutch Ship called the *Morning Star* laden with Sugar bound for Amsterdam and by the Instigacion of the aforesd Jones threw her Lading over board and fitted her for their Service and manned her and the aforesd Anstice was made Comander of her and John Fenn was made Captain of the *Good Fortune*. And amongst the Leeward Islands they took an English Ship called the *Portland* belonging to London (whereof John Lubbock was commander) and forced about 3 or 4 of her men, and particularly Robert Dalton, into their Service and carryed her to Carramaroo in the Windward part of Hispaniola and there took out of her several Pipes of Wine and then restored her to the possession of her commander. And then ye sd two pirate Vessels proceeded to the Island of Tobago and afterwards to the Banks of Newfoundland where they took several English and French Vessels and plundered them and forced many of their men out of them and put them on board the *Morning Star*. That the aforesd Thomas Wiltshire, John Phillips, George Weedon, Cary Crossman, and Samuel Davis and also John Morris, Nathaniel Bird, Jacob Mansell, Thomas Ward, Wm Ingram, John Holladay, Roger Jackson, John Taverner, Michael Ashburnham, Wm Simms als Cook, John Hodges, Stephen Weston, Martin Kendall, George Bradly, John Oram, Claus White, Peter le Motte, Dutch Jack, John Reynolds, Edmund Tiley, Zachary Knowle, Francis Taylor and Montanie went on board the *Morning Star* and continued in her service till she was lost. That the aforesd Hall, Jones, and John White went into her Service for some time and then returned into the Service of ye sd Brigantine and the aforesaid Bridstock Weaver, Old Watkins, Wm. Whelks, Peter Walker, Peter Miller, Old Antonio, Robert Dalton and Daniel Gladdon remained on board the said Brigantine. That from the Banks of Newfound Land the sd Vessels proceeded to Tobago and there watered and there or at Corromaroo the sd Anstice was voted out of the command of ye *Morning Star* and John Fenn was made commander of her and then Bridstock Weaver was forced by the Pirates to be commander of the *Good Fortune* and Wm. Whelks was made Quartermaster and Old South was made mate of her. That from Tobago they went to Testugas and there hove down and cleaned and from thence to the Coast of Crocus where they took 3 Dutch Vessels (to wit) two Ships and a sloop and took out of them some Linnen and woollen Goods and some Money. And each of the Company of the *Good Fortune* then reced thirty pounds or abts as their shares of the Booty. And whilst they were upon the Banks of Newfoundland he the Informant, Cary Crossman, Peter Miller and Wm. Whelks had made an Agreement amongst themselves to run away with the *Good Fortune* and to carry her into the next Harbour and there to surrender themselves.

And the aforesd Old Watkins discovering the same called out to the company of the *Morning Star* and told them that they were going to run away with the Brigantine and thereupon Thomas Jones, John Foster, John White and Wm. Hall came on board of her to prevent the same. And then the sd Vessels proceeded to an Island called the Grand Comander where the *Morning Starr* ran on Shoar and was lost. And the aforesd Fenn was there made Comander of the sd Brigantine and she then proceeded to Rattan to clean and there the sd Bridstock Weaver, John Hodges, John Morris, Montanie, one Nicholo a French Malotto, Samuel Davis and one or two others left her in a boat which they had taken at the Bay of Andoras. And from Rattan the sd Brigantine beat through the Windward Passage where they took the Antelope belonging to New England bound to the Bay of Andoras and took out of her some Bread, Beef and Rum and the next Day they took a French Vessel which came from Hispaniola and was bound to France and they took out of her some Money which was divided amongst them and each Mans Share came to ten or twelve pounds or thereabouts. And then by the Consent of the sd Fenn he the Informt and 18 others of the Company of ye sd Brigantine (to wit) Roger Jackson, John Phillips, John Taverner, Michael Ashburnham, Wm. Hall, Wm. Symms als Cook, Thomas Jones, Thomas Wiltshire, George Weedon, Thomas Ward, John Foster, Nathaniel Bird, Wm Ingram, Jacob Mansel, Wm Patterons, John Oram, Daniel Gladden and Wm Whelks fitted out the sd Ship the *Antelope* and therein came to Bristol Channell under the Comand of the sd Wm Whelks with two Guns mounted and some small Arms. And in their passage thither they met with a small French Vessel and the sd Patterson hailed her and thereupon her boat came on board the *Antelope* and then the sd Patterson and ye sd Phillips, Hall and Foster went on board of the sd French Vessel and brought out of her a basket of Eggs, about ten Gallons of Wine, 2 or 3 Jugs of Brandy and some Fowle and sent on board of her a Negro boy because he should not be discharged by them. And the Informant believes if the French Men had not come on board and had not afterwards delivered ye sd Provisions that the Company of the *Antelope* would by force have compelled them to it. That as they were coming home they agreed to sink the *Antelope* by reason that all of them except ye sd Daniel Gladden were the chief and principal Actors in the aforesd Piracies and were fearfull of being discovered. That he the Informant and eight others of them came on Shoar in the boat at Coome Martin[242] in the Night time. And the Informant was afterwards informed that the rest of the said Persons wilfully sunk the said Ship and came on Shoar.

---

[242] Combe Martin, near Ilfracombe in Devon.

44. Richard Moor

The Examination of Richard Moor, 31 October, 1724. HCA 1/55, ff. 94-97

Quite why Richard Moor gave three separate depositions, two on one day, is not clear, but the wealth of detail he provided on the careers of John Taylor and other captains is to be valued. There is some confusion between Moor's account of the movements of Cocklyn, Taylor and la Buse, and that given by John Matthews [doc. 41], particularly in regard to who was in command of which ship at any given time, but that is not unexpected concerning such confusing events at such a distance in time and need not diminish the general air of reliability that Matthews' and Moor's account possess. Moor's account gives more information about the enigmatic Jasper Seagar (or Seater, as Moor calls him) than any other source, and is also the only known source to explain the final end of Jeremiah Cocklyn.

This Examinate saith that about six years and a half since he went from the Port of London as the surgeon's Mate of the *Comrade* Gally (whereof Thomas Samson was Mar) bound for Barbados and Guinea and from thence to the said Port of London and the sd ship accordingly proceeded to Barbados and from thence to the Coast of Ginea and on the 7ᵗʰ Day of June 1718 the sd Gally being at Anchor about five Leagues to the Leward of Anamaboo to take in fresh water in order to go off of the Coast she was taken by two pirate Vessels the one called the *Speedwell* whereof Jeremiah Cocklin was Comander) and the other the *Duke of Ormond* (whereof Oliver le Boos was Comander). And he the Examinate was

207

forced by the sd Pirates on board and into the Service of ye sd Ship the *Speedwell* and from thence the sd pirate Vessels carryed the sd Gally to Widaw where they took five sail of French and Portuguese Vessels and plundered them and then proceeded to an uninhabited Island called Corista[243] upon the sd Coast of Guinea and there all the sd three Ships were hove down and cleaned. And saith that nine of the company of ye sd Gally at the time when she was taken had bene sent on shoar for Water and were detained there by the Natives upon the Account of some Injury which (As the Examinate was informed) they had reced by one Captain Plummer and the Master and chief mate and two boys had their Liberty and were put on board of a Dutch sloop and one Stephen King the Boatsns Mate was forced with the Examinate into the Service of the said ship the *Speedwell*. And he believes that the rest of the Company (to wit) seven or thereabouts voluntarily entered themselves into the service of the sd Pirates. And saith that from Corista the sd Ship the *Duke of Ormond* proceeded for the East Indias; and about a Month afterwards ye *Speedwell* with the Examinate on board of her weighed anchor in order to follow her and left the *Comrade Gally* at an Anchor there without any Hands on board because they did not like her. And the sd Ship the *Speedwell* about 5 Days after she was come from Corista took a French Vessell called the *Victory* (whereof one Captain Hays was Comander) and plundered her and brought her to Cape Lopez and there fitted her out for their service and manned her with the Company of the *Speedwell* and gave the *Speedwell* to the sd Captain Hays, and from Cape Lopes they proceeded in the sd Ship the *Victory* under the Comand of the sd Cocklin to

---

[243] Corisca, Equatoral Guinea

Madagascar and there halled her on Shoar and cleaned her and took in wood Water and Provisions and were there joined by two other pirate ships called the *Fancy* and the *John Gally* under the Comand of Edward England and there the said Cocklin dyed and was succeeded by Richard Taylor one of her Company. And then they burnt ye *John Gally* and took her men on board the *Victory* and *Fancy*. And then they proceeded to the Island of Johanna and took an East India ship called ye Cassandra[244] (whereof Captain McCreach was Comander) and manned her and made a pirate Vessel of her and gave the sd ship the *Fancy* to the sd Capt. McCreah and from thence the sd Ship the *Victory* under ye Comand of the sd Richard Taylor and the *Cassandra* under the Comand of Jaspar Seater who was made Captain of her in the room of ye sd Edward England (who was turned out of Comand) proceeded to the East India and in their way thither they took two Muscat men laden with horses and plundered them. And in the year 1719 about four of the Clock in the Morning thye met with the Bombay Fleet (which was fitted out to take the Island of Angury inhabited by Pirates[245]) and ingaged them all the Day and fired many Guns at them and chased them till they lost sight of them which was about 12 of the Clock at Night and then the proceeded to a Dutch Fortification called Cochins upon the Coast of Mallavar and there traded for what Goods they wanted and kept their Christmas and being there informed that a Squadron of 7 India Ships were fitted out at Bombay to go in quest of them they proceeded to an uninhabited Island called Morashes and there the *Victory* was hove down cleaned and repaired and from thence both the sd

---

[244] See **docs 55** and **56**
[245] Indian pirates

Ships under ye Comand of the sd Taylor and Seater proceeded to Don Maskareene and arrived there on Easter Sunday 1720[246] and there took a Vessel called the *Guelderland* which had been a Dutch Man of War) with a Portuguese Vice Roy on board of her and another Vessel called the *Greyhound* which was an Ostender and plundered them and the *Guelderland* was reputed to be very rich in Diamonds Rubys and other stones and they carryed the sd Vessels to the Island of St. Mary near Madagascar where they arrived in or about May 1720[247] and there fitted out the sd ship the *Guelderland* as a pirate and the said Richard Taylor was made Comander of her and there the sd Seater dyed and ye aforesd le Boos was made Captain of the *Cassandra* in his Room and the *Greyhound* got away and they burnt the *Victory*. And then hearing Guns fired on the other side of the sd Island of St Mary and believing them to be English Men of War they proceeded to St Augustine at Madagascar and there one of the Natives brought on board the *Guelderland* a Letter which had been left with him by Comodore Matthews for a Capt of one of the English Men of War which had lost ye Company of the sd Comodore. And the sd Richard Taylor opened the sd Letter and read it before all the ships Company giving an Account of the Names of the Squadron of the English Men of War and the Names of their Comanders with the Numbers of their Men and Guns. And from there they proceeded to a place called de la Goa which was a small Dutch Fortification and arrived there in April 1721 and took the sd Fortificacion with a Dutch Vessel that lay there.[248] And there the sd ships the *Guelderland* and

---

[246] This is an error, the capture of the Guelderland took place at Easter, 1721.
[247] 1721

Cassandra were hove down and cleaned, and then went back to Madagascar with the said small Dutch Vessel and there the Company of both the said ships being ordered on board the *Guelderland* it was put to the Vote which of the Men would continue to go a pirating and which of them would go to the West Indias to endeavour to get a Pardon and thereupon the sd Richard Taylor with a hundred and twelve white Men and forty Blacks voated to go to the West Indias and came on board the *Cassandra* to ye Examinate and Thomas Arrett an English surgeon and Mr Snear a Dutch surgeon who did not go on board the *Guelderland* by reason that the Surgeons had no Vote there.[249] And then the *Cassandra* with the said Richard Taylor and the sd hundred and twelve white Men forty Blacks and he the Examinate and the said other two Surgeons proceeded from Madagascar to the Isle of Pointz in the West Indias and there fitted out 2 small Vessels called petty Jagers[250] with 15 Men in each of them. And the sd Richard Taylor was in one of them and he the Examinate was in the other, in order to go to the Grout upon ye Main in the Spanish West Indias to learn whether or no there was any Act of Grace for Pirates and as they were going thither they met with a small Spanish Sloop with 4 Men on board of her who informed them that there was an Act of Grace, and thereupon the sd Taylor hired the sd Sloop of the Spanyards and gave them 50 Crowns to carry the Examinate to ye Grout[251]

---

[248] Delagoa Bay, where Jacob du Bucquoy [**doc. 57**] was employed as an engineer before his capture by the pirates.

[249] This presumably was because surgeons were usually forced men who could not be expected to vote in the best interests of the company, rather than any objection to the medical profession.

[250] Piraguas - canoes

[251] A secure harbour near Portobelo, Panama

to deliver a Petition to the Governour for a Pardon and they accordingly carryed the Examinate on board of his Majesties ship the *Mermaid* at the Grout where he the Examinate delivered the sd Petition to Capt Laws the Comander of the sd Ship which was in April 1723. And the sd Captain Laws asked the Examinate where the sd Richard Taylor was and if he would come on board the *Mermaid* and the Examinate told him that he was about fifteen Leagues off and that he would come on board in case the sd Capt Laws would send his Leiftenant as a hostage for him whereupon the sd Capt Laws sent his own Brother in ye sd Sloop, and the next Day the sd Taylor came on board ye sd Man of War in the sd Sloop and about five Days afterwards the sd Taylor went away in the sd Sloop and the sd Captain Laws's Brother returned on board in the same Sloop. And then the sd Capt Laws at ye Examinate's Request gave him leave to go on board of his Majesty's Ship the *Launceston* at the Grout and he accordingly went on board of her there and from thence proceeded in her to Jamaica, and was there examined and discharged by the duke of Portland and then came home in the sd Ship the *Mermaid* to England.

The Information of the aforesaid Richard Moor, taken as before.

That in the Month of December 1720 he the Informt having been forced into the Service of the Pirates was at the Island of St Mary near Madagascar in a Ship called the *Cassandra* in company with other pirate Ships and he the Informt there saw one Plantin who appeared to be and was (as ye Informt believes) intimately acquainted with many of the Pirates and eat and drank and caroused with them and owned and confessed that he had been a pirate belonging to the *Dragon* under the Comand of Edward Condon and the Informt heard him the sd Plantin and others of the Pirates say that their Share of the Booty of the Moor Ship (meaning as the Informt apprehended a Juda Man which (as they declared) they had taken in the said Ship the *Dragon* off of the back of Bombay) came to nine hundred pounds for each man.

The farther Information of the aforesaid Richard Moor, 5/11/1724

This Informant saith that about Christmas 1721 he the Informt being by force and Compultion a Surgeon on board of a pirate Ship called the *Victory* (whereof Richard Taylor was Comander) at a French Island called Don Maskareen in the East Indias he the Informt then and there saw one Edward Condon (who had been commonly reputed to be Comander of a pirate Ship called the *Dragon*). And saith that he the sd Condon and many other (who were reputed to have been part of the Crew of the sd Condon on board the sd Ship the Dragon) then lived on Shoar upon the sd Island. And he the said Condon and many others of them then declared that they had got Riches enough (by pirating) to maintain them hansomly as long as they lived and that therefore they had broak up, meaning that they had left off pirating and that they had left one Plantin and the rest of their Crew at St Marys near the Island of Madagascar.

45. Edward Evans

The Information of Edward Evans, 10 October, 1723. HCA 1/18, f. 37

The testimony of Edward Evans, brief though it is, is illuminating because of the details about pirate punishments which are its focus, and it is included here for that reason. Punishment, as described by Evans, was both formal,in its use of a trial and twelve-man jury, but at the same time arbitrary, with different punishments handed down for the same offence.See also **doc. 46.**

The Informt saith That he was Carpenter of the Ship or Vessel called the *Little York* of Bristol aforesaid (James Philips Comander) in her then homeward bound Voyage from Virginia to the Port of Bristol aforesaid in prosecution whereof the said ship or vessel was on or about the seventeenth day of July in the year of our Lord one thousand seven hundred and twenty taken by a Pirate ship of six and twenty Guns and a sloop of Eight Guns Comanded by John Roberts[252] about seventy leagues to the Eastward of Newfoundland in the Latitude of forty three and the Informant together with severall others of the said *Little York's* Crew were forced on board the said Pirates for about eleven months, in which time this Informt and three others of his Comrades endeavouring to make their escape from the said Pirates were all four taken by the said Pirates and tried by them for their lives by a Jury of Twelve men belonging to the said Pirates, one of which twelve men was the person now in Custody in Bridewell charged with Piracy giveing his name Thomas Lawrence Jones[253] who then seemed as active

---

[252] 'John' was Bartholomew Roberts' given forename. When or why he changed it to Bartholomew is unclear.
[253] See **doc. 32**

and cruell as any of the said Pirates and two of the said four persons were by the said jury ordered to be shott to death which was immediately executed on them and this Informt and one James Watts the other two persons then tried by the same jury were ordered to receive five hundred Lashes each (with a Log line) or thereabouts which they received the same night as the other two persons were shott, and the said Informt further saith that the said Thomas Lawrence Jones was one of the Pirates who lashed this Informt in manner as aforesaid.

46. William Whelks

The Information of William Whelks, 22 April 1723. ADM 1/4104, ff. 76-77

William Whelks was probably forced into the service of Anstis' company because of his skill at navigation.

This Informant upon his Oath saith that in April 1721 he set sail from Bristol in the *Hamilton* Frigate Joseph Smith master and himself second mate bound for Jamaica that on the 22nd day of June the same year he was taken by the *Good Fortune* Brigantine a pirate ship about fifteen Leagues to the Westward of Cape Cruize by Thomas Anstis mar and that he was Detained on board the said ship by force by the sd master for the span of Twenty months and compelled to sign their articles, and that during that time the said Thomas Anstis took diverse ships both French Dutch English and Spanish and plundered them of whatsoever he found necessary for their use, some of whom after they had put the men on shore they burnt or sunk, this informant further saith that there was on board the sd Pirate ship about Eighty white men and about twenty black and that also this Informant with two other men of the Crew endeavoured to make their Escape from the said Thos Anstis in the Island of Tobego but was levied again by some of their crew and carried onboard the said Pyrate ship again and tried by their Jury for Desertion for which they were severely whipp'd and this Informant upon his Oath further saith that in January last (to the best of his Memory) they took a Spanish Sloop about fifty tons and carried her to Tobego aforesaid, landing her crew there and put on board sufficient Number to sail her of their own Crew at which time the said Pyrate ship commanded by Anstis aforesaid was Careening and her Guns out which this Informant observing he with Joshua Underwood, Daniel Gleddon, Wm. Simner, Zach: Knowles, Stephen Weston, John Hamons, Peter Miller, Bridgstock Weaver,[254] John Barker, Nathan Burd and John Oaram thought it a proper time to make their Escape from him and accordingly seized the sd Spanish prize and bro[ugh]t her for England under the Command of Joshua Underwood aforesaid, and arriving at Padstow in Cornwall he this Deponent with Danl Gleddon, Wm. Simner and John Oaram aforesaid were put on shore near Padstow aforesaid when the sd Joshua Underwood told this Informant that he intended to go round for the other Channel. This Informant also saith that at their Leaving the sd Pyrate ship they shared about Twenty pounds apiece more or less, how the sd

[254] See docs. **42** and **61**

Spanish prize came to be foundered after they were on shore this informant knows not.

47. John Fillmore's narrative

Narrative of the Singular Sufferings of John Fillmore and Others on board the noted Pirate Vessel commanded by Captain Phillips: With an Account of their daring Enterprise, and happy Escape the tyranny of that desperate Crew, by capturing their Vessel (Aurora, 1837).

John Fillmore is one of the great unsung pirate memorialists. His account of his time as a forced man in John Philips' company is one of the most readable and most enlightening accounts surviving from the 'golden age', and is certainly the fullest single source on life aboard John Philips' ship, the Revenge. *Yet the narrative is frequently overlooked, and for that reason it is included here. The narrative was not published until 60 years after the death of its author, and its survival makes one wonder how may other narratives written by forced men or captives might have been lost, or not yet found. John Fillmore himself is of passing interest as the great-grandfather of U.S. Presdent Millard Fillmore.*

The depravity of the human mind is so universally acknowledged in the present enlightened age, and the belief of the universal presidency of Providence over the affairs of men so evidently established, as to need no argument to enforce the reception of a narrative in which both are peculiarly manifest.

Convinced of the truth of the above sentiment, I shall proceed in my narrative, endeavoring on the one hand to avoid tedious repetitions, and on the other to omit no incident that may afford entertainment to my courteous reader.

My father dying when I was young, my mother put me apprentice to learn the trade or occupation of a carpenter. On the other side of the road, opposite to the house where I lived, there dwelt a tailor, who had an apprentice named William White, with whom I was intimate during the time of his apprenticeship; but he was out of his time, and went to sea some time before I was free, being about three years older than myself.

White did not return as was expected, nor do I remember that I ever saw or heard of him afterwards till I found him among the pirates.

From my youth I had an almost irresistible desire for undertaking a voyage to sea, which I resolved at all events to gratify, as soon as I obtained a right to dispose of myself. In establishing this resolution, a love of novelty, joined to a secret delight I enjoyed in hearing sailors relate the curiosities they met with in their voyages, doubtless had a great effect, and the older I grew, stronger became the impression.

But however strong my desire was to follow the sea, a sense of duty I owed my surviving parent, so far overbalanced my inclination, as to occasion me to form a determination not to gratify it until I should be of age, unless I could gain her consent. The propensity, however, was so strong, as to induce me at the age of seventeen, to apply to my mother, and request her liberty to go a voyage to sea. My mother was very uneasy at the request, and used every art of persuasion that maternal tenderness could dictate, to induce me to relinquish the design ; expressing some surprise that I should entertain any idea of following the sea, as it was a life most evidently attended with innumerable fatigues and dangers ; urging as a particular reason for her disapprobation of the measure, the melancholy fate of my father, who, being a seafaring man, was taken by a French frigate, on a voyage homeward bound, and carried into Martinico, a number of years before, where he underwent all the hardships of a close and cruel confinement, and although ultimately redeemed with many others, was supposed to be most inhumanly poisoned by the French, on board the cartel, as they principally died on their passage home.

However strong an argument this might have appeared to my mother, it failed of its desired effect on me; it only lulled my desire for a while, but by no means eradicated it. I waited, however, with a great degree of patience about two years longer, when I again asked leave to go a voyage to the West Indies, and my mother finding my resolution unabated, concluded she could as well part with me then as when I became of age, after which she imagined she should not be able to detain me. Upon the whole, she told me she was unwilling I should go to the West Indies, but that the sloop, *Dolphin*, Capt. Haskel, was then in the harbor, fitting out for a fishing voyage, and if I would go with him she would give her consent. To this proposal I readily assented.

I accordingly shipped on board the sloop, and had a tolerable passage to the fishing ground ; but soon after our arrival there, we were surprised by the appearance of a ship which, from external signs, we suspected to be a pirate. We were not by any means prepared to oppose so formidable an enemy, and she was so close upon us before we suspected her, as to render it impossible for us to escape by running away, we were therefore obliged to abide our fate peaceably, let the consequence be what it would.

The pirate soon came up and sent a boat on board our sloop, demanding who we were, and where we were bound? To which our Captain gave a direct answer. By this boat's crew we learned that the noted pirate, Captain Phillips, commanded their ship. This intelligence, it will readily be conceived, gave us great uneasiness, most of our crew being quite young. Having often heard of the cruelties committed by that execrable pirate, made us dread to fall into his hands.

The pirate's boat soon boarded us again, demanding the name of every hand on board. In this boat came WHITE, the tailor, with whom I had been acquainted during his apprenticeship, as before mentioned. I was greatly surprised to find him employed in so criminal a course of life, though. I said nothing of the matter to him. On the return of the pirate's boat with a list of our names, White, as I was afterwards informed, acquainted Phillips of his knowledge of me, informing him, that if he could engage me in his service, he would gain a good, stout, resolute fellow, every way, he supposed, such a hand as he wanted.

On receiving this information, as he stood in need of a hand, and found we had no property he wanted on board, he sent his boat once more, with orders to Capt. Haskel, to send me on board his ship, and the rest of his crew, with the sloop, may go free. My worthy commander, with much visible concern in his countenance, took me aside, and informed me of Phillips' orders, adding, that although it would be exceedingly disagreeable and painful to him to let me go, yet we were entirely in the power of a bloody, merciless ruffian, and had no hopes of escape, but by giving me up, I believe, says he, you must go and try your fortune with him.

The thought of being sacrificed, as it were, to procure liberty for the rest of the crew, operated greatly upon my spirits, and the conclusion I drew up was, that I would not, on any conditions, agree to go on board the pirate. I therefore told my Captain that I had ever been faithful to his interests and commands, that I had always wished to do my duty punctually and well, but that I was determined not to go on board the pirate, let the consequence be what it would. Our conversation ended here, for that time, and the boat returned without me.

Phillips was greatly incensed when the boat returned without me, and sent again, with orders to bring me either dead or alive. My Captain took me aside again, and told me the pirate's resolution and message, adding, that he believed I should do well to go with them, for if I refused to go, and made resistance, it would be inevitable death to me, and probably to our whole crew. He urged further, that my submitting would prove the certain release of the rest of the crew, and there would be at least a probability of my making an escape from them at some time or other; but if I could not find a way to escape, it was not impossible but Phillips might discharge me, for he had sent word that if I would agree to serve him faithfully for two months, he would then set me at liberty.

Those only who have been in similar circumstances can form any adequate idea of the distress I experienced at this time. If I obstinately refused to join the pirates, instant death stared me and my comrades in the face; if I consented to go with them, I expected to be massacred for refusing to sign the piratical articles,[255] which I had fully determined never to do, though I should be put to the extremity of torture for refusal. Into so critical a situation had my bad fortune plunged me

---

[255] The articles belonging to John Philips' company are one of the few sets to have survived. Their source is unclear but they were published in Charles Johnson's *General History of the Pyrates*:

1. Every man shall obey civil Command; the Captain shall have one full share and a half in all Prizes; the Master, Carpenter, Boatswain and Gunner shall have one Share and quarter.

2. If any man shall offer to run away, or keep any Secret from the Company, he shall be marroon'd with one Bottle of Powder, one Bottle of Water, one small Arm and shot.

3. If any Many shall steal any Thing in the Company, or game, to the Value of a Piece of Eight, he shall be marroon'd or shot.

4. If at any Time we should meet another Marrooner that Man that shall sign his Articles without the Consent of our Company, shall suffer such Punishment as the Captain and Company shall think fit.

5. That Man that shall strike another whilst these Articles are in force, shall receive Moses' Law (that is 40 stripes lacking one) on the bare Back.

6. That Man that shall snap his Arms, or smoak Tobacco in the Hold, without a cap to his Pipe, or carry a Candle lighted without a Lanthorn, shall suffer the same Punishment as in the former Article.

7. That Man that shall not keep his Arms clean, fit for an Engagement, or neglect his Business, shall be cut off from his Share, and suffer such other Punishment as the Captain and the Company shall think fit.

8. If any Man shall lose a Joint in time of an Engagement he shall have 400 pieces of Eight; if a limb 800.
9. If at any time you meet with a prudent Woman, that Man that offers to meddle with her, without her Consent, shall suffer present Death.

that inevitable destruction seemed to stare me in the face from every quarter.

I took the matter, however, into serious consideration, and after the most mature deliberation determined to venture myself among them, rather than bring the vengeance of the pirates upon my comrades; I therefore went with them, seemingly content, and the Captain renewing his promise to set me at liberty in two months, I engaged to serve him to the best of my abilities during that term.

I was likewise agreeably disappointed in their not urging so strenuously as I expected, the thing I most of all dreaded, viz., the signing of the articles. To induce me to join them, they used more arguments of a persuasive than a compulsory nature, judging, I suppose, that youth would be more easily enticed than compelled to join in sharing their ill-gotten gain.

When I first went on board the pirate, their crew consisted of ten men, including the Captain; and the whole of them I think, as stout, daring, hardy-looking fellows as I ever saw together. As I was then the only hand on board who had not subscribed to their articles, the Captain assigned me the helm, where I kept my station during the greatest part of the time I stayed with them.

No captures of any consequence were made during the first two months. Some small vessels were taken, but their loading was too inconsiderable to satisfy the insatiable disposition of the pirates.

The period being now arrived, when I had a right according to agreement, to demand my liberty, I thought it a proper season at least to remind the Captain of the manumission he had engaged me. For this purpose I went to him, and in language the least offensive that I could frame, reminded him of his promise and requested him to fulfill it. Phillips, in tolerable good humor, replied, that we had done but little business since I came aboard ; that he could not well spare me yet, but if I would stay with him three months longer, he would then set me at liberty, upon his honor; and I was obliged quietly to comply with his demands, and trust to his honor, though it turned out in the end that he did but mock me.

Nothing of importance occurred during these three months. Some few small vessels were taken and plundered; their cargoes were of no great value, and their hands were dismissed with their vessels, except two or three robust, stout looking men, whom Phillips picked from among them, and compelled to sign his articles.

When the three months were expired, I went to the Captain, and once more reminded him of the expiration of my servitude, and handsomely requested him to set me ashore, according to his promise, that I might go to my mother, who had not heard from me since my first Captain returned from his fishing voyage.

'Set you at liberty! damn you; you shall be set at liberty when I'm damned, and not before,' replied Phillips, in a rage more compatible with the diabolical disposition of an infernal fiend, than a being endowed with a rational soul, susceptible of human sensations.

It is evident, and experience daily evinces, that persons by habituating themselves to any particular vice, become so familiarized thereto, as to be unable to distinguish it from a real virtue; and in such case, conscience ceases to alarm the

224

understanding, and suffers the culprit to pursue it to its extremity. This was undoubtedly the case with Captain Phillips, who was not addicted to one particular vice, but to every vice.

Having now lost all hope and probability of being liberated, there was no alternative more eligible for me than to sustain my servitude with as much patience, resolution, and fortitude as possible. Although the Captain had asserted that I should not be set at liberty till he was damned, I was still in hopes that we might be taken by some vessel, or that we might take more prisoners, who, in concert with myself, might be able to contrive some plan whereby we might take the ship, and thereby incapacitate Phillips to determine whether I should obtain my freedom before he received his final doom or not.

As we were sailing one day, we came within view of a fine merchant vessel, the appearance of which pleased the Captain much, who swore by Heaven he would have it. I was ordered to bear off for her as direct as possible. Phillips, being extremely anxious for taking this vessel, walked the deck with his glass in his hand, viewing her the greatest part of the day, and damning me because, as he said, I did not steer so well as I might.

Eleven holes he cut through my hat and the skin of my head, without the least provocation, with his broad sword. But the merchantman being light built, and completely rigged, left sight of us before night. Phillips exclaimed in a horrid rage, that the loss of that fine ship was all my damn'd doings; adding, that he wanted the damn'd thing just long enough to sail to hell in.

We had several prisoners on board, Frenchmen and negroes; we had also an American, with whom I had been intimately acquainted when young, and whom the pirates could not persuade or compel to sign their articles. Thus fortune had sent me one friend with whom I could sympathize under my almost insupportable calamities; though our sympathy was chiefly confined to looks and private gestures, for we durst not complain in the hearing of the crew.

About the end of the seventh month from my entering on board, we took a merchantman belonging to Boston, Captain Harridon commander, a young man about twenty-two years of age. The father of this young man was a merchant in Boston, and had given his son the education requisite for a mariner, and sent him to the West Indies, Captain of this vessel, in which he was returning home when we took him.

All except Harridon, James Cheeseman, a ship carpenter, and a Spanish Indian, who was taken with Harridon, the friend alluded to above, and myself, had been compelled to sign the pirate's articles. We had been enjoined to sign them, but had utterly refused, choosing rather to be killed by the villains than to be taken, condemned and executed, for being their associates. But I suppose they thought we might be serviceable to them, and therefore deemed it best not to dispatch us yet.

One day we took a large vessel after considerable trouble in chasing, but found nothing on board worthy the attention of the pirates, except their provisions and water, which being in some want of, Phillips stript of it entirely, took out one or two of their hands, and let them go.

Some of the pirates having been sent on board of Harridon's vessel, there remained only six of the old pirates on board, besides those who had been forced to sign their articles; and as there were five of us who wished to escape from them, we began to think and even suggest trying some scheme to effect that purpose. There was no time that we could confer together without being discovered, except in the dead of night, and even then we durst not be all together, and consequently could not, without great difficulty succeed in forming any regular plan to effect our escape. One day we came in sight of a merchantman which Phillips imagining would prove a valuable prize, gave orders for chasing. His orders were put into execution immediately, but the merchantman being light built, and a prime sailor, we chased her three days before we were able to capture her. Having made what disposition he pleased of the hands, &c, he found on board the new prize, Phillips ordered one Fern, a daring, resolute fellow of the old pirate crew, to go on board of her, and take command, taking some of the old crew along with him.

Phillips had now become so extremely arbitrary as to be hated by his own crew, but they stood in such dread of him that they durst no more contradict his orders than they durst to die. Soon after night came on, Fern proposed to the pirates with him, that as they were now in possession of a fine vessel, every way fitted for a cruizer, and as good sailor as Phillips', if they would join him, he would put out his lights and steering by the light of the old pirate, make their escape from the tyranny of Phillips, and set up for themselves. The crew accordingly joined, and they began to execute their plan, but Phillips suspecting their design, on finding they darkened their ship, put out his own light, and endeavored to follow them; in which design he succeeded so well as to be in sight of them the next morning. We continued to chase the new pirate till the third day, before we came up with her, when a fierce engagement ensued; but Fern soon finding himself overpowered, and no hope of escape, sent word to Phillips, that if he would grant him pardon, he would strike to him, and once more serve him faithfully; but if not, they would all fight till they died. Phillips immediately complied with their demand and sent orders for Fern to come aboard his ship, which he did; and Phillips, not regarding his engagement to pardon, immediately ran his sword through his body, and then blew his brains out with his pistol, and thus glutted his own vengeance, and ridded us of a desperate enemy.

I mentioned before, that there were five of us who had not signed the pirate's articles; and as Phillips, by killing Fern, had left but five of the old pirate crew alive, we began to conceive it a proper opportunity to make our escape. We were, however, exceedingly cautious, and had not yet an opportunity to communicate our plans to my New England friend before mentioned; yet conscience made the pirates suspicious of something of the kind being in agitation, and from the consequent murderous procedure of Phillips, we had reason to apprehend they had in reality discovered our intentions.

My friend, the American before mentioned, being on board the vessel lately taken from Captain Harridon, Phillips ordered out a boat, and went on board, where he accused him with joining a plot, assisted by me, to kill him and all his crew, and take the vessel. My friend solemnly denied the accusation, and declared he knew nothing of such a plan, (which was in fact the case; for I afterwards learned that there had been nothing said to him about it). This reply, however true, did not mitigate the Captain's passion in the least, for he damned him, and swore he would send him to hell, and instantly ran him through the body with his sword, in such a manner that he twisted the point of it off, leaving it in his back bone.

My friend, I suppose, not being conscious of having received his death wound, still denied the charge, and with great earnestness begged that his life might be spared; but the Captain, whose insatiable thirst for slaughter was not sufficiently gorged, damned him, presented his pistol and shot him through the head, exclaiming, 'I have sent one of the devils to hell; and where is Fillmore? he shall go next.' I was then ordered to go aboard Harridon's vessel.

My long familiarity with, and constant apprehension of death, rendered its near approaches less terrifying than formerly; but I did not receive this sentence without heart rending sensations, and thrilling emotions of trepidation and fear. But Phillips was completely despotic and there was no such thing as evading his commands; I therefore drew up a resolution, that if I found he was bent on my death, I would sell my life as dear as possible, and endeavor to kill him first. With this resolution, and as much fortitude as I could muster, I went on board to Phillips, and stood by a handspike that lay on the deck. Phillips charged me, as he had done my friend, with contriving to betray him, and take the ship. The accusation was true enough, but I concluded a lie was warrantable in that case, and consequently replied, that I knew nothing of any conspiracy either against him or his crew. I had prepared to make resistance, in case he offered any abuse; but he had a pistol concealed under his coat, which he presented to my breast, and snapped it, before I had time to make any evasion; but happily for me it missed fire. He drew it back, cocked, and presented it again, but I struck it aside with my hand, so that it went off by my side, without doing any injury.

I thought of knocking out his brains with the handspike that lay near me, but I knew it would be instant death for me, and therefore concluded if he would leave me, I would not meddle with him at that juncture. He then swung his sword over my head, damned me, and bid me go about my business, adding, that he only did it to try me. These last words raised my spirits one degree higher than they had been before; for I confess I thought that snapping a loaded pistol at a man's breast, was a harsh mode of trial, and such an one as I had by no means been accustomed to before. I stopped to take up the handspike, thinking to try him with the butt end of that; but upon a moment's consideration, concluded to let the matter rest a little longer, and watch for a more convenient opportunity to resent the injury. The pistol missing fire when snapped at my breast and then going off by my side, was a strong indication to me that Providence had interposed graciously in my preservation, that our final deliverance from the barbarity of the savage Phillips, and his abandoned banditti, might be more speedily effected.

A few weeks now ensued which were spent in tolerable good humor and peace among all hands on board, and myself and friends put on the semblance of content as much as possible, though we were incessantly seeking opportunities to confer with each other upon some mode of escape; but no proper opportunity occurred, nor indeed were our measures properly concerted as yet.

Again we were called upon to sign their flagitious articles, and become willing members of the piratical band, with menaces of immediate death in case we still refused; but we had heard their threats too often to be frightened into compliance with them now.

A short time after this, being about nine months after I was taken, and about two from the time we fell in with and made prize of the vessel on board of which Harridon was taken, the crew, in commemoration of some signal advantage which they had obtained, had a grand carouse, eating and drinking, and spending the day in such diversions as their gross inclinations required. A favorable opportunity now seemed to offer to extricate us from our suffering, and we determined to improve it if possible. Cheeseman was ordered by Phillips, to bring some tools on deck, and do something towards repairing the ship early next morning, and the master was ordered to take an observation next day at noon, to find out where we were. Thus far Providence seemed to favor our design, and we felt firm in the determination of executing it the next day.

It was late in the evening before the pirates retired to rest, and White and one more of the pirates got in the caboose, as drunk as beasts, and lay down before the fire; a favorable opportunity now seemed to offer for us to improve in conferring upon some means for our escape. We got together, held a consultation, and concluded to risk our lives in trying to work our deliverance, concluding that we had better die in so just a cause, than share the fate of our New England friend, which we had no doubt would soon overtake us, if we persisted in our determination never to sign their articles or share in their unlawful gain.

When I mention that we had determined on an immediate execution of our design, I would inform the reader that there was but three of us, Cheeseman, myself, and the Spanish Indian before mentioned; for poor Harridon declared, that his heart was broken, his resolution and courage gone by a series of ill usage, and that he durst not engage to assist, but would not discover our plot. Thus there remained only three of us to engage the whole crew, and the Indian we felt rather dubious about, though we gained a confidence in him from his having firmly refused several times, though threatened with immediate death, to subscribe the piratical articles. However, I must do him the honor to say he was true to his trust; and had it not been for him, our plot would most probably have failed in the execution.

Cheeseman, the Indian, and myself, got together, and agreed that Cheeseman should leave his broad axe on the main deck when he had done using it, and when I saw Cheeseman make ready to grasp the master, I was to catch it up, and make the best use of it I could, cutting and slashing all that offered to oppose me, while the Indian was to stand ready to help, as occasion might require. And each one of us, in the mean time, was to do everything he could think of to forward the design.

Our plan being thus concerted, I went down into the caboose, where White and John Rose Archer, a desperate fellow who had been taken in one of the prizes, and immediately joined the pirates, laid on the floor, as before mentioned, drunk as beasts. I took fire and burnt these two villains in the feet, while they lay senseless, so badly as to render them unable to be upon deck next day. There were only four now left of the old pirate gang, and five who had joined them since, besides the two I had rendered incapable of injuring us.

We were up early in the morning,[256] and Cheeseman used the broad axe, and left it as agreed. It was very late in the morning, and the pirates were none of them up, and we were afraid they would not arise until too late to take an observation, and our plan of consequence must fall through. To prevent this, about ten o'clock I went to the cabin door and told the Captain the sun was almost up to the meridian. 'Damn you', said he, 'it is none of your business.' This was all the thanks I got, and indeed all I expected for my service. However, it answered the end designed, for the Captain, Master, Boatswain, and Quarter-master, came upon the deck, a little after eleven o'clock. Enquiry was made for White and Archer[257] and their burns imputed to accident. Harridon was nearly dead with fear, and the Indian became so near as white as any of us. Phillips took notice of Harridon's paleness, and I cloaked the matter by informing him, that Harridon had been sick all night, and I believed a dram would help him. Phillips told me to go to his case and get a bottle of brandy; which I did, and we all drank heartily except the Indian, who refused to taste a drop, though something apt to drink at other times.

---

[256] Harridon testified at the subsequent trial of Fillmore and Cheeseman that he was captured on 14 April, 1724. The rising against the pirates thus occurred in mid-June.

[257] Charles Johnson claimed that John Rose Archer was quarter-master of Philips' company, but this passage seems to contradict that. It is possible that there were two quarter-masters, though that would be surprising in such a small company.

The important crisis drew near, when three of us were to attack the whole crew; the Master prepared to take his observation, and Cheeseman was walking the deck with a hammer in his hand. The Quarter-master was in the cabin, drawing out some leaden slugs for a musket, and the Spanish Indian stood by the cabin door. The Captain and Boatswain stood by the mainmast, talking upon some matters, and I stood partly behind them, whirling the axe around with my foot, till my knees fairly smote together.

The Master being busied, I saw Cheeseman make the motion to heave him over, and I at that instant, split the boatswain's head in twain with the broad axe, and dropped him upon the deck to welter in his gore. Before the Captain had time to put himself in a posture of defence, I gave him a stroke with the head of my axe, which partly stunned him; at which time Cheeseman having despatched the Master overboard, came to my assistance, and gave the Captain a blow with his hammer, on the back side of his head, which put an immediate end to his mortal existence.

The Quarter-master hearing the bustle, came running out of the cabin with his hand up to strike Cheeseman with his hammer, and would probably have killed him, had not the Indian catched him by the elbow, as he was bringing the hammer down, and there held him, until I came up and gave him a blow on the back side of his head, cutting his wig and neck almost off, so that his head hung down before him.

We had now despatched all the old pirates except White, and demanded a surrender of the vessel, which was granted, and the poor Frenchmen and negroes came to us and embraced our legs and feet, begging for their lives.

We carried the vessel safely into Boston, where White, Archer, and one more of the pirates were tried, condemned and executed; the three other pirates were sent to England, with the vessel, with whom my friend Cheeseman and the Indian went likewise, whom government liberally regarded for their services, and gave Cheeseman an honorable berth in one of the king's shipyards;[258] the three pirates who went home with the vessel, were hung at execution dock, and the vessel was made a prize of by government.

I never saw any of the human species more spiteful than White was, from the time he was taken till he was executed. I believe he would have killed me at any time in that interval, had it been in his power.

The honourable court which condemned the pirates gave me Captain Phillips' gun, silver hilted sword, silver shoe and knee buckles, a curious tobacco box, and two gold rings that the pirate Captain Phillips used to wear.

When we came in sight of the castle near Boston, we hoisted our pirate's colours and fired a gun, as a signal for them to come off to us. At this time some of the pirates were on deck, and one of them asked leave to fire another gun, which being granted, he would not swab the gun out nor have the vent stopped, but put in the cartridge, and stood directly before the muzzle to ram it down, by which means the cartridge took fire and blew him into pieces; it is supposed he did this purposely, in order to escape the punishment which he knew must be his lot in case he was carried into the harbour.

---

[258] Cheeseman was appointed Quarter-master of the Dockyard at Portsmouth, and held the post until his death.

48. Nicholas Simmons

The Memorandum of Nicholas Simmons.

Of all of the 'golden age' pirates, probably more and better detailed evidence survives relating to the company commanded successively by Edward Low, Francis Spriggs, and Captain Shipton, than any other company. In addition to two trials of members of the company, in one of which Simmons appeared as a defendant [doc. 62], at least three fairly full accounts were written by men forced to join the company: Philip Ashton's Memorial is the fullest and is available elsewhere, the accounts written by Nicholas Simmons and his companion Jonathan Barlow ('Barno' in Simmons account) have not been reprinted since the 1920s. Simmons' and Barlow's accounts follow more or less the same tale, but Simmons' is the fuller of the two and so was selected for inclusion here.

A Memorandum of my Transactions since I sailed out of Newport in November 1723 in a Brigantine belonging to Capt John Login of Boston loaded with Mellasses I my self being Master of sd Brigantine not long after we arrived at Boston the owners of which Melasses were Mr Joseph Whipple and Mr Christopher Almy. Then I being discharged from sd Brig Ship'd my self on Board of one Capt Robt Pete Commander of the Ship *Grayhound* as Mate (The owner of sd Ship was Mr Hoof of Boston) bound for Jameca and the Bay if Opportunity Prevents the Ships not going to the Bay and I having a mind to go thither came to an Agreement wth sd Pete and was discharged from him by Consent of both then Shipping my Self on Board of one Capt Macmanus Commander of the Sloop *Dinkbee* bound for the North Side of Spaniola which Voyage I performed then being discharged from sd Macmanus Ship'd my Self on Board of Capt Macfashin bound for the South Side of Spaniola having performed our Voyage & Coming homeward at the West end of Spaniola we saw a Ship of two and Twenty Guns which prov'd to be Pirates one Spriggs being Commander & a Pirate Sloop whose Commander was one Shipton. They ordered us to hoist out our Boat & to Come on board, accordingly we did. I coming over the Side saw a Man whose Name was Jona Barny of Rhode Island I had not Oppertunity to talk with him but was directly ordered into the Cabbin of sd Ship which Spriggs was Commander of. Whereupon I went and there being there only sd Spriggs and the Doctor & my Self, Capt Macfashin being at the Door, they treated me very plentifully and having Eat and drank enough to satisfy me They discovered their minds unto me & perswading me to Sign their Articles which I refused, he said he would fill my Belly with other Sort of Diat and he sent the Boy to Fetch two Candles in a Plate which he made me eat. After so doing he told me I might go to the Devil he would force no Man he leaving me the rest of the Company fell upon me and beat me some saying I should go with them and some saying I should not and leaving me for a while I saw some of them have Sticks in their Hands with Neadles in the Ends, I asked sd Barny or Some of the Company what they were for and he told me to swet People. I asked them the meaning of that and they told me to run round the Mast and they to prick me as I ran round. I hearing that went to the Main Chains desiring the

Lord to receive my Soul & jumpt overboard, the Capt seeing a Man overboard and not knowing who it was sent the Boat to take me up which accordingly they did and carried me on board the Sloop wch sd Barny was taken in whereof was Commander Capt Shipton a Pirate. He having no one on board Capable of Navigating or taking Charge as a Navigator forced me in his Absence to take Charge of the Sloop which I did by force, then parting with sd Spriggs wee met again at Rattan and they hearing that the Ship *York* was at the Bay of Hondoras with other Shipps agreed to go and take her, Which they did. I had not Opportunity to go on Shore being Confin'd as a Prisoner on Board. In a few Days came down the *Diamond* Man of Warr wch Oblidging them to run then we left Spriggs and going out from the Bay we met a Ship which they took & burnt and then sending away w[ha]t Prisoners they thought fit in a Bay Craft. And calling a Consultation where to go they concluded to go through the Gulf and so on the American Coast to the Northward & from thence to Ruby and there to heave down and Crean[259] at the Pitch of Cape Florida we were cast away. I myself with two more came away wth a small Craft for fear of the Indians, who were one Jona Barno & one Pirate, we were at Sea four Days and the fifth Day at Night came to an Anchor at the North Keys where wee met with the Pirate again & forcing us with him again then keeping Company with him as forced to the West End of Cubee,[260] and they finding there a Small Craft put me with the other two on board sd Craft & carried us seven Leagues from Land then having bad weather being fast to their Stern they cut us loose & left us to our own Discretion.

---

[259] Careen – clean the vessel's hull of weed and barnacles.
[260] Cuba

In two Days we arrived at Cape Catoach and the third Day as wee lay hid there we saw the Pirate pass by us, and there we Continued seven Days that She might be gone Clear in hopes to see her no more and the eighth Day wee made Sail for the Bay in hopes to get Deliverance from sd Pirates. Recking[261] my self ten Leagues to ye Eastwd of the Bay, wee met them again, the Capt rejoyced to see me and told me he would never part with Me again. The next Day they Came to an Anchor in the Bay near Camegal where they sent the Boat with three hands to fish they returning gave an Account of two Vessells the one being a Sloop commanded by Ebenezer Kent and the other a Ship Commanded by one Capt Glin which they took, and taking possession of sd Vessells left me in the Craft & ordered me to follow where they come to an Anchor.

Wednesday the 23d of December then I being put or forced on Board the sd Ship called the *John & Mary* of Boston as Navigator or Commander, by Command of the sd Capt Shipton a Pirate, with three Pirates & one forced Man whose Name was Jonathan Barno who was forced either to go with me or to be shot, my Orders were to follow Ebenezer Kent's Sloop. It being Clear weather at 8 in the Morning we weighed Anchor wth Kent's Sloop and a Petteorgar[262] in Company steered our Course Southward. Then I discover'd my Mind to the Mate Mathew Perry, the Capt of ye Ship being on Board Kents Sloop, I said to him that if he and the Company of the Ship would Stand by me that I and Jonathan Barno would destroy those Blood thirsty Pirates that were on Board.

---

[261] reckoning
[262] Piragua

Thursday 24th, With much Rain now plying among the Keys the wind blowing very hard at North West, at 8 At Night the Sloop tack'd and made Signals for us to tack but I being in hopes to weather away the North End of Glovers Reaf I thought it not proper to tack with the Consent of sd Perry and the Ships Company, but the Wind came to the Northward so that we Could not weather the sd Reaf at 12 D[itt]o we tacked & stood to the Westward ye Wind blowing very hard at NNW at 8 the next Morning saw the Sloop three Leagues to Leward of us but being dirty weather we lost Company with the Sloop.

Fryday 25th D[itt]o this Twenty four hours hard Gailes of Wind at WNW with Squalls of Rain still to the Westward of sd Reaf still remaining my Self & Jonathan Barno and the Ships Company in the same Mind.

Saturday 26th D[itt]o this 24 Hours Fresh Gailes of Wind at WNW at 2 this afternoon saw the Island of Ntillee[263] and being ordered by the Capt of the Pirate to go there if lose Company from the Sloop I should find them there, but I being in hopes to get Clear of them thought fit with Perry & the Ships Company to go for Banaccar, and there by some Opportunity to Destroy the Pirates that are on Board of us. They being so Armed with Small Arms & Pistols and Swords and other Arms that it could not be done without some Pollycy I thought to perswade some of them to go a Shore to hunt or Shoot Fowls.

Sunday 27 D[itt]o This 24 Hours the Wind at West, at 4 this Afternoon Anchored at the South Side of Bannacar under Skinners Key where we found the Pirates at an Anchor in

---

[263] Presumably one of the Antilles, possibly Puerto Rico

Kent's Sloop in Company with another Ship which they took this Day. Then the Capt of the Pirate came on Board of us with some other Pirates & Some forced Men the which one of them was Kent's Mate and I discovered my Mind with him & said to him if the Ship's Company would Assist me I would be in Boston or some other English Port as Soon as possible I could, he Shook hands with me & wished me well. So they plundered the Ship and took what they had a Mind to take & then gave orders to Arm our Selves, the which by force I did to take Care of the People that were in the Ship & likewise if the Wind was fair in the Morning to make the best of our way to the Island of Rattan but if the Wind was not fair he would take what was fitting for their use and then to set the Ship on fire and also the other Ship that they had Taken this Day and take all the Prisoners on Board Kent's Sloop and Carry them to Rattan where his Consert Capt Spriggs lay having a Ship of two & Twenty great Guns then having five Prises with him that he took in the Bay of Hondoras. At Seven in the Afternoon Jona Delivered one of the Pistols that he was forced to Keep with him to the Mate Mathew Perry, he taking his Opportunity In the Steerage snapt at one of the Pirates that had three or four Pistols about him then but his Pistol did not go off, whereupon he retreated back. I being in the Cabbin with one of the Pirates and hearing him Snap his Pistol at Perry I said 'Now in the Name of his Majesty King George let us go on with our Design', I shot him that had the four Pistols through ye Body and said to the other if he did move in resistance he should be a Dead Man, whereupon Jonathan and the Rest of the Company killed him, then Directly Loosing our Sailes made the best of our way to an English Port.

241

Jan. 30th 1724/5 Arrived in ye sd Ship *John & Mary* at Rhode Island. [264]

---

[264] The date and nature of the last six paragraphs suggest that Simmons used a journal to refresh his memory.

3. PIRATES' VICTIMS.

The victims of piracy, whether fore-mast seaman or officer, often provided vivid accounts of their experiences at the hands of pirates. Frequently, like forced me, they detailed the tortures and barbarities committed against them [**docs 52, 53**], but in other accounts the pirates come across as fairly restrained in their treatment of their captives [**docs 50, 51**], and others still show a mix of violence and restraint [**docs 55, 56, 59**]. Even in the accounts written by pirates' victims there occur elements of self-exoneration: ships' masters must justify to their employers the loss of their ship or cargo, and even the humble seaman must excuse himself for not having resisted the pirates harder.

49. Mutiny on the ship *Adventure*

A TRUE RELATION Of a most Horrid Conspiracy and Running away with the SHIP ADVENTURE, Having on Board Forty Thousand Pieces of Eight, *and other Goods to a great Value. Together with the Cruel and Barbarous leaving and turning ashore upon the Island* Naias, *in the* East-Indies, *the Captain, and three Merchants which were Passengers, and Sixteen honest and able Seamen, Eight whereof miserably perished by Hunger and Hardship, and but Four of the Remainder yet come to* England. *Together with some short Account of what passed at the Trial and Condemnation of those who Committed that Fact* (London, 1700)

The following account of the seizure of the ship Adventure *by Joseph Bradish and his supporters is full enough to stand on its own with little introduction. Bradish and his men were captured in New England and shipped back to London with the infamous Captain William Kidd. Bradish's fame has been far eclipsed by Kidd's, but to other pirates of the 'golden age' they were both notorious.*

The Ship *Adventure*, of which Thomas Gullock was Commander and Supra-Cargo,[265] bound to Borneo in East-India, broke ground from Graves-End on the 16th of March 1697/8. and toucht at Brava one of the Cape de Verdy Islands, and having there got plenty of Refreshment, Fowls, Hogs, Goats and green Trade,[266] proceeded on their Voyage, and in the Month of August fell in with the Coast of Sumatra,

---

[265] Supercargo, the agent of the freighters or owners.
[266] Presumably fresh vegetables

went to Padang to get Refreshment for the Ships Company, lay there five days, bought there four Bullocks, Fowls, Fruit, green Herbs, Potato's, &c. which was equally divided to the Ships Company, also about a Tun and half of Rice, and half a Butt of Arack, got one Boat-load of Water, and sail'd thence; about 20 days after, being by calms and currents driven near Naias,[267] an Island inhabited by a barbarous sort of People who have no Commerce with any Europeans, came to an Anchor, the Captain order'd the Long boat on shoar with empty Cask to fill Water, under the charge of Mr. William Hill his second Mate, with 24 Men well arm'd, with orders that if a Gale of Wind should spring up, or that they should see any Natives or tracks of them upon the Sand, then immediately to repair on Board without Water, being in no great want of it, but thought that the best use could be made of the time whilst lying at an Anchor. After the Long-boat was put off, the Captain was in great perplexity lest the Boats-crew might be destroyed by the barbarous Natives, therefore went on shoar himself in his Yaul after them, and stay'd at the watering place, being two or three hundred yards distant from the Boat, until Mr. Hill sent him word the Water-cask were full; the Captain then sent him orders to send the Long-boat on board with fifteen Men; Joseph Bradish Boatswains mate desired Mr. Hill to let him have the Yaul to tow the Long boat off from the shoar, which he agreed to, intending only the Security of the Boat, but they continued to tow much farther than necessary, and then cast off the Tow-rope, laying the Yauls Head to the shoar, with only two Men as appear'd in her; when the Long boat was near the Ship, two Men more rose out of the Yauls hull, and

---

[267] Nias, Indonesia

245

then with four Oars row'd directly onboard the Ship getting both on board together; then did Joseph Bradish, John Lloyd, Thomas Hughs and others, seize Mr. Abraham Parrott the chief Mate, telling him he was their Prisoner, and the Ship and all that was in her was their own. He asked them what was the matter, and what they thought would be the end of it? They answered he need not trouble himself about that, they were for A short Life and a merry one.[268] The Conspirators being immediately arm'd, made themselves Masters of the Ship, cut her Cable, loosed her Sails, and run away with her, leaving the Captain and 14 Men upon the said Island, exposed to inexpressable Miseries and Dangers, not only from the barbarous Natives, but Tygers and other wild Beasts, &c. without any manner of Provisions, Moneys or Cloaths, except the worst, which they had on their backs, or any prospect of returning to their Native Country, or indeed of so much as preserving their Lives.

Soon after the Ship was under Sail, they turn'd the Yaul away, and in her five Men, viz. Mr. Dru Hacker, Rex Kempson, George Reyner, Jonas Grizley, and Francisco an Indian, being such as would not joyn with them in their Villainous Design, not giving them one Bisket Cake, or any Sustenance, but refused to let them go to their own Chests to put on a Coat, Hat, or 2 Shoes, insomuch that three were turned ashoar without Coats or Hats, and two without Shoes, and being forced to travel over sharp Rocks, they, with others whose Shoes soon wore out, had their Feet torn and mangled,

---

[268] This phrase was later attributed to Bartholomew Roberts by Charles Johnson, in his *General History*. Roberts himself alluded to the relatively obscure Bradish on another occasion, so it may be that Roberts has read this very account at one time or another.

and bled in such a miserable manner, that they desired to lye down and dye there, rather then to have gone on, if the Captain had not over perswaded them.

The number left in this deplorable state were 16 of their fellow Seamen, with the Commander and three Merchants, who, besides the extream danger of perishing there, were rob'd of what they had aboard, frustrated of the fruits of their Voyage, and their poor Wives and Children left to starve at home. Eight have since perished by hunger and hardships, who, if they were present, would more livelily set out the horrid Cruelty of those unmerciful Men who run away with the Ship, and left them in that miserable and wretched Condition.

This distressed Company being thus left, without any thing to eat, did remain so from Saturday morning the 17th of September till Thursday evening the 22th.

But tho' the Barbarity of their fellow Seamen left them in such unspeakable distress, yet it pleased God wonderfully to bring about Means for the Preservation of a few of them to be Witnesses of so horrid a Villany; for there happened to come two Boats to the said Island, which the Captain did hire with the Promise of 500 Pieces of Eight to pursue his Ship, and was on Munday the 19th within 4 or 5 Miles of her, but by a sudden Storm was forced ashoar, and both those Boats staved to pieces, only himself with 5 Men in the Yaul escaped that Ship-wrack. But it pleased God none of them lost their Lives, but all came by Land to a Creek or Cove, whither the Captain with much toil and difficulty got in the Yaul; the Number was now by these Atcheeners[269] encreased to 42 Men, and no

---

[269] Seamen from Aceh (formerly Achin), Indonesia.

Boat or Vessel but the Yaul, which could not carry in the Sea above Eight or Ten. The Atcheeners seem'd most afraid of the Natives, begging the Captain to stand by them, or else the Natives would either kill or make Slaves of him and them; for they said there was a Boat of Atcheen which came there the Year before, the Men of which the Natives had knockt on the head, and halled the Boat up above Highwater mark; this Boat was survey'd and found much rent with the Sun, but that the Malayers undertook to stop, and did so, with Moss, Bark, &c. whilst the Captain took care to get the Sail and some other things of one of the wrack'd Boats, and did Launch her that day, (tho' whilst they were about it they were attack'd by 200 of the Natives, all arm'd with Swords, Targets, and Launces, who made a fierce onset, but by firing Twelve or Fourteen shot were put to flight) and with her and the Yaul got off to small Islands call'd Maroos, where they got some Coker Nuts, and from a Boat they met at those Islands got some Rice which had been wet with Salt water in the same Storm when the two Boats were lost, and was heated and stank abominably, but was eaten heartily: This Boat pretended to belong to Padang, so that the Captain agreed with the Master for transport to Padang, giving the launch'd Boat to the Acheeners in lieu of their two Boats, which was all the Recompence he could then possibly make them. Going with this Boat toward Sumatra they were chased with a Malaya Pirate, who came up with them, but seeing them stand to their Arms bore up round, and stood away without one word. Coming near Pariaman there is a Shoal upon which the Malayar ran his Boat; and when the Boat was on ground, the English-men all leapt over Board to go to a dry Spot not far distant, but many had like to have been drown'd by holes in the Rocks, which dipt them over head and ears, but others who could Swim assisted and got them safe to the dry Spot. The Captain went on shoar with the Yaul, and begg'd the Assistance of the Dutch Corporal, who sent a Boat with Natives, which brought the Men all off from that Spot, which not long after was overflown with the Tide, otherwise they must have been drowned; for the Malayar, after they jumpt out, got his Boat off, and went away without staying to expect his Freight, for what reason we know not. Two days after they went to Padang, where being ill treated, and labouring under great Want and Sickness, three soon died there. But it pleased God to raise them up there a Friend indeed, Mr. Antony Gillis a Native of India, who pitied their Miseries, relieved their Wants, and (under God) saved their Lives; whose inexpressible and almost inimitable Charity, extended to the Dead and Living, shrowding the one, and succouring the other, which is here mention'd to his honour, and in gratitude to him.

The remaining part of this distressed Company got their Passage to Bencoolen, whereof one died by the way, and some remain'd there, of which three more soon died, and it is to be fear'd several of the rest which staid there are since dead, for only six of the Company proceeded to Batavia, where, after a languishing Sickness, died one more, viz. George Rayner, from which place the Commander and three more got passage to England.

The foregoing Account is given, not only by the Commander and poor surviving Seamen, but was (long before the taking of any of the wicked Crew who run away with the Ship) written from Padang in a Letter to the Owners by Mr. Robert Anby and Mr. Ralph Peck, two Gentlemen, who, with some

249

others, were to have staid at Borneo to have settled a Factory; which Letters, with two others from Mr. Nixon and Mr. Parrot at Batavia, may be seen at Mr. Crowches a Bookseller at the Corner of Popes head-Alley in Cornhill, out of which, for Vindication of the Commander from the base and unjust Aspersions of his ill usage of the Seamen, the Owners have permitted the following Paragraphs to be printed with this Narrative.

'Now, honoured Sirs, we humbly crave your leave to do our worthy Captain Justice, by acquainting you of his particular care of the Ships Company, in respect to the health both of their Souls and Bodies; we never failed of Morning and Evening Prayers in publick upon the Quarter Deck, when the Weather would permit, our Commander daily endeavouring to suppress all manner of Vice, and to encourage Vertue. As to the health of their Bodies, he was as tender as a Mother to any that were sick, daily minding the Doctor of his charge; and when he had fresh Provisions at his own Table, would ask the Doctor who was sick, and always sent them some. Those that were in health he endeavoured to keep so, by refreshing twice or thrice a day in bad weather with Drams. In fine, God Almighty knows our hearts that we speak the truth; he is the most religious, sober, careful and kind Commander that we knew or heard of ever.

Robert Anby. Ralph Peck.

Padang the Twenty Third of October, 1698. Old Style.'

Mr. Samuel Nixon Chirurgeon,[270] in his Letter to the Owners from Batavia, Nov. 27th. 1698. writes thus:

'I Do declare that I never saw in any of his Majesty's Ships, or any other where I have been, better Victuals or Victualling, nor never so much care taken, nor kindness shewn, both toward Soul and Body, as was by the Commander, both to well and sick; for tho' it pleased God to bless us with so healthful a Passage, that we never had any Man lay down three days together, yet hath the Captain often circumvented me in sending Broth or other fresh Provisions to sick Men from his own Table, and hath sundry times ordered Fowls to be kill'd expresly for them only, and hath also several times in the Voyage given of his Fowls to the whole Ships Company, and never kill'd a Hogg, but a great part was given them; and the same by his Parsnips, Carrots, Pumkins, &c. allowing for the sick Men Water grewel with Fruit, Sugar and Spice, such as I thought fit. Insomuch that I am ready to give Oath, I have heard them say sundry times, that they never saw so good Victualling, nor a Commander so kind and careful of his Men.

'Also he so husbanded the Brandy allowed for them that they had Drams always when wet, and at the turning out of the Watches. And the Ships Company drank all Beer until near the Southern Tropick, and to the Eastward of the Cape, and then Beer and Water to the very last, giving the Seamen sometimes strong Beer. As for Abuses I never saw any or less striking in any Ship where I have been, the whole amounting to the punishment of four or five Persons, and that for great Faults, as Thievery, etc.'

Mr. Abraham Parrott Chief-mate, in his Letter to the Owners, gives the same account of Victualling and Punishments, &c.

---

[270] Surgeon.

adding, That after the Seisure of the Ship it was freely discourst, William Griffeth the Trumpeter had taken upon him to have shot the Captain.

And now to return, to give some Account of the procedure of those who ran away with the Ship, taken from Three who by force were with them the whole Voyage, and gave Evidence upon Oath thereof, at their Tryal, viz. John Westby, Robert Amsden, and William Saunders; the Captain only giving Evidence that the Prisoners were aboard the Ship when it was run away withal.

After they had seised the Ship, and turned ashoar the five Persons before-mentioned, they sailed about 50 Leagues to Sea from the Island, and then turn'd away in the Long Boat Mr. Abraham Parrott the Chief Mate, William Whitesides the Boatswain, and Richard Heath Armourer [Note, These 3 poor Creatures were 23 days at Sea, and had there perish'd if they had not by accident met a Dutch Ship bound to Batavia, who carried them thither.], to each of whom they gave a Certificate in the following words; the Original whereof was produced and sworn to in Court, viz.

'Septemb. 21. 1698.

Not willing to venture our selves near any Factory, and unwilling to keep any to breed Faction among us, have turned to Sea in the Long-Boat all such as were not willing to stay, except John Westby to act as Chirurgeon, and Robert Amsden Carpenter, Servant, which two per force we keep; the others, viz. Abraham Parrott, William Whitesides, and Richard Heath we forced away detaining likewise William Saunders.

Joseph Bradish.

John Lloyd.

John Peirce.

Andrew Marten.'

This being done, they began to divide the Clothes and Moneys of those whom they had so left and turn'd ashoar, and some time after divided the Pieces of Eight belonging to the Owners, weighing to each Man his Proportion by the Stillyards, which came to about Fifteen hundred Pieces of Eight a Man.

When they came near the Coast of New-England they agreed to destroy all the Journals and Writings aboard, which they did by putting them into a Bagg, and sinking them with Shot, saying, They should not rise up against them.

After this, near to Block-Island, they disperst themselves into several Sloops, taking with them their Moneys, &c. and were not contented with that, but fired five Guns through the Ships bottom, and sunk her in deep Water, with the Cloath, Lead, Iron, and other Commodities aboard; all which, as well as the Ship, were thereby irrecoverably lost.

Notwithstanding their separating themselves into several distant Parts, Divine Justice has pursued them, and they have all been taken but one, who is suppos'd to be kill'd, and were brought to their Trial on the 21st of June last at the Old-Baily, where what they said for themselves, as to the Matter of Fact, was frivolous and inconsistent, but endeavoured to extenuate their Crime by charging the Commander with

Severity and Ill usage, from which the Court was pleased to give the Commander an opportunity to vindicate himself, which he did upon Oath in the manner following, to the Satisfaction of the Court, Viz.

That he was sorry to see so many Men so remorsless, as to endeavour the excusing one Villany by committing another, as not content to have rob'd him of his Ship and Cargo, expos'd himself and 19 more to those inexpressible Hardships and Miseries, whereby the King lost eight of his Subjects by untimely death, and no more than three besides himself return'd to England, of the 20 left on shoar,) but farther endeavoured to Murther his Reputation with most unjust, and base Aspersions. As for the Victualling of his Ship, he said, that on Sundays, Tuesdays and Thursdays they had every Mess a piece of good Beef and a Pudding of two pound and a half of Flower with ¼ of Suet, besides Butter or Cheese for Breakfast. That on Mondays and Fridays they had Pork and Pease, with Breakfast as before: On Wednesdays and Saturdays Fish and Burgoo; and they had Burgoo for Breakfast, with Butter and Sugar, on those days. That they had three Cans of Beer a Mess every day till far beyond the Cape of good Hope, and after that two Cans of good Beer and Water; and when they drank Water, there was a Cask with a Scuttle or Hole cut at the Bung enough to put a Cup in and drink when they pleas'd, lash'd fast to the Main-mast upon the Main-deck, fill'd as often as there was occasion. Also that they had 28 pound of Bread per Week every Mess, until John Lloyd desired the Captain to let him put two bags of Bread about 50 pound each, (which his Mess alone had saved out of their Allowance) into the Bread-room, which was done accordingly. That then they were at no Allowance for a

Fortnight or three Weeks, but had the Bread in an open Cask in the Steerage, to eat when and what they pleas'd, until they left it greasie up and down where they eat, and then 'twas retrencht to 25 pound per Week every Mess, and never less by his order or knowledge. Also that they had Drams Morning and Evening when fair, and as often as the Watches was chang'd when wet, never letting them go to their Hamocks wet without a Dram, to be sure of which he did not suffer the Steward to give it them below, but constantly his own Servant at his Round house door. Also that every Mess had on Sundays a Can of strong Beer; and when about the Cape in cold raw weather, they have often had, both Morning and Evening, Burgoo, and sometimes Fowls for the whole Ships Company, with a very particular regard to all sick Men.

The same Account John Westby, Robert Amsdem, and William Saunders upon Oath confirm'd; except that Mr. Westby and Amsden said, they once heard or saw that one Mess had but Sixteen pound of Bread one Week, which the Captain said he never heard any Complaint of, for if he had, he should have as readily redrest it as he did the only Complaint was ever made him of Victuals, which was by William Griffeth, who brought him a piece of Pork very small, which he order'd his Servant to take from him, and give Griffeth a piece from his own Table in exchange for it; the truth of which was confirm'd by the Witnesses, and cannot be deny'd by the Prisoners themselves, unless they will run the hazard of going from Man's Judgment to the most tremendous and eternal Judgment of God with guilt.

As for Chastisement, he did acknowledge that Ham Edgell and Wetherell had been punished; Edgell because that he being a Quarter-Master, working in the Lazaretta,[271] did break open a Box, and stole about a dozen pound of white Suger; the next day the Captain demanded at once all Keys of Chests, and did find the Sugar in his Chest: which Felony he thought fit publickly to punish, especially in him, who being a Quarter-Master, might have the opportunity of the same Fact in Goods of far greater value, and that it might prove exemplary to the whole Ships Company.

Edward Ham purely for the welfare of those who complain against it, because that he after many checks, and some blows, continued nasty to that degree, that upon a complaint of the copperishness of the Pease, the Captain himself went into the Cook-room, and took off the sides of the Copper a great quantity of Verdigreese, for which the Captain beat him with a Japan Cane, but not to that degree as at all to wound or break his Skin, as the Chirurgeon's Mate, Mr. Westby confirmed upon Oath. And Witherell was beaten for striking the Boatswain of the Ship. And if Correction in such Cases be not used aboard Ships, no order can be maintain'd, but all would run into Confusion.

And these very Men themselves, sometime after Seisure of the Ship, did seise the same Edward Ham to the Gang-way, and severely beat him for the same Crime.

The Names of the Prisoners which were Condemned, were Joseph Bradish, John Lloyd, Thomas Hughs, Ellmore Clarke, Edward Ham, Thomas Dean, William Griffeth, Robert Mason, Thomas Edgell, Francis Read, Cornelius Larking, Thomas Simpson, Tee Wetherell, Robert Knox, Thomas Davis, Andrew Marten, Rowland Marten, John Peirce.

---

[271] Sometimes used to describe a sick-berth.

The Names of those left on shoar, Capt. Thomas Gullock, Mr. Robert Anby, Mr. Ralph Peck, Mr. Drew Hacker, Edward Watts, Rex Kempton, George Reyner, Jonas Grizley, William Hill, Samuel Nixon, John Baker, John Hire, Daniel Gravier, Henry Barnet, Giles Brown, Thomas Barrow, John Templer, one Frenchman, and one Dutchman.

Names of the Dead are Rex Kempton, Henry Barnet, Giles Brown, Daniel Gravier, Robert Anby, Ralph Peck, Edward Watts, George Reyner.

50. Israel Phippany and Peter Freeland

The Affidavit of Israel Phippany and Peter Freeland, 31 March, 1705. Printed in *The Case of Captain Thomas* Green (London, 1705), pp. 13-14

The case of Thomas Green is one of the most scandalous in Scottish legal history. Green, captain of the East-Indiaman Worcester *was forced by bad weather into the Forth at a time when anti-English feeling was running particularly high. A few years earlier English merchants had been held to blame for the disastrous Darien expedition, and by the time Green and the* Worcester *arrived in the Forth Scotland was waiting eagerly for the return of the Darien Company's last hope, a ship called the* Speedy Return *which had been sent with virtually all of the Company's money invested in it on a trading voyage to the East Indies. The* Speedy Return *had not returned speedily, and rumours circulated around Edinburgh that she had been taken by an English pirate. It did not take long for the act to be fastened onto Green and the crew of the* Worcester, *who were arrested, tried, and found guilty of the piracy. Much to the dismay of the Edinburgh mob, their execution was postponed at the request of the Privy Council, and scheduled to take place one week later. During that week, Israel Phippany and Peter Freeland, seamen belonging to the* Speedy Return, *arrived in England and testified Green's innocence. The documents were rushed to Edinburgh and presented to the Lord Advocate, but to appease the mob who had already been denied the execution once, Green and two of his men were hanged. The mob having been satisfied, the rest of the crew of the* Worcester *received a pardon for a crime they had not committed.*

Be it known unto all Men by these Presents, That upon the One and Thirtieth Day of March, Anno Dom. 1705. Before John Vineing Esq; Mayor of the said Burrough and George Huish, Gent. Notary and Tabelian Publick, dwelling in Portsmouth, personally came and appeared; Israel Phippany and Peter Freeland, now belonging to the *Raper-Galley*, lately arrived there from the East Indies, and did solemnly declare upon the Holy Evangelist; that they the said Appearers did both formerly belong to a Ship called the *Speedy Return*, belonging to the Scotch Company, Trading to Affrica and the East Indies[272] (of which Capt. Robert Drummond was Commander) and that on or about the Twenty Sixth Day of May, which was in the Year 1701 the said Ship the *Speedy Return* sailed from Newport Glascow in Scotland in Company with the *Content* Briganteen, Capt. Stewart Commander, and afterwards Arrived at Bangole in Guinea, from thence sailed to the Cape of Good-Hope, and

---

[272] The proper full name of the Darien Company

from thence to the Island of St. Marys in Madagascar, where the said Ship the *Speedy Return*, and the said Briganteen took on board Negroes, which were Transported to Don Mascarenhas; from thence they sailed to the Port of Maritan in Madagascar aforesaid, where the said Capt. Drummond went on Shoar; and about Nine or Ten Hours after his going on Shoar, Five several Persons who afterwards appeared to be Pirates armed with Pistols, Swords and other Weapons, came on board the said *Speedy Return* with a pretence to buy something, and taking the Advantage of the said Capt. Drummond, Andrew Wilky his Surgeon, and several of the said Ship's Company being Ashoar, and others working in the Hold, the said Five Persons by Force of Arms took Possession of the said Ship, and immediately made a Signal, upon which about Forty or Fifty other Pyrates came on board the said Ship, and then took the said Briganteen (which was afterwards burnt) and the said Pirates forced these Appearers, and the other Persons on board the said Ship the *Speedy Return* to sail in Her till such Time as she Arrived at Rajapore, and Place so called, where the said Ship the *Speedy Return* was also burnt, and then these Appearers and the other Men that did belong to the said *Speedy Return* went on board a Moca Ship, called the *Deffiance*,[273] which some time after touched at the Island Mauritius, where the Appearers made their Escape; and the said *Raper-Galley* soon after arriving there, the said Appearers went on board her, and are since arrived at the Port of Portsmouth.

And the said Appearers did farther Declare, That at, or after the time of taking the said Ship *Speedy Return*, neither the

---

[273] A pirate ship commanded by Nathaniel North

said Capt. Drummond, nor any other Persons belonging to her were Killed or Wounded; neither was she ever Attacked by a Ship called the *Worcester*, Capt. Green Commander, or any other Ship, Sloop or Vessel whatsoever. In Testimony whereof, the said Mayor hath hereunto set his Hand, and caused the Seal of the Office of Mayoralty of the said Burrough to be hereunto Affixed the Day and Year first within Written.

51. George Weoley

George Weoley to Mr Pennyng, 7 November 1703. Printed in The Case of Captain Thomas Green (London, 1705), pp. 18-21

George Weooley's account, though written well over a year before Green's trial, was presumably not available to the court. Yet, it firmly ascribes the seizure of the Speedy Return *to John Bowen, who subsequently took over the ship and used her as his pirate vessel. Weoley's account is perhaps most interesting for the light it sheds on the relationship between pirates and colonial society in the Indian Ocean.*

Worshipful Sir,

Yours of the 5th reach'd my Hands, this Morning the 11th Hour; it being impossible for me to give you an Account at large of every Thing relating to the Actions of the Pirats, but here send you the Heads of what I saw, and what I had from their Mouths in Discourses at several Times, viz. That Three Years past, one Capt. Merrino, a French Man, and French

Company, took a Ship belonging to Surat, off, or near Cape Aden, and made a Prize of her; wherein was considerable Riches, and quitted her after they had taken her Moneys and other Things out of her, and sailed for the Island Mascarenha, a general Randezvous for Pirats, where the said Merrino is now settled, and actually become an Inhabitant. This Relation I had from some of his own Ship's Company, which are French Men, and belonged to the Ship I was Imprisoned in. The same Year was taken off St. Johns a Surat Ship, by the ship *Speaker*, whose Company consisted of all Nations to my certain Knowledge, the major part being now in the Pirats on the Coast, and the same Commander John Bowen, here near Callequilon, they took Capt. Conaway from Bengall, selling Ship and Goods in Shares, viz. One Third Part to a Merchant of Callequilon; another Third to a Merchant of Porca; the other Third to Malpa the Dutch Broker of this Place, which Relation I had from Capt. Bowen and several of his Company; then left the Coast, and sailed for the Island Madagascar; but in the way was lost on the Island Maritius, on St. Thomas's Reef where they were most courteously [re]ceived and feasted; their Sick carried into their Fort and cured by their Doctor, and a new Sloop sold them, and supplied with all sorts of Necessaries for their cutting her, and making her a Brigantine, which they performed by the middle of March, and took their leave of the Governour, giving him Twenty Five Hundred Pieces of Eight, their Vessels and Necessaries; leaving their Lascars with him to be conveyed for Surat; and being invited to make it a place of Refreshment, sailed for the Island of Madagascar, where, at a Place on the East side, called Maritan, the Captain with a Gang settled themselves till two

Scotch Ships or Vessels falling in the Port, were both surprised and taken by them,[274] by another Gang which settled at St. Augustine, the Ship *Prosperous* was taken, the Remainder went for New Mathelage, where they gave the King their Brigantine, where I saw her and left her when the Pirats sailed from thence; The Pirates having these Three in their Possession in searching after one another, lost one of the Scotch Vessels, but at last two met at Mayotta, where it was my Misfortune to fall into their Hands, and detained by them after they had slain my Chief Mate, and another European, and plundered what they pleased, let the Ship go, and sailed for Mathelage; from thence to the Islands Mayotta and Johannah; from thence to the High-land of St. Johns, off which, and at Surat's River-mouth, they took Two Sail of Surat ships from Moca; she at the Rivers-mouth was taken by Thomas Howard in the *Prosperous*, the other by John Bowen in the *Speedy Return*, a Scotch Ship: Having took the following Sums out of each Ship, viz. Out of her taken at the Rivers-mouth, One Hundred Sixty Eight Thousand pieces of Eight, counting each piece of Gold two pieces of Eight. In the other Ship was taken Eighty Eight Thousand pieces of Eight; At the same reckoning, one Ship they left a Drift off Daman without Anchor or Cable, the other they carried to Rajapore. Thus by the help of our Friend's Brigantine, have been taken six Sail of Ships, and hundreds Ruined: Here in Rajapore was both the Pirate's Ships burnt, and both Companies transported on board the Surat Ship, detaining about seventy Lascars mounting fifty six Guns, and one hundred and sixty four Fighting Men, of which part are forty three English, the better part of the Company French, the rest

---

[274] Clearly this refers to the capture of the *Speedy Return*.

Negroes, Dutch, etc. Nations that cries Yaw; from whence they sailed for the Coast of Mallabar, and about Three Leagues to the North-ward of Cocheen they Anchored and fired several Guns, but no Boat coming off, the Quarter-Master went near the Shoar, and had Conference by Boat with the People, who supplied them next Day with Hoggs, etc. Refreshments. And from Malpa the Dutch Broker came a Messenger, who advised of the Ship *Rhimæ*, her being in Mudbay, and that if the Pirates would take her he would buy her of them: This I heard my self, and that they should be supplied with Pitch, Tarr, and other Necessaries. I took an Opportunity to ask the Messenger, who sends the Things on board, not knowing but that I was one of the Pirates, told me the Dutch, but he should be sent off with them; but before he brought them on board I got clear of the Pirates. There had been several Dutch on board, before I got Ashoar; and since my Abode here for my Health, I have seen no difference between a Pirate and a Merchant Ship: Both Black and White flocking off with all sorts of Merchandises and Refreshments, Jewels, Plate, and what not, returning with coffers of Money; And Malpa the Broker has been so impudent as to offer them to sail a small Ship which they want, and asked one Thomas Punt to carry her off to them, who denied him, telling him, now he was not ashamed to show his Face; but should he be guilty of so base an Action, he must never see the Face of his Countrymen, which made the Gentleman change his Countenance.

Thus are those Villains Encouraged by our pretended Friends, which Auga Rhimee cannot chuse but see; and if at his Arrival at Surat will speak the Truth, must declare the same. I would have waited on him to that Purpose, but so feard of being taken notice of, and loose the Benefit of the Physician, which at present am in great need of, I dare not do it.

These being the Heads of what I remember, and what I heard, and had from their Mouths in Discourses at several Times, from the Reports of the Pirates on Board them in my seven Months Imprisonment, having omitted nothing but the many Hazards of Life and Abuses received from those Villains. I conclude with my Humble Service to your Self etc. Gentlemen of Calicut, I remain,

Your Worship's Most Humble Servant,

George Weoley

52. Edward North

The Deposition of Edward North, 22 May 1718. CO 37/10, f.37

Charles Vane was one of the most prominent of the Flying Gang pirates, and became their leader after 'Commodore' Henry Jennings accepted a pardon. Though Vane also accepted the pardon of 1718, and surrendered himself to Captain Pearse [doc. 69], he left Nassau in a defiant and ostentatious manner just as new governor Woodes Rogers was arriving. He continued his piracy but was captured and executed in Jamaica in 1720. This document is included because the torture it describes, in terms of both severity and frequency, contrast with the popular idea of the egalitarian and essentially friendly sanitized pirate.

Saith, That on the fourteenth day of Aprill last past the Deponent being in and Commandr of a Sloop called the *William and Martha* of these Islands,[275] was come up with and taken nigh a place called Rum Key one of the Bahama Islands by one Charles Vain Commandr of a Pirate Sloop called the *Ranger*: mounted with six Guns and had on board (as this Deponent was informed) sixty men who took from him seventeen pistols and an half (being all the money that was on board) Ten ounces of Ambergreese or Thereabouts one Negro man, and severall Necessaryes and barbarously treated this Deponent with all his Company by beating them and using other cruelties particularly to one, who they bound hands and Feet and ty'd (upon his Back) down to the Bowspritt with Matches to his eyes burning and a Pistol loaded (as he supposes) with the Muzzle into his mouth, thereby to oblige him to Confess what money was on board, which said Pirates did (the same day, about three hours after they had taken this Deponent) take one John Tibby master of a sloop belonging to these Islands from whom they took one Negro, a considerable sum of money, cut away his mast and Bowspritt, burnt his Vessell and beat him with all his Company, at which time they also took one Samuel Vincent of New York whom they (for some days) Detained with his Vessell and Company to tend on them: And (as they informed this Deponent) had also (about a week before) taken Daniel Stiles and James Basden both of this place from whom they took some of their sails, all their Negroes, cut away their Masts, beat them and one of their men, all which severities were practiced (as they Informed this Depot) upon the Accot of one Thomas Brown who was some time

---

[275] Bermuda

detained in these Islands upon suspicion of Piracy, and that the said Thomas Brown had subscriptions of hands to the number of Seventy in order to go out under his Command upon the Account of Piracy and would give no Quarters to Bermudians; and this Deponent further saith that during his Continuance on board the said Pirate sloop the Expressions following (Vizt) 'curse the King and all the Higher Powers', 'Dam the Governour' were Generally made use of by them; and other Expressions at Drinking was 'Damnation to King George': And this Deponent further saith that on or about the Three and Twentieth day of the said Month of Aprill lying at Anchor at Exumer one of the Bahama Islands in Company with one John Peniston Comandr of a sloop of these Islands was (together with him) again taken by the said Charles Vain, who Carried us to a place called Ratt Island in order to Careen by us, where we were detain'd about four days, in which time they took from this Depo[nen]t some Ballast and other Necessaries which Remain'd on board after being the first time taken by them, as also from the said Peniston some Provisions and severall Necessaries (he having no money on board) and informed this Deponent that they had taken a Ship belonging to New England, two sloops of Jamaica, one of these Islands, some of whom they acknowledged to have used very barbarously by beating them and using other Inhumanities and took all their money, and such Necessaries as they could find that were usefull to them, and that they had increased ten in their Number of men in about the space of nine days, and this Deponent further saith that about a Fortnight before he was (the first time) so as aforesaid taken he met with a ship belonging to New England the Comandr whereof inform'd him that he had been (a short time before) taken by a French Pirate sloop of[f] the Coast of Spaniola which had on board about thirty men who took some of his Provisions (haveing no money) and beat him with all his Company, and forced the mate and some others thereof to Continue and Proceed with them. And further this Deponent saith not.

53. Thomas Grant

The Information of Thomas Grant, 28 April, 1721. HCA 1/54, ff. 119-120

It was unfortunate for Walter Kennedy that he took such an interest in Thomas Grant when Grant was a prisoner of Roberts' pirates. Had not Kennedy bullied Grant, it is possible that Grant might not have recognised him so easily, and subsequently reported him. Grant's testimony gives a vivid picture of the capture of a merchantman and the pirates' subsequent treatment of their captives.

This Informant saith that on the 27th day of July in the Year of our Lord 1719 he the Informant being on board the sd Ship[276] bound from the Coast of Guinea to London within two Leagues of Cape Lopez one Degree South a Vessel came up with him and fired two Guns over the Informant's ship, at which time the sd Vessel was about half a mile to the windward of the Informts said Ship and she then hoysted a

---

[276] The *Experiment*, of which Grant was the captain.

black Flag at her Mast head and some or one of the Crew
called to the Informant and told him that if he did not strike
he should have no Quarter. And thereupon the Informant's
Colours were struck, and the Crew of the Vessel ordered the
Informant to go on board which he did and then found her to
be a pirate Vessel called the *Royal Rover* and one
Bartholomew Roberts was Commander of her, and one of her
Company immediately speaking to the Informant said Damn
You Where's your Money? And he the Informant told them
what there was on board. And then 8 or ten of them went on
board in the Informant's Yawle and then cut the said Yawle
adrift. And many others of the Crew then went from the said
Vessel on board the Informant's Ship and carried part of her
Cargoe on board the said Vessel and one Walter Cannady[277]
(who the Informant saw yesterday before Justice Steavens)
then speaking to the Informant in the Cabin of the said pirate
Vessel said Damn Youn I know you and will sacrifice you
and then with his Fist struck the Informant with great
Violence upon his Mouth which occasioned his Nose and
Mouth to bleed and the Informant believes that ye sd
Cannady would then have murthered him if some of the Crew
had not ordered the Informant out of the way. And saith that
he the sd Cannady then ran about in the sd pirate Vessel with
a naked Cutlass in his hand to seek for the Informant. And
the next Day he the said Cannady with the quarter master of
the said Vessel went on board the Informant's Ship and
ransacked her and when they returned into the sd Vessel they
brought with them fifty Ounces of Gold, 16 moidores, ten
Guineas, and all the other moveables of value which he the
Informant then had in his cabin, and all her Cargoe except the

---

[277] See **docs 24** and **25**

wood and Teeth was also taken out of her. And when he the Informt had been detained on board the said pirate Vessel three Days the said Cannady and eleven others of her Crew were chose by her said Crew to determine whether the Informts said Ship should be kept of burnt and they all voted her to be burnt and she was burnt. And farther saith that the said Cannady acted as Boatswain's Mate of the sd pirate Vessel. And they afterwards carried the Informt to Brazil where they took two Portugal Ships and the sd Cannady at that time was Leiftenant and commanded upon the main Deck and had part of the Gold and other things which were taken out of the Informant's Ship and the said Portugal Ships.

54. Edward Green

The Information of Edward Green, 29 April 1721. HCA 1/54, f.123

Edward Green was captured earlier than Thomas Grant, but also remembered Walter Kennedy. Like the previous documents, Green gives an account of his experiences which is vivid and terrible.

This Informant saith that on or about the 2d Day of Febry in the Year of our Lord 1718, the ship *Loyal Merchant* (whereof Mathew Golding was then Comander and he the Informant Chief Mate) being bound from Liverpool to the Isle of May and in sight of the said Island he the Informant observed a sloop lying about a mile and half from the said

269

ship in the Road near the said Island. And about half an hour afterwards the said sloop came up with the said Ship and hoysted up a black flag with a Death's head and fired several Guns a the said Ship and took her within Sight of the said Island. And the said sloop was called the *Duke and Duchess* and was commanded by Howell Davis and mounted with ten Guns and had 70 Men on board or thereabouts. And they immediately commanded the Informant on board their sad sloop, where Walter Cannady and several others of her Crew examined the Informant concerning the Goods, Money and Effects on board the said shp and as to hiding and concealing the same and how she sailed. And he the Informant thn refusing to make any Discovery he the said Walter Cannady and others of the said Crew beat and wounded him in a barbarous manner and obliged him to go with them on board the said Ship and to discover where he the Informant had concealed his Money and other things, and they then took from him the Informant a silver Watch of the value of five pounds and fourteen pounds seventeen shillings and six pence in Money, all his Cloaths to the value of ten pounds, twelve hats or thereabouts and several other Goods to the value of ten pounds more and carried the said Watch, Money, Cloaths and Goods on board the said pirate Sloop, and threatened to hang the Informant and then put a Rope about his Neck and drew him up under the main top and kept him hanging there about a Minute and let him down again and then put a Rope round his Head and tyed it cross his Ears and twisted it until he was almost blnd and insensible. And two or three Days afterwards or thereabouts they forced him to go on board of a New England Ship which they had taken and to heave out ballast and doe other work. And several of the

Crew of the said Pirates afterwards manned the said Loyal Merchant and made use of her as a pirate ship. And afterwards the aforesaid sloop near the said Island took another Vessel called the *Robert and Jane* (whereof Mr John Bennett was Commander) and put the Informant on board of her and there left him whereby he got his Liberty.

55. Captain Mackra's ship taken by Edward England

The Post Boy, 25 April and 27 April 1721

The capture of the Cassandra by pirates under the command of Edwaard England was not only one of the most significant events in Indian Ocean piracy of the 'golden age',but was also one of the few pitched-battle engagements between pirates and a heavily armed opponent in whch the pirates won a clear victory.

The Substance of a Letter from Capt. Mackra, dated at Bombay Nov. 16, 1720, giving a more particular Account of the Action between him and the Pyrates mention'd in this Paper of the 18th Instant.

We arrived the 25th of July last, in Company of the *Greenwich*, at Juana, (an Island not far from Madagascar) and putting in there to refresh our Men, we found fourteen Pyrates, that came in their Canoes from the Island Mayotta, where the Pyrate-Ship, to which they belong'd, viz. the *Indian Queen*,[278] of two hundred and fifty Tons, twenty eight Guns, and ninety Men, commanded by Capt. Oliver de la

---

[278] See **doc. 41**

Bouche, bound from the Guinea Coast to the East-Indies, had been bulged and lost. They said they left the Captain and forty of their Men building a new Vessel to proceed on their wicked Design. Capt. Kirby and I concluding it might be of great Service to the East-India Company to destroy such a Nest of Rogues, were ready to sail for that purpose the 17th of August, about Eight o' Clock in the Morning, when we discover'd two Pyrate-Ships standing into the Bay of Juana, one of thirty four and the other of thirty Guns. I immediately went on board the *Greenwich*, where they seemed very diligent in Preparations for an Engagement, and I left Capt. Kirby with mutual Promises of standing by each other. I then unmoor'd, got under Sail, and brought two Boats a-head to row me close to the *Greenwich*; but he being open to a Valley, had a Breeze, and made the best of his way from me; which an Ostender in our Company, of twenty two Guns, seeing, did the same, tho' the Captain had promised heartily to engage with us, and I believe would have been as good, as his Word, it Capt. Kirby has kept his. About half an hour after Twelve, I called several times to the *Greenwich* to bear down to our Assistance, and fired shot at him, but to no purpose. For tho' we did not doubt but he would join us, because when he got about a League from us he brought his Ship to, and look'd on, yet both he and the Ostender basely deserted us, and left us engaged with barbarous and inhuman Enemies, with their Black and Bloody Flags hanging over us, without the least Appearance of escaping being cut to pieces. But God in his good Providence determin'd otherwise; for notwithstanding their Superiority, we engag'd 'em both above three hours, during which the biggest receiv'd some Shot betwixt Wind and Water, which made her keep off a little to stop her Leaks. The other endeavour'd all she could to board us, by rowing with her Oars, being within half a Ship's Length of us above an hour; but by good Fortune we shot all her Oars to Pieces, which prevented them, and by consequence saved our Lives.

About Four o' Clock, most of the Officers and Men posted on the Quarter-Deck being kill'd and wounded, the largest Ship making up to us with all diligence, being still within a Cable's Length of us, often giving us Broadside, and no hopes of Capt. Kirby's coming to our Assitance, we endeavour'd to run ashoar; and tho' we drew four Foot water more than the Pyrate, it pleased God that he struck fast on a higher Ground than we happily fell in with; so was disappointed a second time from boarding us. Here we had a more violent Engagement than before. All my Officers and most of my Men behaved with unexpected Courage; and as we had a considerable Advantage by having a Broadside to his Bow, we did him great Damage, so that had Capt. Kirby come in then, I believe we should have taken both, for we had one of them sure; but the other Pyrate (who was still firing at us) seeing the *Greenwich* did not offer to assist us, he supply'd his Consort with three Boats full of fresh Men. About Five in the Evening, the *Greenwich* stood clear away to Sea, leaving us struggling hard for Life in the very Jaws of Death; which the other Pyrate that was afloat seeing, got a warp[279] out, and was haling under our Stern; by which time many of my Men being kill'd and wounded, and no hopes left us from being all murder'd by enraged barbarous Conquerors, I order'd all that could get into the Long Boat

---

[279] A cable fixed to an anchor which is dropped by boat some way ahead of the ship. As the capstan winds the cable in the ship moves up to the anchor.

under Cover of the Smoak of our Guns; so that with what some did in Boats and others by swimming, most of us that were able got ashoar by Seven o' Clock. When the Pyrates came aboard, they cut three of our wounded Men to pieces. I, with a few of my People, made what haste I could to the King's Town, twenty five Miles from us, where I arrived next day, almost dead with Fatigue and Loss of Blood, having been sorely wounded in the Head by a Musket Ball.

At this Town, I heard that the Pyrates had offer'd ten thousand Dollars to the Country People to bring me in, which many of them would have accepted, only they knew the King and all his Chief People were in my Interest. Meantime, I caused a Report to be spread that I was dead of my Wounds, which much abated their Fury. About ten days after, being pretty well recover'd, and hoping the Malice of our Enemies was nigh over, I began to consider the dismal Condition we were reduced to, being in a Place where we had no hopes of getting a Passage home, all of us in a manner naked, not having had time to get another Shirt, or a Pair of Shoes.

Having obtain'd Leave to go on board the Pyrates, and a Promise of Safety, several of the Chief of them knew me,[280] and some of them had sailed with me, which I found of great Advantage; because notwithstanding their Promise, some of them would have cut me, and all that would not enter with them, to Pieces, had it not been for the Chief Captain, Edward England, and some others I knew. They talk'd of burning one of their Ships, which we had so entirely disabled, as to be no farther useful to them, and to fit the *Cassandra* in

---

[280] According to Johnson, Mackra and England had actually gone to school together.

her room; but in the end I managed my Tack so well, that they made me a Present of the said Shatter'd Ship, which was Dutch-built, call'd the *Fancy*, about three hundred Tuns, and also a hundred and twenty-nine Bales of the Company's Cloth,[281] tho' they would not give me a Rag of my own Cloaths.

They sailed the 3d of September; and with Jury-Masts, and such old Sails as they left me, I made a shift to do the like on the 8th, together with forty three of my Ship's Crew, including two Passengers and twelve Soldiers, having but five Tuns of Water aboard; and after a Passage of forty-eight days, I arrived here October 26, almost naked and starv'd, having been reduced to a Pint of Water a day, and almost in despair of ever seeing Land, by reason of the Calms we met with between the Coasts of Arabia and Malabar. We had in all thirteen men kill'd, and twenty four wounded, and we were told that we had destroy'd about ninety or a hundred of the Pyrates. When they left us, they were about three hundred Whites and eighty Blacks in both Ships. I am persuaded, had our Consort, the *Greenwich* done his Duty, we had destroy'd both of them, and got two hundred thousand Pounds for our Owners and selves; whereas to his deserting us, the Loss of the *Cassandra* may justly be imputed. I have deliver'd all the Bales that were given me into the Company's Warehouse, for which the Governor and Council have order'd me a Reward. Our Governor Mr. Boon, who is extreme kind and civil to me, had order'd me home with this Paquet; but Captain Harvey, who had a prior Promise, being come in with the Fleet, goes in my room. The Governor hath promis'd me a

---

[281] The pirates later regretted this kindness, see **doc. 56**

Country Voyage to help to make up my Losses, and would have me stay to go home with him next Year.

56. Richard Lazenby, a prisoner of John Taylor

The Narrative of Richard Lazenby, of London, Second mate of the Cassandra, *Captain James Macrae, Commander, taken by the Pirates Seagar in the* Fancy *and Taylor in the* Victory *at Johanna in the Comoro Islands in July 1720.*

276

*Lazenby, as his narrative tells us, was a master's mate, that is to say, a navigating officer. Yet there is no mention in the account of his being forced to navigate for Taylor's pirate company, and over all, the narrative suggests that he was a prisoner rather than a forced man. Taylor's reasons for keeping Lazenby prisoner aboard his ship after the fight with the Cassandra [**doc. 55**] are unclear, but it is worth noting that Lazenby was not the only 'idle' prisoner taken by Taylor: Jacob du Bucquoy [**doc. 57**] was also kept on board by Taylor without being forced to work, and was treated somewhat better than Lazenby.*

On the morning of the 3rd September 1720 the Pirates unmoored and hove short for sailing. Captain Macrae came aboard and interceded for me to be set free, but to no purpose. Soon after they got under sail designing to proceed to India where they arrived sometime in October. The day before they made the land they saw two ships to the eastward which they took to be English. Whereupon the Captain called me to him and told me he would cut me in pieces if I did not immediately tell him the private signals agreed upon between us and our consorts from England. I made him answer that I knew of none whereupon he abused me, calling me scurrilous names shook his broadsword at me, and said he would plague me like the dog I was, unless I told him.

They came up with the ships which proved to be two small Moors ships from Muscat with horses which they took by firing a gun or two. They brought aboard their captain and merchant and put them to torture to confess their money. They continued all night rifling and tormenting the people and in the morning made the land, and at the same time saw a fleet in shore plying to the north. Instantly they held a council what to do with the beforementioned ships. Some were for sinking them, horses and all and others for only throwing their sails overboard, and all for fear of being discovered on the Coast. After their debates were over, they brought the ships to an anchor in 35 fathoms, throwed all their sails overboard and cut half way through the masts.

When at anchor one of the beforementioned fleet bore down upon them and hoisted English colours to which the Pirates replied with Red. The rest of the day they employed in taking all the water from the Moors ships, and at night weighed with the sea wind, and left the two Moors ships, they standing to the northward after the fleet with which they came up about four the next morning just as they got under sail with the land wind. They made no stop but ran right through them firing their small arms and both broadsides as fast as they could load and fire until daylight having all the time taken them for Angrias Fleet.[282] When they discovered their mistake, they were in great consternation not knowing what to do, whether to run from them or pursue, they being so much inferior in strength, having no more than 300 men in both ships, and 40 of them negroes.

The *Victory* had four pumps going and must have sunk but for the pumps they got from the *Cassandra*. In the end, observing the indifferency of the fleet they took courage to chase, rather rather than run, which they accordingly did when the sea breeze came in, but keeping to leeward about a gunshot, some ahead, and some astern of the Company ships, which took them for fireships. About sunset the great ships

---

[282] A powerful Indian pirate force

commenced to gain upon them and kept this same course all night. The smaller ships of the Company's fleets cut away all their boats and thus gaining on the Pirates were out of sight saving only some gallivats[283] and a small ketch.

The Pirates bore down on the ketch, which perceiving their intent embarked all their people on a gallivat, and set fire to the ketch. The gallivat being too nimble for them the Pirates left off the chase. About an hour after, they sighted another gallivat to the northward which they chased and took, finding her to be laden with cotton in bales bound for Calicut. The Pirates questioned the men concerning the fleet they had seen, but they denying they had seen either ship or boat since they left Gogo they threw all the cargo overboard, and squeezed their joints in a vice to extort confession. The next day the Pirates put the poor creatures in a boat with nothing but a trysail and four gallons of water half of it salt and they out of sight of land.

They then cruised to the southwards and the next day between Goa and Karwar hearing guns, they sent out their boat to discover what ships were in the roads of Anjediva near by. About two in the morning the boat returned with word of two grabs lying at anchor in the road on which the Pirates weighed and ran down till daylight giving the grabs sight of them, they ran under the walls of the Castle wronging the Pirates. The Pirates held a council to see what they should do whether to make a descent or continue their voyage, and agreeing on the latter they went down to the southwards.

---

[283] A small gunboat fitted with sail and oars.

The next morning they came to Honawar Bay wherin they spied a ship at anchor which they took, it having no one aboard but a Dutchman and two Portuguese, the captain being ashore with his officers. They sent to him to acquaint him that he could have his ship again if he would supply them with fresh provisions and water and the master returned for answer that if they would deliver him possession over the bar, he would comply with their request. This proposal the Pirates thought was but a trap, and the mate who honestly entered with them, being of the same opinion, they resolved to go for the Laccadives, first burning the ship.

The same day of their arrival they took a small Manchew near the Island of Amendivi. They then sent their boat ashore which returned giving a good account of abundance of water and a large village. But, at the sight of the ships, the inhabitants fled off in boats to the neighboring Islands leaving abundance of women and children hidden in the bushes, which the Pirates found and forced to their barbarous inclinations. Afterwards they destroyed all the coconut trees and everything else they met with and then burnt the houses and churches. Whilst there they had a great gale which drove them off the island, after losing several anchors and leaving 70 people and their water casks ashore.

It was ten days before they again made the Island and took aboard their men and their water. They then went to Cochin to be supplied with provisions by their good friends the Dutch. Three days later they took a small ship belonging to Governor Adam off Tellicherry, John Fawke, Master, who was brought aboard very drunk. He giving them an account of Captain Macrae's fitting out a fleet[284] which put them all into a tempest of passion. 'The Villain,' says they, 'that we treated so civilly as to give him a ship and other presents, and now to come armed against us? He ought to be hanged, and since we cannot shew our resentment on him let us hang the dogs who wish him well if clear,' says the Quartermaster, 'Damn England!'

Then the Quartermaster told me to prepare, for the next day he would hang me like a dog, not doubting that I would take the first opportunity to fight against them as Captain Macrae was doing though they had so civilly used him as to give him a ship to go from Johanna. They next proceeded to Calicut where they endeavoured to take a large ship from out of the roads, but were intercepted by guns fired at them from on shore. At this time I was below, but the Captain and the Quartermaster were so malicious as to order me to the boom in the hope I should be shot. The Quartermaster told me that if ever he knew me off the deck in time of action he would shoot me through the head.

I told him he had better do it at once than keep me in misery there, at which he begged the Captain to correct me, he being lame of his hands. According to his desire Captain Taylor fetched his cane and began to belabour me so unmercifully that in the end some of the people hindered him and said he should be ashamed to so abuse me, telling him they would have me put ashore at Cochin. The next day they came up with a Dutch Galliott laden with limestone bound for Cochin aboard of which they put Captain Fawke. Some of the people told the Captain he might as well let me go, but he answered

---

[284] This rumour was not true

that if they had a mind to let a dog go that had heard all their designs for the ensuing year, he would never consent to it.

This occasioned a strong debate, and so far enraged the Captain that he swore if I went he would first have a limb of me to his own share. The next day they arrived off Cochin and in the afternoon ran into the road with the sea breeze and anchoring saluted the fort with eleven guns each ship, the Fort returning the same, gun for gun. At night there came a great boat laden with fresh provisions and liquor sent them by one John Trumpett, a Dutchman, which boat told them to weigh and run further south where they would be supplied with all they desired. At night there came aboard the said John Trumpett, bringing a large boatload of arrack which they received with abundance of joy, demanding more.

He said he had procured for them all that the place yielded which was about 90 leaguers.[285] With this came 60 bundles of sugar cane. The second day they sent ashore a fine table clock from the *Cassandra* and a large gold watch presents to the governor as earnests of what they would pay if all their demands were satisfied. When they had all on board, they paid Mr. Trumpett to his satisfaction, it was computed, £6,000 to £7,000, and gave him three cheers, fired eleven guns from each ship, and threw ducatoons into the boats by handsful for the boatmen to scramble for.

That night, being a little wind, they did not weigh, and the next day, John Trumpett returned with more arrack, piece goods and ready made clothes. At noon they saw a sail to the southward, on which they immediately weighed and stood after her. But she, having a good offing, got away, and

---

[285] Cask containing around 20 gallons

anchored under the walls of Cochin Fort. In the morning they had sight of her, and came into the roads, being assured by the aforesaid John Trumpett and the Fiscal of Cochin, that they might take her without any molestation, and if they did, they would buy her from the pirates for as good a price as any.[286]

They stood boldly in to board her, but when within a cable's length, the Fort fired her guns, at which the Pirates instantly bore out of the roads and made sail to their former berth. At night a great boat with water came from John Trumpett, and intimation that if they would wait a few days longer there would come by a very rich ship belonging to the brother of the Governor of Bombay. They spent the night getting in the water, and in the morning continued their cruise. When at sea, they held a council, at which some were for going forthwith to Madagascar, others to stay and cruise for a rich Moors ship.

The latter they at last agreed upon, on which they plied to the southward, where they saw a ship lying in shore, but she having the wind of them, they could not get near her. The night coming on, they separated, thinking in the morning to have her between them, but in this they were disappointed, for when day broke they were very near five sail, which made signals to them to bear down. This put them into great confusion, by reason that their consort was three leagues to the southward, so they immediately stood towards her and joined company, the fleet chasing them all the time. At first

---

[286] Compare George Weoley's encounter with Dutch merchants in the East Indies [**doc. 51**]

they were very dejected, thinking this the fleet under Captain Macrae, sent out after them, and made all sail possible.

After three hours, finding none of the fleet coming up with them, except a grab, which came half way and went back, they began to rejoice, and in the morning, finding the fleet completely out of sight, were very rejoiced, desiring none of Macrae's company. Thinking themselves now out of danger, they caroused, and kept their Christmas in a most riotous manner, destroying most of the fresh provisions they had aboard, of which quite two-thirds was wasted. After three days of such debauchery and waste, they decided to go to Mauritius to repair the *Victory*, which was now in a very bad way. In their passage thither, they expected her to founder every day, and were several times going to quit her, were it not for scarcity of water and provisions, and that there was still a quantity of arrack aboard.

At this time, they were reduced to one bottle of water per man, and two pounds of beef, and a small quantity of rice for each a man for ten days, though the water came every day. Had it not been for the arrack and the sugar, most of them must have perished of hunger and thirst. In this condition they arrived at Mauritius in the middle of February 1721, finding there good provision of all sorts, and materials with which to repair and re-sheath their leaky ship. Having completed their arrangements they sailed for Mascarenhas, on the 5th April , and arrived there at eight in the morning of the 8th inst. They found lying there a large Portuguese ship of 70 guns, which they took with small resistance, by reason she had lost all her masts and all save 21 of her guns in a great storm in latitude 13.

She had on board, when they tooke her, the Viceroy of Goa, and several other gentlemen that were passengers, and had gone ashore, came aboard the Pirate ship in the morning, believing she and her consort were English Company ships. After they had taken the Viceroy and his ship, the Pirates had account of an Ostender that lay to the leeward of the Island, so they made their way thither and took her. There now happened a great cabal amongst the Pirates on the Viceroy's account, some being for carrying him to Mozambique for a great ransom, and others saying 'twere better to take a smaller sum there than to be troubled further.

At last they compounded for 2,000 dollars for the ransom of the Viceroy. At this place, I, John Lazenby, begged earnestly to be put ashore, which in the end was granted, and on the 10th instant, I went ashore with the Viceroy and all the other prisoners. The Governor of this place interceded with the Pirates to leave a ship to carry away all those landed from the Viceroy's ship, they being more than the Island could properly support. With smooth promises, the Pirates said they would call a council to see what should be done. But instead, they sailed away during the night, carrying with them the best of the sailors taken in the two ships, besides 200 Mozambique slaves taken from the Viceroy's ship.

They designed to go for Madagascar and there to clean the *Cassandra*, and sell their negroes, and from thence to the Red Sea. If they met no success in the Red Sea they would then go to Cochin to sell their Dutch friends the diamonds taken in the Portuguese ship, which the Viceroy since told me were of the value of three or four million dollars.

57. Jacob du Bucquoy describes life in the company of John Taylor

Extract from *The sixteen-year voyage in the Indies made by Jacob du Bucquoy, full of remarkable adventures, notably those which he experienced during his mission to the Delagoa River* (Harlem, 1745)

Jacob du Bucquoy's memoirs of his time as a prisoner of John Taylor is probably the fullest and most detailed of all of the published memoirs written by pirates' captives, but the fact that it has never been published in English has also made it one of the most overlooked sources. Most of the account consists of a narrative account of Taylor's activities in the Indian Ocean, much of which can be gleaned from **docs 41, 44, 55** *and* **56***, as well as other documents not included here. But unlike other captive memorialists, most of whom included some interesting insights into pirate social mores as collateral information to bulk out their narrative accounts, du Bucquoy included a deliberate examination of the nature of pirate society, and the fullest single eye-witness character sketch of any pirate of the 'golden age'. Du Bucquoy's full account is far too long to include here, but these elements of his account are too good not to include. This is the only document in this collection that has not been presented in full.*

Imagine a crew of wretches, devoid of manners, fugitives from prisons, capable of anything, hardened to evil, having of their own will left all humanity in the lands of their birth from which they had been cast out. Such is the collection of utter evildoers who, like wolves, never eat each other while in pursuit of prey. Their chiefs, appointed by election, are worthy of them, being their superiors only in intelligence and competence.

Their first estate consists of a captain and a quartermaster, under whose orders are a boatswain and petty officers. The captain is responsible for the running of the ship and above all for command in battle. The quarter-master, who is the principal agent on board, leads the crew whose spokesman he is with the captain. He maintains discipline, allocates rations, is the custodian and distributor of booty, convokes general meetings, controls the captain's decisions and very often dictates instructions to him in the name of the men.

Each band or association has its laws and statutes, which are agreed by consensus and signed by the interested parties who intend to uphold them by placing, in the English fashion, two fingers on a bible.

When a crime has been committed by a member of the band, the quarter-master proceeds against him in the name of the law in front of a jury of a dozen members, of whom half are chosen by the accused. The latter, having presented his defence, retires, and the jurors pronounce judgement which the quarter-master executes with fairness and impartiality. He is not always so scrupulous when it is a question of punishing other infractions of the sworn law.

The first article of their code declares as enemies all those who are not part of their association, permits the use of force or guile to take their goods, commands each man to give no consideration or mercy to anyone and to put to death any who resist or defend themselves, even his own father.

The following article obliges each man, under pain of death, to keep faith and to give assistance to any brother danger.

A further article allows the looting of prizes, but everything taken must be delivered up to the quarter-master, under pain of flogging and confiscation into the common pool of all the possessions of the guilty party.

The code is very severe against violence committed on women travelling on prizes, who must be taken to land as soon as possible and, if no land is in view, must be left to the hazards of the sea.

Deserters are condemned to have the nose and ears cut off and to be cast away, naked, on desert isles.

It is forbidden on pain of death to kill or wound in cold blood anyone who has surrendered (it should be noted that this article is not generally applied to pirates who are drunk.) It is also commanded to set ashore the crews of captured ships, which must be sent to the bottom if they cannot be used.

It is not permitted to force any prisoner into the association against his will.

In order to preserve the peace and union necessary between members of the brotherhood, quarrels and insults are forbidden, likewise religious disputes; for the same reason, gambling for money is also forbidden.

Such are the main provisions of the code which aims to maintain peace on each vessel and to promote courage and vigour against the enemy. The pirates were utterly committed to these obligations, even though they had accepted them voluntarily.

When, in spite of these precautions, quarrels arises on board, and the offence requires settling by force of arms, the quarter-master and the captain preside over the duel, which ends only with the death of one of the antagonists. A flag is then waved over the head of the victor.

At sea, duties are carried out in an orderly fashion, better even than on the ships of the India Company; the pirates take great pride in this. They exercise continually at target practice and at scrimmaging with wooden sabres or rapiers. Meanwhile their musicians play such melodies that the days pass most agreeably. They eat but once a day and always with a good appetite, for hunger makes the best cook; they are usually short of rations.

When they have finished a cruise, they usually come to recuperate at Madagascar, where they divide of spoils which they dissipate in no time. This division is made by the quarter-master, overseen by four crew members. Here are the proportions by which the shares are allocated: a sailor receives one share; the captain, first boatswain, first master gunner and first master pilot each have a share and a quarter; men who are not counted among the crew have a half share and the boys a quarter share. The quarter-master gets only one share, but everyone adds something for his trouble.

These men, who lead a gross or even bestial existence, live and die like animals. In all the time that I, to my great displeasure, spent with them, I never saw them engage in the visible practice of any religion whatsoever. They take oath on the Bible, but they never read it. The only custom they observe which seems to show any respect towards God was that whenever they are able they rest on Sundays. When one of them dies they chant a psalm or canticle while escorting the body, but that is rather a custom left over from their earliest education than a sign of their submission to God.

In the ordinary course of life, Captain Taylor was easily angered and became beside himself with fury. But, faced with imminent danger in combat or in the struggle with the sea, he was not at all the same man; his calm, his self-possession and his personal courage in dangerous situations won him the admiration of his companions. I have been witness to the skill with which he settled his discontented crew, when he feared a revolt, and to the audacity and courage with which he quashed and overcame a revolt when it burst out, throwing himself boldly into the midst of mutinous pirates whom he struck left and right by point or flat, as if he had no more to do than scatter pigeons in a courtyard. In spite of the severity that he deemed necessary, he was well loved by his people, to whom he endeared himself by his affability and friendly manners, often discarding his prerogatives as captain by coming down into the 'tween-decks to converse, play, eat from the common pot or drink with them.

For the rest, he was a skilful politician; so, the better to assert his authority, he divided his men into squads of seven men, consisting, for example, of a Frenchman, a Swede, a Portuguese and three or four Englishmen, so that the English, on whom he could depend, were always in the majority, and could warn him of all that was done or said on board.

He was polite towards prisoners and received the officers at his table, advising them to resign themselves to their fate and sometimes warning them not to whisper amongst themselves, so as to avoid the ill-will of the crew.

58. Andrew Kingston taken by Bartholomew Roberts

Daily Post, 22 June, 1721

The capture of Andrew Kingston's vessel was typical of the mass of seizures by pirate, frightening for those involved certainly, but unspectacular and unheroic.

Extract of a Letter from Capt. Andrew Kingston, Commander of the *Lloyd* Galley, carrying 12 Guns and 18 Men, who sail'd in February last from London for the Island of Jamaica

St. Christophers,[287] April 24, 1721

Sir,

I am sorry to give you this Account of my great Misfortune in this Voyage: On the 26th of March, I made the Island of Deziada about 11 a-clock at noon, and soon after I saw two Sail standing the same Course as I did. I made the best of my Way from them; but about 8 at Night they came along Side of me: I was then about four Leagues from Antegoa; they fir'd at me, being Pyrates, one a Ship of 36 Guns, 250 Men and 50 Negroes, the other a Brigantine of 18 Guns, 46 Men and 20 Negroes; these I could not withstand. They had been but two Days upon that Station before they saw me, and are both under the Command of John Roberts. They carry'd me into Bermuda,[288] there kept me 5 Days, and what of the Cargo was not fit for their Service, they threw over-board: They took away most of my rigging and Sails, all my Anchors,

---

[287] St. Kitts
[288] Probably Barbuda

Blocks, Provisions, Powder, small Arms, etc. and 12 of my Men, and then carry'd me to the Northward, that I might not come into these Islands to give an Account of them; and the 1st of this Instant they left me in a very sad condition.

The next Day I met a French Pyrate Sloop of 6 Guns and 63 Men;[289] they took my Ship from me with the rest of my Men, and most of the Passengers, and put me, my Boy and 7 Passengers into a Sloop they had taken about 6 Hours before: That Sloop landed me upon the Virginia Islands,[290] where I staid 5 Days before I could get a Passage to this Place.

In coming hither I met the *Rose* Man of War, and gave the Commander an Account of these Pyrates, who went in search of the French-men, but could hear nothing of them; so that after having been eleven Days on board the *Rose* I was landed here.

I hope the Ships bound from London to Jamaica soon after me, may escape the said Roberts; for he design'd to keep that Station, and destroy all the Ships that come to these Islands which may fall into his Hands. They left me without any Manner of Clothing; and Roberts brought my Brother (chiefe Mate) to the Gears,[291] and whipt him within an Inch of his Life, by reason he had conceal'd two Gold Rings in his Pocket. This is the dismal Account I am to give of this Voyage.

Yours etc.　　At Kingston.

---

[289] Probably Montigny le Palisse
[290] Virgin Islands
[291] Jeers, tackle used for hoisting a yard

P.S. At this Place are several Pyrates in Prison, which run away with Merchant Ships Boats from Antegoa, and taken at Santa Cruz an Island not inhabited: Its thought they will not be hang'd, which makes a great many Pyrates about these Islands.

59. Richard Hawkins' account of his capture by Francis Spriggs

The British Journal, 8 August, 1724 and 22 August, 1724.

Hawkins' account of his time as a captive of Francis Spriggs' company is often quoted by historians, but is difficult to find in full. The first instalment reached the public when the letter he wrote to his employer was published in the British Journal. *On his return to England, discovering that his letter had stirred interest, he was moved to write a fuller account of his experiences, published a fortnight later. It is interesting two compare the two versions of Hawkins' account, which are an excellent example of the way in which one witness can tailor the same story to suit two different audiences – both may be true but they will not be the same. In Hawkins' first account he included all of the details that he believes his ship-owner employer would be interested in and understandably does his best to excuse himself for the loss of his ship. In the second account, written for public consumption, he was much more interested in providing lurid details of life among the pirates than self-exoneration, though the tales of the pirates' barbarity must have contributed to his saved reputation to some extent.*

The British Journal, 8 August, 1724

Sir, in the utmost Confusion and Anxiety of Mind do I now write you an Account of my deplorable Condition, and your great Loss: I shall endeavour impartially to relate to you my Misfortunes, in order as they happen'd. As to my Passage to Jamaica, I wrote you thence; as likewise, that I was charter'd one Half for the other: I winded it down to Leeward, for I never had a Passage wherein I was so much crossed with contrary Winds; I was three Weeks on my Passage: At the Bay I hired a Craft of the Freighter at ten Shillings per Ton as customary, and thirty Shillings a Trip to the Steersman. I had on board ninety Ton of Logwood on Freight, five Tons for the Owners, some spare Cordage, a Box of Candles, two Kegs of Salmon, and two Barrels of Beef. When I was loaded I discharg'd three Extra Men at four Pounds a Month, to ease the Ship of Wages: On the 15th of March I sail'd for Jamaica; and on the 22nd was taken by Captain Spriggs in the *Delight* (formerly a Man of War.) He kept me a Prisoner on Board ten Days, took away my new Sheet Anchor and Cable, cut away my best Bower, and vered the Cable over-board; cut my small Bower in pieces, took my new Hawser, and, in short, every Thing that pleased them not they threw over-board. All my Compasses, Instruments, Books, Escritoire, Binnacle, and, in short, every individual Thing they destroy'd; broke all my Windows, knock'd down the Cabbin, seized all my small Arms and Ammunition, and then deliver'd me my Ship in a despicable Condition.

Mr Burridge telling me in the Bay, he could not proceed with me farther than Jamaica, I shipp'd another Man upon the same Footing with my Foremast-men, titled him second Mate, with a Promise he should succeed Mr Burridge: Both he and Mr Burridge enter'd on board the Pyrate, and they forc'd every one besides, except the Boatswain and Father George, nay, they would not even let my poor Boy escape, that I was to leave with you: They put on board me all their Prisoners, which were a Master of a Sloop that they had burnt, and three of his Men; and then took away all my small Sails, Runners, and Tackles, and Part of my running Rigging; after which I was set at Liberty. They burnt an unknown Quantity of Logwood.

I lost Company of her in four Hours; for she sail'd primely well. On the 2d of April, turning to Windward among the Keys, I spy'd a Sail, and fearing it was a Spaniard (believing the Pyrates to be a long Way to the Northward of us) I run for Life, lost Sight of them in the Night, and they of us: But happening to be in the Wake of the Planet Jupiter, who then very much blazed, they again descrie us, came up with me, and discharg'd two Broad-Sides, (double, round, and partridge)[292] with two full Vollies of Musketoons, Blunderbusses, Muskets, and Pistols; and on hearing us make a lamentable Cry for Quarter, they ceased firing, and order'd me on board. I went in a Canoe, that the Pyrates had given me in Lieu of my Boat, and found him to be my old Chap that took me before. As soon as I was over their Side they were so incensed that I was not a Spaniard, or some other Vessel to their Purpose, that I was surrounded by fifteen Men with keen Cutlashes in their Hands, who all made at me, and

---

[292] The mixture of 'round shot' (plain rounds cannon balls) and 'partridge shot' (multiple small balls like a shotgun) suggests that the prate aimed to cause maximum damage to both ship and crew.

soon laid me on the Deck, some giving me the Edge, others favour'd me with severe Blows with the Flat. Here I should certainly have expir'd, had it not been for Mr Burridge, who flew among the thickest of them, and begg'd earnestly to save my Life, adding that he would never beg for another. Whereupon, he being so well belov'd, they ceas'd beating me.

He conducted me to the Quarter-deck. The Pirates being then very merry, as it customary for them at that Time of Night, they unanimously agreed to set my Ship on Fire; and in less than three quarters of an Hour she was all of a Blaze, and down she went. After this they wanted a little more Diversion, for Mischief is their sole Delight: I was sent for down to the Cabbin to Supper; what should be provided for me but a Dish of Candles, which I was forc'd to eat, they having a Pistol at my Head, and a naked Sword to my Breast, whilst others beat me with Swords call'd Tucks.[293] After that I had eat to their Satisfaction, I was buffeted and thump'd forwards to the Bag, among the rest of the Prisoners, who had much the same Fare with myself.

Then they consulted for more Diversion, which was to sweat me: It was agreed on and all Preparations made thereto. The Manner of a Sweat is thus: Between Decks they stick Candles round the Mizen-Mast, and about twenty five Men surround it with Points of Swords, Penknives, Compasses, Forks, etc. in each of their Hands: Culprit enters the Circle; the Violin plays a merry Jig; and he must run for about ten Minutes, while each Man runs his instrument into his Posteriors. In I was called, in order to enter the Ring; but Mr Burridge

---

[293] Tuck, a long, thin, double-edged sword

advance'd among them, with the Captain, Mr Cole, the Surgeon, and a Prisoner on board, who had formerly been Gunner of her, these, with one Joseph Cooper,[294] did intreat earnestly for me, alledging, That I never did any Man any ill; that I had done them no Injustice; and they had already ruin'd me; wherefore they begg'd I might be voted clear of any farther Punishment; otherwise Mr Burridge, who is their Master, said, He would be content for their Diversion to be sweated in my stead: Hereupon a general Reprieve was unanimously agreed on. On the 4th of April they anchored at Ratan, an uninhabited Island; here was I turn'd out with three of my People (one of whom was a Passenger, who cou'd not undergo the Muroon Life, and I buried him,) and Captain Pick, and four of his People. I had an old Hat, Shirt, Drawers, and Shoes; and they gave me a Cutlass, and Musket, and twenty Loads of Powder and Ball. The next Day they sail'd. You may conjecture to what hard Shifts we were put, the Thoughts of which even now so affect me, that I beg to be excus'd for not mentioning them: Providence so order'd it, that one James Farmer, who had three Times escap'd from the Spaniards, with a Man that escap'd from the Pirates, came to us in a Canoe, and carry'd us to another Island, and were a great Assistance to us in providing fresh Provisions, such a Guana's and wild Hogs.

The Bay (of Honduras) being afterwards taken, the *Merriam* Sloop, Captain Jones having escap'd, put in here with the *Mary and Betty*, Captain Wyat, who happily sav'd his Person, though he was so unfortunate as to lose your Ship as well as myself. It was with Concern I read your Letter in a Place

---

[294] Cooper becmae the last captain to command the company that had originated with Edward Low

where I could not be capable of serving him, or you; but to me he was very kind, sparing what Cloaths he well could; for which I stand oblig'd. Being of Opinion that I ought to go to Jamaica to meet my Freighter, and make legal Protests, etc. occasion'd my going on board Captain Allen, who was bound there. There I must settle Accounts with Captain Montgomerie. I am very much oblig'd to Captain James, who offer'd me very friendly my Passage to you: I intend to stay some Time at Jamaica, 'till I have the Happiness of hearing from you; for, being so unfortunate a Fellow I cannot entertain Hopes of being in your Service again, though I am conscious to myself I did the uttermost for you Interest. Shortness of Paper makes me conclude, with a thousand Thanks for all your undeserv'd Favours; and am, with sincere Respect,

Dear Sir, Your most Obliged, Most Afflicted, and Ruin'd Humble Servant,

Richard Hawkins.

The British Journal, 22 August, 1724

To the Author of the *British Journal*,

Sir,

I was not a little surpris'd, upon my coming to England, to find my Letter expos'd to the Publick in your Paper; However, as it was thought proper to print the same, I shall be glad if it may be in any Way instrumental toward the Security of our Merchant Ships. But as the Publication of that Letter occasions my being frequently ask'd many Questions, both in relation to the Pyrates, and my particular Misfortunes,

I desire you would give this also a Place in your Paper, which will, I hope, fully satisfy all Enquiries.

The Ship which Spriggs is in, sail'd from England under the Command of Captain Hunt, and was taken by Loe, on the Coast of Guinea: Spriggs was then Loe's Quarter Master, and was put on board with eighteen Men, to keep Possession of the *Delight*; at which Time the following Accident happen'd. A Man was killed on board of Loe in cold Blood; which being contrary to their Articles, Spriggs insisted upon having the Murderer hang'd. Upon Loe's refusing this, Spriggs run away with this Ship, and was by the rest made Captain of her; and they detain'd on board Mr Cole Wyeth, the surgeon, and a Negroe Free-Man, the Cook, who are the only two Prisoners I saw on board. The Pyrates do not insist upon these two Persons signing their Articles.

There is one Thing I can't pass over in Silence, that is, concerning the Mate of Captain Pike, who was forc'd to sign. It had been observ'd, that he kept himself sober and grave; which being taken notice of by the whole Company, it occasion'd them to interrogate him, whether he chose to stay with them, or go on board with me: The poor Man was fearful to make answer to this Question; but they insisted upon his declaring himself directly, he scratch'd his Head, and with a demure Look told them, that since he had a Family, and a small Estate, (tho' he has neither,) he would chuse rather to go than stay: Yes, yes, they said, you shall go, and we will give you your Discharge on you Back; whereupon he was sentenced to receive ten Lashes with a Mannatie Strap from every Man and Boy in the Ship, which was rigorously executed.

This deters the forc'd Men from seeming inclinable to leave them; and tho' there may be a greater Number of forc'd Men than Pyrates, it is not likely they should attempt to rise against them; for should any two of these be seen to whisper together, and, upon Examination, should differ in the Account of what they whisper'd about, they would be set ashore, as I was, on an uninhabited Island.

Mr Burridge, my first Mate, and Mr Roger Stephens, the second Mate, were at first forc'd; but I have Reason to believe they turn'd Pyrates afterwards. About Eleven of the Clock one Night, after the whole Crew had been some time assembled in the great Cabbin, I heard three Huzza's, and then they all came upon Deck, and hoisted Jolly Roger, (for so they call their black Ensign, in the Middle of which is a large white Skeleton, with a Dart in one Hand, striking a bleeding Heart, and in the other an Hour-Glass.) When this was hoisted, they fir'd all the Guns in the Ship, with repeated Shouts. I ventur'd to ask the Reason if this Joy, and was told, that Mr Burridge had enter'd. He is now their Master, or Pilot. When they fight under Jolly Roger, they give Quarter, which they do not when they fight under the Red or Bloody Flag.[295]

I was much concerned to find Mr Burridge to have enter'd after his being forc'd; but it may happen well to many a poor Sufferer; for he makes it his Interest to have the poor Prisoners us'd like Men. Spriggs himself is well inclined thereto, but is over-power'd by Votes, he having but two: Mr Cole Wyeth is a great Mediator for kind Treatment; as are

---

[295] Other sources suggest the opposite was sometimes also true, and that some pirates used red and black flags indiscriminately without attaching particular meaning to either.

also Joseph Cooper and James Stapleton: To these Men was I indebted for being preserv'd from the Sweat.

When they first took me, they had twelve Guns, and thirty seven Men. I observed two Irish, one Sweed, and one French Man; the rest, I believe, are English. They said they intended to take to the Bay for the sake of more Men and Guns.

The Captain seems to have no Manner of Command, but in Time of Chace or Engaging: then he is absolute: The Quarter Master is chief Director. If any one commits an Offence, he is tried by the whole Company. In the Morning they enquire who was drunk the last Night, and whosoever is voted so, must either be at the Mast-Head four Hours or receive a Ten-handed Gopty, (or ten Blows in the Britch) from the whole Watch. I observ'd it generally fell on one or two particular Men; for were all to go aloft that were fuddled over Night, there would be but few left to look out below. They seldom let the Man at Mast-Head cool upon it, but order him to let down a Rope to hawl up some hot Punch, which is a Liquor every Man drinks early in the Morning. They live very merrily all Day; at Meals the Quarter-Master overlooks the Cook, to see the Provisions equally distributed to each Mess; whether they were drunk or sober, I never heard them drink any other Health than King George's.

Captain Pike of Rhode Island, the Master of the Sloop which they burnt while I was with them, said he was inform'd in Jamaica, that the King was dead. On this they immediately hoisted Jolly Roger half Mast, and drank his Royal Highness's Health by the Name of George the Second.[296] They doubted not of an Act of Grace[297] in a Year's Time,

---

[296] George I did not, in fact, die at this time.

which they said they would readily embrace, and come in upon it; but if they should be excepted out of it, they declar'd they would murder every Englishman that should fall into their Hands. They have no Thoughts of ever being taken; but sware, with the most direful Imprecations, that if ever they should find themselves over-power'd they would immediately blow their Ship up, rather than do Jolly Roger the Disgrace to be struck, or suffer themselves, to be hang'd like Dogs.

The Manner of our living on the Island was tolerable considering our Circumstances; for we were sent away empty handed, having some Flower, Beef and Brandy, most part of the first was spoil'd by Rain; the Beef lasted about ten Days, and the Brandy a Week. The second Day of our being ashore, two of the Sailors, taken in the Sloop, gave us Encouragement not to despair, by telling us they were no strangers to such a Kind of Life, and question'd not but they should kill every Day as much wild Hog as we could eat: Next Day they went with my Consent on the hunt, taking with them the Musket, Powder, Shot , and the Cutlash; but, to our great Disappointment, saw 'em not again for many Days, and they having all our Arms and Ammunition, we were oblig'd to search along the Sea-Shore for such Shell-Fish we could find, which were Concks, Wilks,[298] etc. We constantly kept a Fire; and after having cleans'd the Fish in the Sand, and wash'd them, we boil'd them in a Pewter Bason, (of which we had four) with muddy Water, which we season'd with Salt Water: the Liquor we esteem'd good Broth.

---

[297] Pardon
[298] Conches and whelks

In my Letter, before publish'd, I mention'd one James Farmer, who, with his Consort, came to us in a Canoe, in which he convey'd us, at several Times, from Ratan to a little Island not so big as Lincolns-Inn Fields, leaving Captain Pike's two Men wand'ring in the Woods. On this Island we were visited frequently by an ugly Vermin call'd Ticks: I have seen of them in other Places, but none so venemous as these; for they almost cover themselves in the Flesh and raise a large Bump, and cause continual Itching for ten or twelve Days. Here I found some wild Pursley, which is good Food either raw or boil'd. From this Island we remov'd to another, for there a great many lie contiguous. In this we could meet with no fresh Water, but some black stinking Rain, reserv'd by old Farmer, which we pallated pretty well. The Provision we chiefly fed on was Soldiers, a Creature about the bigness of a Wilk, with one Claw, the Tail of which is a Bag of Oil almost as large as one's Thumb. They are very bitter, but wholesome, and we had of them in great Plenty. On this Island we shot several Guayanas, which are not unlike to an overgrown Lizard, which we skinn'd and boil'd, and they are as sweet as any Rabbit; for this Entertainment we were obliged to the old Man, who was provided with Fire-Arms and Ammunition; but we had not the good Fortune to kill one wild Hog.

From this Island we removed to another, within a Mile of Benacca. Here we found a Well of good fresh Water, Soldiers and Guayanas; and from Benacco we fetch'd Plenty of Cocoa-Nuts. We saw several Fish swimming about us, but we were very uneasy, not knowing how to come at them: At length Tobias Martin, my boatswain, (who is come home with me,) found a Tenpenny Nail in the Canoe; this he crook'd like a Hook, and made it fast to a Line of the old Man's, and therewith caught a Rock-fish as large as a Cod; which, with the Broth made us a good Meal. Some Days after, we shot at another of them with a single Ball, which being in Shoal Water, and among the Rocks, we had the good Fortune to take.

On the 12th Day of our being there, (which was the 29th from being sat ashore,) we espied a Sloop off at Sea: We made a large Smoke; she came in, and prov'd to be the *Merriam*, Captain Jones, who had escap'd from the Spaniards when the Bay of Honduras was taken; and the next Day came to us the *Mary and Betty*, Captain Allen, who received me on Board, and carried me to Jamaica: Captain Pike, with his Mate, and two others belonging to his Sloop, were taken on board the *Merriam*, and sail'd for Bermudas. I saw Captain Pike's two Men, who left us the second Day of our being ashore, a few Days before I came away. They had lost their Firelock in the Woods, and broke their Cutlash. I left them with old Farmer, to help him turn Turtle, it being near the Season of the Year when they come ashore to lay their Eggs.

I arriv'd here from Jamaica in Sunday last, coming over in the *Beckford*, Captain Anthony Wilks. I take this Opportunity publickly to acknowledge his kind Treatment in complimenting me with my Passage; and also to the two worthy Gentlemen, Passengers on Board, who entertain'd me at their Table, and supply'd me with Cloaths.

I am Sir, your humble Servant,

Richard Hawkins.

4. TRIALS

During the 'golden age' several dozen trials for piracy were held, and records of some twenty or more have survived in manuscript or published form. Of these, the trials of Roberts' and John Augur's companies were included in Captain Johnson's *General History of the Pyrates*, and the trials of various members of Phillips' company (including John Filmore [**doc. 47**]) were printed in Jameson's *Privateering and Piracy*. The original printed trials of members of Golden's, Every's, Kidd's, Green's, Quelch's, Bellamy's, Bonnet's, Rackham's, Low's, Jedre's and Fly's companies have been reprinted in Joel Baer's *British Piracy in the Golden Age*. The trials of Anne Bonny and Mary Read, and William Kidd, have been published as single volumes.

The three trials included here have all been selected because they have not previously appeared in print, and because each has an interesting or significant feature. The trial of Gibbens and Bournal [**doc.60**] is interesting because it gives some insight into the plight of pirates who retired tried to settle ashore. Gibbens was a member of the company commanded by James Fife, who is known from a number of newspaper articles about his activities and from a brief mention in Charles Johnson's *General History of the Pyrates*, but about whom very little is known. Bournal was a pirate aboard the *Rising Sun* under Captain Moody for a time, and it is a great pity that he pleaded guilty and so robbed future generations of the detailed testimonies that a trial was likely to produce. It does, however, clear up one point: there were several pirates named Moody during the 'golden age', and there is some confusion as to which of them commanded the *Rising Sun*, this document makes it clear that it was William Moody. The trial of Weaver and Ingram [doc.61] is the only trial included here to have been conducted in England rather than the colonies, and it includes a number of intrinsically interesting details. It also provides the final chapter to the story told in docs 29, 32, 42, 43 and 46. The final trial included here is a good example of one of the peculiar aspects of piracy trials in the eighteenth century, the phenomenon of trials staged with the deliberate intention of acquitting the defendant, either because he was required as a witness in another trial, usually of his shipmates, and would not be eligible to take the stand if currently under arrest on the same charges, or to ensure that an innocent man was acquitted while defence witnesses were available so that he could not subsequently be arrested and tried at a time and place when his witnesses might not be available.

At the beginning of the 'golden age' piracy trials were conducted under a statute of 1536, which made no provision for the trial of pirates in the colonies. This had been less of a problem when most piracies committed in the waters around Europe, but as piracy began to flourish further afield, and 'local' piracy began to diminish, the mechanism became unwieldly. Pirates captured in the colonies had to be sent to London for trial, often at the expense of the colony, and the cost and delay made prosecuting pirates an unattractive business. Jamaica passed an Act in 1681 enabling piracy trials in that island, and other colonies were encouraged to follow suit, but three years later a jurisdictional flaw was discovered which meant that colonial courts were unable to try Admiralty cases. The Navigation Act of 1696 required colonies to establish Vice-Admiralty courts, which were first used to deal with prizes captured by colonial privateers and settle maritime disputes. In 1700 a new piracy law was passed, enabling Vice-Admiralty courts to try piracy cases, and from that time onwards the number of piracy trials held in the colonies overtook the number held in London.[299]

---

[299] Joel Baer, *Pirates* (Stroud, 2007), pp. 23-26, 164-167

60. The Trials of Aaron Gibbens and William Bournal

Proceeds of the Court of Admiralty relating to Aaron Gibbens and Wm. Bournal accused of Piracy, 1720. CO 37/10, ff. 165-171

Pirates of the 'golden age' tended to end their careers in one of three ways: many were killed or died in the course of their piracy; many were captured and tried; and some tried to slip ashore and return to legitimate society. Of these, little is known about the experiences of the last group who, if successful, have left little documentary evidence. The trial of Aaron Gibbens, whom the court were prepared to believe was truly a forced man, gives us an interesting example of the kind of experience retired pirates had ashore. No sooner had Gibbens returned to his home than multiple applicants visited him in hopes of having their money returned., and it was not until more than a year later that he was actually brought to trial. James Fife's company, like those of William Moody[300] and Captain Thompson mentioned in William Bournal's indictment, flit across the pages of history without emerging from obscurity, and these two trials signfcantly add to our knowledge of these pirates.

At a Court of Admiralty held at the Sessions House in St. George's on Wedneday the Seventeenth day of August in the Seventh Year of His Majesties Reign, Annoq Dom: 1720

Present

His Excelly Benja. Bennet Esqr. Govenor

---

[300] There were several men called Moody who were active as pirate during the 'golden age', and this trial clears up the question of which of them was the notorious Captain Moody of the *Rising Sun*.

President

Capt. Thomas Brooke	Capt. Leonard White
Coll. John Trimingham	Majr Henry Tucker
Samuel Sherlock Esqr	George Tucker Esqr.
Lieut. Coll. Wm Outerbridge	Secretary

Commissioners Appointed by His Majesties Especial Commission for the Tryal of Pirates.

Proclamation being made as Usual to Command Silence.

The Reg[ist]er opened and read His Maties Commission Impowering the Commissioners above named to hold Courts of Admiralty for the Tryal of Pirates.

Then His Excellency the Govr Presidt and the Rest of the Commissioners took the Oaths Appointed by the Act of Parliament.

Then the Court adjourned till the next morning at Seven of the Clock.

Thursday morning August the 18th 1720, the Court met according to Adjournment.

Present.

His Excelly the Govr Presidt

Capt. Thomas Brooke	Lieut. Coll. Wm Outerbridge
Coll. John Trimingham	Capt. Leonard White
Saml Sherlock Esqr	George Tucker Esqr.
Lieut. Coll. Sam Smith	Secretary

Lieut. Coll. Saml Smith one of the Commissioners appointed being not present yesterday did this day take the oath according to Act of Parliament.

Richard Tucker was sworn Register.

Then the Court adjourned till Tuessday nexy being the Twenty third instant at Seven of the Clock in the Morning.

Tuesday Morning August 23d 1720, the court met According to Adjournment.

All the Commissioners aforesd beng Present.

Proclamation was made that all Persons that had any thing to do at this Especial Court of Admiralty were to draw near and give their Attendance.

Then Aaron Gibbens was Ordered to the Bar, who was accordingly Brought.

Memorandum. That when Aaron Gibbens was Brot to the Bar, George Tucker Esqr, One of the Commissioners, arose from his seat being an Evidence against the Prisoner.

Presidt: Register turn to the Prisoner and read the Accusation against him.

The Register reads,

You Aaron Gibbens of these Islands mariner stand here accused of Piracy Robbery and Felony for the you the said Aaron Gibbens not havng the fear of God before your Eyes but being led and seduced by the Instigation of the Devil not well Weighing Your Duty and Allegiance to Our Sovereign Lord King George that now is nor the severall Treaties Friendships and Alliances between the Crown of Grea Britain and divers other Kings Princes and Potentates not

311

regarding nor the severall Punishments and Penaltes by the Laws of Great Brtain to be inflicted on such Offenders but designing and Piratically intendind to take seize pluder rob steal and run away with their Ships Vessel money wares Goods and merchandizes and so hurt injure lessen harm and destroy as well the persons of the subjects of his said Sacred Majesty as of other Forreign Kings Princes and Potentates in League Amity and Allliance with the Crown of Great Britain and in open Breach and Violation of the same thereby to Acquire to your self great wealth and riches did on or about the twenty second day of February in the year of Our Lord 1718 at Turks Islands and at divers other times and places after join with or enter your self on board a sloop whereof one James Fyff a noted Pirate was Commander and did then and there in a Piraticall manner associate your self and remain with the said Fyff Cruizing in and about the West Indies and did with the rest of the said Fyff's Company in a Piraticall manner did then and there by force of Arms take seize Rob and spoil divers Vessells belonging to the Subjects of his Sacred Majesty aforesaid Inhabtants of these Islands and other his Majesties Dominions in America and particularly Nathl. Tynes Master of the sloop *Elizabeth*, Capt. Harris in a shp belonging to New England, two sloops belonging to Rhoad Island, in the taking Whereof you were actually Instrumental and Piratically aiding and assisting by being Armed and acting as a Pirate upon the high seas in as ample manner as any of the said Fyff's Company, and other Grievous Enormities then and there Piratically did against the Peace of his said Majesty his Crown and Dignity to the Evil Example of others in the like case offend and against the Laws and Statutes in such cases made and Provided.

Register. How say you Aaron Gibbens are you Guilty or are you not Guilty of the Piracy Robbery and Felony which you stand here accused of?

To which the Prisoner pleaded not Guilty.

Then Proclamation was made that if any Pson or persons not summoned could give Evidence against Aaron Gibbens the Prisoner at the Barr to draw near and they should be heard. None appeared.

President. Register, who is the first Witness you would have called?

Register. Andrew Fleming who being duely sworn said (Vizt.)

That on or about the Twenty second day of Feburary in the Year 1718, the said Deponent together with Aaron Gibbens the Prisoner at the Bar being on board and belonging to a sloop called the *Elizabeth and Mary*, Pert. Spofferth of these Islands then Master, were surprized and taken by one James Fyff Commander of tha Pirate sloop with four Guns mounted and Ten men on board who forced him the said Deponent and Gibbens to go on board the said Pirate sloop where they were detained and carry'd with the said Piate and on or about the Twenty fourth of the said Month the said Fyff took a sloop called the *Elzabeth* belonging to these Islands whereof Nathaniel Tynes was master which he kept as a Cruicer and afterwards took to sloops belonging to Rhoad Island, and a shp commanded by one Capt. Harris belonging to New England, and in the Month of March following the said Pirate sloop being at Porto Rico and severall of the said Piraes gone into a Boat in order to Chace a Canoa, the said Fyff, Gibbens (the Prisoner at the Bar) the said Depont. and others put under Sail and bore away for these Islands leaving the Boat and People behind. And the said Deponent further said that some time before their bearing away as aforesaid the Company of the said Pirate sloop shared money (the sum he knows not) and in their way to these Islands the said Fyff shared some Amber-greece which money and Amber-greece were taken from the said Tynes and Spofferth, and part thereof given to the said Aaron Gibbens, and further said not.

Presidt. Andrew Flemming, did the Prisoner at the Bar seem to be troubled or Lament at his being kept on board the Pirate sloop?

Andrew Flemming. Yes Sir, very much.

George Tucker Esqr Secretary of these Islands being duely sworn said Vizt.

That in or about the Month of May 1718, the said Depont went (by Order o his Excelly the Govr) to the house of Aaron Gibbens the Prisoner at the Bar (who arrived into these Islands in the sloop Elizabeth, then Commanded by one James Fyff a Pirate) in order to inquire after some anbergreece which (as this Dept was informed) the said Fyff's Company (one of whome was the Prioner at the Bar) had shared, which Ambergreece (being to the best of the sd. Deponent' remeberance about five Ounces) the sd Gibbens delivered to him, and further said not.

Perient Trott of Hamilton Tribe[301] Esqr being Duely sworn said Vizt.

---

[301] Tribe, a name given to geographical divisions, much like counties, in Bermuda

That in or about the Month of Aprill in the year 1718 the said Deponent beng informed that Aaron Gibbens the Prisoner at the Bar arrived into these Islands in the sloop *Elizabeth* with James Fyff a reputed Pirate, and that the said Fyff's Company (one of whom was the said Gibbens) had shared some money, part wereof belonged to the said Deponent at the time of its being taken, he went to the house of the said Aaron Gibbens in Company wth George Tucker Esqr Secretary of these Islands and asked the sad Aaron Gibbens to deliver what money he had who immediately answered he had five Pistoles that were given him and that he would deliver them to the said Depont, and upon his second Demand the said Gibbens answered that one Mr Perient Spofferth of these Islands had lost money and seemed to suspect his own Safety in Delivering the said money to the said Deponent fearing it may be afterwards demanded by some other person, which money or any part thereof the said Dept. Averred he never received and further said not.

Presidt. To the Prisoner: Have you any Witnesses to produce on your behalf?

Prisoner. Yes Sr, Robert Gibbens, who being sworn on behalf of the Prisoner said Vizt.

That on or about the Twenty second day of February 1718 he the said Deponent together with Aaron Gibbens the Prisoner at the Bar beng on board and belonging to a sloop of these Islands Pert Spofferth Master, at Turks Islands, were surprised and taken by one James Fyff then Commander of a Pirate sloop who took the said Aaron Gibbens by Force and carried him on board the said Pirate sloop where the said Depont (some time after) went and saw the prisoner at the

Bar very much Grieved and Lamented at his being detained on board against his will and further said not.

Presidt. You the Prisoner, have you any other Witness you'd have called in order for your Defence?

Prisoner. No Sir

President. Marshall clear the Court and take away the Prisoner.

               Which was accordingly done.

Presidt. To the rest of the Commissioners, Gentlemen, You have heard the Evidence both for and against the Prisoner, you are now to condiier and to Debate the Circumstances of his case, which was accordingly done, and the Judgement of the Court being drawn up, the Prisoner was brought to the Bar.

Presidt. Register, turn to the Prisoner and read the Judgement of the Court.

The Register reads:

It is resolved by this Court that you Aaron Gibbens are not Guilty of the Piracy Roberry and Felony whereof you stand Accused and this Court doth accordingly acquit you of the same.

             Rich. Tucker, Reger of the Court of Admiralty.

Then William Bournal was ordered to the Bar and accordingly Brought.

Presidt. Register turn to the Prisoner and read the accusation against him.

The Register reads:

You William Bournal late of Exeter in Devonshire Great Britain but now in these Islands mariner stand here accused of Piracy Robbery and Felony for the you the said William Bournal not having the fear of God before your Eyes but being led and seduced by the Instigation of the Devil not well Weighing Your Duty and Allegiance to Our Sovereign Lord King George that now is nor the severall Treaties Friendships and Alliances between the Crown of Great Britain and divers other Kings Princes and Potentates not regarding nor the severall Punishments and Penaltes by the Laws of the Realm of Great Brtain to be inflicted on such Offenders but designing and Piratically intending to take seize pluder rob steal and run away with their Ships Vessel money wares Goods and merchandizes and so hurt injure lessen harm and destroy as well the persons of the subjects of his said Sacred Majesty as of other Forreign Kings Princes and Potentates in League Amity and Alliance with the Crown of Great Britain and in open Breach and Violation of the same thereby to Acquire to your self great wealth and riches, Did in the Month of June in the year 1718 at the Bay of Handorus and within the jurisdiction of the Admlty of Great Britain and at divers other times and places after, join wth or enter your self on board a ship called the *Rising Sun* whereof one William Moody a noted Pirate was Commander and did then and there in a Piraticall manner associate your self and remain with the said Moody Cruiceing as Pirates in and about the West Indies for the space of two Months and there entered on board a sloop called the *Eagle* whereof on Joseph Thompson another noted Pirate was Commander and did then associate your self as aforesaid and with the rest of the said

317

Thompson's Company in a Piraticall manner by force of Arms did seize Rob and spoil divers Vessells belonging to the subject of his said Majesty Inhabitants of these Islands and other his said Majesties Dominions, particularly one Capt. Sandys Commander of a ship of London, Capt. James Seymour of these Islands Commander of a sloop called the *Hopewell,* John Steed Comr of a sloop called the *Seeker,* and John Stamers Comr of a sloop called the *Frances and Elizabeth,* in the taking and Robbery Whereof you were actually Instrumental and Piratically aiding and assisting in as ample manner any of the said Thompson's Company, and other Grievous Enormities then and there Piratically did against the Peace of his said Majesty his Crown and Dignity to the Evil Example of others in the like case offending and against the Laws and Statutes in such cases made and Provided.

Rich. Tucker Regr of the Admiralty

Register. How say you William Bournal are you Guilty or are you not Guilty of the Piracy Robbery and Felony which you stand here accused of?

To which the Prisoner pleaded Guilty

Presidt. Marshall clear the Court and take away the Prisoner, which was accordingly done.

Presidt. To the rest of the Commissioners,

Gentlemen, you have heard the Prisoner plead Guilty to the Accusation against him, Therefore the next thing is the Judgement, which being drawn up, the Prisoner was brot to the Bar.

Presidt. Register turn to the Prisoner and read the Judgement of the Court.

The Register reads:

You William Bournal the Prisoner at the Bar having Pleaded Guilty to the accusacion which you stood Charged with, It is Thereupon the Judgement and Opinion of this Court that you are Guilty of the Piracy Robbery and Felony which has been laid upon your Charge. Therefore you are to return to the place from whence you came and from thence to the Place of Execution, where you are to be hanged by the Neck until you be Dead, Dead, Dead, and the Lord have mercy upon your soul.

B. Bennett

Tho. Brooke

Jna Trimingham

Saml Sherlock

Wm Outerbridge

Leond White

Geo Tucker

Rich Tucker Regr of the Admlty Court

Memorandum. That the said William Bournal was Executed on Fryday the second day of Septer 1720, at Gallows Island in the Harbor of St. George's.

61. Bridstock Weaver and William Ingram

The Proceedings on the King's Commission of Oyer and Terminer, and Goal Delivery for the Admiralty of England, held at Justice Hall in the Old Bailey, on Wednesday and Thursday, being the 26th and 27th Days of May, in the Eleventh Year of his Majesty's Reign. (London, 1725)

Bridstock Weaver [**doc. 42**] *and William Ingram* [**doc. 29**] *were the only two members of Anstis' company to be tried in England, and the only two whose trial has survived. Anstis' successor, John Fenn, and some of the company were tried in Antigua, but their trial has not survived. Other pirates and forced men of Anstis' company reached England, and several voluntarily surrendered to the authorities, but were not tried. Thomas Lawrence Jones* [**doc. 32**] *would certainly have been tried, probably alongside Weaver and Ingram, had he not died in prison before he could be brought to trial. See also* **docs 43** *and* **46.**

Before the Honourable Sir Henry Penrice, Judge of the High Court of Admiralty, Mr Justice Tracey, and Mr Justice Reynolds.

The Jury

Richard Bridgman	William Sedgwick
James Shorter	Thomas Soulter
Nicholas Venoist	William Laws
William Goddard	John Casbourn
Edward Pink	Samuel Ellsworth

Peter Prate   Benjamin How

The Proceedings were as follows, viz.

Bridstock Weaver and William Ingram, of London, Mariners, were Indicted for Felony and Piracy, for that they on the 10th of August in the Ninth Year of His Majesty's Reighn, on the High-Seas, near the Coast of Crocas, and within the Jurisdiction of the Admiralty of England, did invade, ascend, break and enter a certain Dutch Ship belonging to Persons unknown, and the Master and Mariners of the said Ship did assault and put in fear, and the said Ship, with its Apparel, Tackle and Furniture, value 300 l. 100 Pieces of Holland value 800 l. and 1000 Pieces of Eight value 250 l. the Goods of Persons unknown, did feloniously and piratically steal, take and carry away.

They were a 2d Time indicted, for that they on the 10th of April, in the 8th Year of the King, on the High-Seas near the Island of Barbadoes did invade, ascend, break and enter a Ship call'd the *Morning Star*, and the Master and Mariners of the said Ship did assault and put in fear, and the said Ship value 400 l. and 200 Hogsheads of Sugar value 500 l. feloniously and piratically did steal, take and carry away.

They were a 3d Time indicted, for that they on the 20th of November, in the 8th Year of the King, on the High-Seas near the Island of Barbadoes did invade, ascend, break and enter a Ship call'd the *Dolphin* of London, William Haddock, Master, and the said William Haddock and Mariners of the said Ship did assault and put in fear, and the said Ship with her Apparel, Tackle and Furniture value 300 l. 300 Pieces of Eight value 75 l. 40 Gallons of Rum, and other Things, the

Goods of Persons unknown, did feloniously and piratically steal, take and carry away.

They were a 4th Time indicted for piratically on the High-Seas taking away the Ship call'd the *Don Carlos*, belonging to Lot Neekins value 300 l. and 400 Ounces of Silver value 100 l. 50 Gallons of Rum value 30s. two Ingots of Gold value 100 l. 1000 Pieces of Eight 100 Pistoles and other Things, the Goods of Persons unknown, on the 21st of September, in the 8th Year of the King.

They were a 5th Time indicted for piratically taking in the High-Seas near the Leeward Islands, a Ship call'd the *Portland* value 200 l. and 10 Pipes of Wine value 250 l. on the 22d of April in the 8th Year of the King.

Ezekiel Davis thus depos'd. On the 20th of November 1721, the Ship call'd the *Morning Star* (in which I was then a Sailor) was taken by a Pyrate Brigantine call'd the *Good Fortune*, of which Thomas Anstis was then Captain; in this Brigatine I saw the two Prisoners. I was kept five Months on Board of her, and then was out again into the *Morning Star*, and continued there for five Months and eleven Days longer. Captain Anstis was made Commander, and the Prisoner Ingram made gunner of the *Morning Star*, and the Prisoner Weaver was made Captain of the *Good Fortune*, in the room of Captain Anstis. We took between 50 and 60 Sail of Ships in the West-Indies, and by the Banks of Newfoundland. In particular, when I was on Board the *Good Fortune*, (of which Weaver was then Master)we took the Ship call'd the *Portland* Commanded by Captain Levit. Weaver was pretty active, and assisted without shewing and sign of being compell'd to it. Some time after that, when I and Ingram were put into the *Morning Star*, we attack'd two Dutch Ships and a Sloop on the Coast of Crocas: In this Engagement Ingram handed the Powder thro' the Scuttle, and appeared very willing and forward to do it; and after the Prize was taken he (as being an Officer) receiv'd for his Part of it one Share and a quarter, which came to about 25 l. At another Time we took the Ship *Dolphin*, and then Captain Anstis openly declar'd That he would keep no Man against his Inclination, and if any one was willing to go away, no body should hinder him; but if they thought fit to continue in his Service they should be treated with Civility. Hereupon six or seven Sailors went off, but both the Prisoners tarried with us. Weaver indeed has often told me that he was a forced Man, and I cannot say but that his Behaviour was very civil, insomuch that without any fear, I have frequently talked with him freely about leaving the Ship. But as for Ingram, he was so far from being unwilling to hear us Company, that he did what he could to prevent any Man from getting from us. Once I remember, while we were at Cuba on Board the *Good Fortune*, we had a Portuguese with us, his Name was Mayork: This Fellow desir'd leave to go a-shore, which being granted him, he took his Gun with him and went; but Ingram had a mistrust that he intended to escape, and therefore he presently follow'd him. We lay so nigh the Shore that I could plainly see Mayork run off, and in running he dropt his Gun, which I believe he did designedly that he might make the more haste. Ingram ran after him with a drawn Cutlass in his Hand, and coming to the Gun he took it up and fir'd it at him, but the Portuguese made his escape without receiving any Hurt. Ingram return'd to the Ship in a great Rage, and swore if he could have catch'd him he would have cut him in two for offering to run away. At another Time one Benjamin Sapes was very desirous to leave the Ship and go home, all the Company voted in his favour except Ingram, and the Man was detain'd upon his Opposition alone, for every single Man among us had a Power to hinder any other from going away.

Henry Treehill thus depos'd. About the Year 1721, when the Ship *Hamilton* (in which I was a Sailor) was taken by the *Good Fortune* Brigantine, within twenty Leagues to the Leward of Jamaica, I was put on Board the *Good Fortune*, Thomas Anstis was then Captain of her, and Weaver was Master, he steer'd her and look'd after the Watch. As the Brigantine lay at a Cape to take in Water, Ingram came Voluntarily on Board and Sign'd the Articles. The *Good Fortune* afterwards took the *Morning Star*, which Captain Anstis went on Board of, and then Weaver was made Captain of the *Good Fortune*: Though he seem'd unwilling to accept of the Post; but he could not well refuse it, because he was Voted to it by the Crew on Board the *Morning Star* which was the Commodore. I continued in the Brigantine about 16 Months, in which time we took above 50 Ships, and in taking of all which, Weaver was present, and assisted according to his Place. Among the rest we took three Dutch Ships on the Coast of Crocas, but it was with some Difficulty, for they made great Resistance: Weaver had orders from the Commodore, to Board the smallest Ship, but in attempting it, he ran the *Good Fortune* Ashore, and might then have made his Escape, as several others did, for he was under no Confinement. The Goods taken on Board the Dutch Ships were distributed, and I saw him receive a Share and a Quarter, which was about 40 l. for his Part. He might have been discharg'd when the Captain declar'd on Board the

Dolphin, that every Man should be at his Liberty to stay or go. At last Captain Anstis, upon some Quarrel betwixt him and his Crew, was turn'd out of his Place, which was afterwards fill'd by John Fenn.

The Prisoners then made their Defence: Said Weaver, I never received any Part of the Plunder. I did nothing but what I was forc'd to: I declined being Captain of the *Good Fortune*, but the Quarter-master of the *Morning Star* compell'd me to it; and if I could have made a present of four Hogsheads of Cyder to Captain Joseph Smith, he would not have apprehended me. Then Ingram, thus. I was cutting Logwood in the Woods when the Pirates Boat came on Shore and Prest me into their Service: When I came on Board the *Good Fortune*, they gave me their Articles to Sign, setting me (with a Bible to Swear upon) before a large Looking-glass, and placing two Men behind me with loaded Pistols to Shoot me if I refused, so that I was terrified into a Compliance. I made two or three Attempts to get away, but was disappointed; one of them was with Mayork, and another when Captain Anstis left every Man to his Liberty; for then I went on Shore, but in three Days, was fetch'd on Board again by one Thomas Jones.

William Watts thus deposed: About four or five Years ago, I was on Board the *Royal Fortune*, which was then Commanded by the great Pirate, Captain Roberts. We were lying at the Island of St. Christophers, and had English Colours hanging out; Weaver (as he afterwards told us) took our Ship to be a Bristol Vessel, and was coming with some other Sailors in a Boat, to enquire what News from England: When they were within Pistol Shot of us, we hoisted up a Black Flag, upon which they were turning back; but we fir'd upon them, and oblig'd them to come on Board, and drink with us. Weaver began to Cry, for which one of our Sailors lick'd him with a Rope; and Damn ye, says he, do ye Cry? You're a pretty Son of a Bitch to make a Mate of – Here! Take the Cann, and Drink, ye Dog!

Weaver desir'd them to let him go, and they promised him that they would the next Day, but they were not so good as their Word. I met with very ill Usage from them; they gave me 100 Lashes while I was on Board, which was but eleven Days, for as we lay in the Harbour, I took an Oppertunity of Running away with one Robert Davis: But Weaver could not Escape at that Time, because he was off at Sea in another Ship. Tis common for the Pirates to make any Man an Officer on Board, whether he will or no, and to force him to Fight; for if he refuses, they often either kill him or Maroon him, that is, they put him upon a Rock in the Sea, with a Bottle of Water, a Bottle of Powder, and a Gun, and so leave him to Shift for himself.

William Grace thus deposed: on the 21st of June, 1721, the Ship, the *Hamilton* (in which I then Sail'd) was taken by the *Good Fortune*; on Board of which, I was put with several more of our Ships Crew. Some of the Pirates bid Weaver take his Share of the Cloaths that were taken out of the *Hamilton*, but he said, He had neither bought them, nor paid for them, and therefore would have nothing to do with them; and so went away into his own Hammock. I have heard the Pirates say, that Weaver was a disaffected Person.

William Parker thus depos'd. I have heard Weaver declare, that he would have no Share of the Booty; and several of the Pirates have told me, that he was a forced Man. I was very much abused in the time that I was on Board the Good Fortune, which was about ten or eleven Weeks. The Pirates beat me several times; they put burning Match betwixt my Fingers; and twice I was thrown Over-board: But Mr. Weaver took my Part, and was always very Civil to me; for which he gain'd the Ill-will of some of the others: Indeed, I can't say but that he was one that boarded our Ship; tho' at the same time he spoke very kindly to me: Well, Doctor, says he, (for you must know, I was the Surgeon) what do you think of it? How shall ye like to be a Prisoner? Why, truly, (says I) I can't say that I have any great liking to it: But – a – Since it is, as it is. What must be, must be. You say very right, Doctor, (says Weaver) for I am a Prisoner as well as you; but your Ship fell in our way, and we were oblig'd to speak with ye; and therefore as you have run your Hand into the Lyon's Mouth, your best way will be to draw it out again as easily as you can. So I was taken on Board the *Good Fortune*; but I had no Liberty there, but what was by Compulsion. Howsomever I can't say that I ever received any Clandestine Usage from Mr. Weaver, or ever saw any such thing by him.

Thomas Smith thus depos'd: I have known Weaver, nine or ten Years. In May, 1723, he came, in very ragged Condition, to my house in Bristol, and tols me that he had been taken by the Pirates, and had made his Escape from them. I assisted him with some Money, and Captain Edwards lent him 10 l. more to buy Cloaths and other Necessaries. I provided him a Lodging at the Griffin, a Publick Inn; and he walk'd openly about the Town. In a few Weeks he went to see his Friends at Herteford, where he was Born, and return'd from thence with his Sister to my House, where he continued till about Michaelmas, and then he was taken up by Captain Joseph

Smith, who was Commander of the *Hamilton*, when she was taken by the Pirates. He was a Man of a Sober Character: He was Born to a good Fortune, but was sent to Sea by some of his Relations, because he stood in the Way.

Elizabeth Taylor thus depos'd: I heard Captain Joseph Smith say to Weaver's Sister, as they were talking about her Brother at my House, I expect some Restitution: Let him send me four Hogsheads of Cyder, and I'll give him no farther Trouble.

Sarah Edwards thus depos'd; One Day as I was talking with Weaver in the Street, who should come by, but Captain Joseph Smith: How do ye do, Mr. Weaver, says he? O your Servant, Captain your Servant, says Mr. Weaver: Sir, says the Captain, I am very glad to see you; Pray let us go and take a Bottle together; with all my Heart, says Mr. Weaver: And your Servant Mrs. Edwards, says he; your Servant, Madam, says the Captain; and your Servant, Gentlemen, said I, and so they went to the Tavern. By and by the Captain sees me again, and follows me up Allhallows Lane: Mrs Edwards, says he, when I was taken by the Pirates, this Mr. Weaver boarded my Ship, indeed he was very Civil to me, but I lost a great deal of Liquor, and as I hear, that he has got an Estate: I expect some Satisfaction; and if he'll send me four Hogsheads of Cyder, I won't hurt a Hair of his Head.

Several Persons of Credit, who had known Weaver from a Child appeared in his Behalf, and gave him a good Character. But the Indictment being plainly prov'd against both the Prisoners, the Jury found them both Guilty. Death.[302]

---

[302] Ingram was executed, along with John Gow [doc. 34] and several of his crew who were tried for piracy by the same court and immediately after Weaver and

62. The Trial of Nicholas Simonds and others

The Trials of Nicholas Simonds et al, Rhode Island, 24/2/1724. HCA 1/99

During the 'golden age' a number of piracy trials were held with the intended purpose of acquitting the defendants. This was done

---

Ingram, on Friday 11 June, 1725. Weaver was reprieved pending evidence of his voluntary surrender to the Mayor of Bristol which, arriving in July, enabled him to successfully obtain a pardon. *Mist's Weekly Journal,* 12/6/1725; *London Journal,* 7/8/1725.

for two reasons, either to establish formally the innocence of a man required as a witness in another trial, or to ensure that an innocent man suffered no further harassment because of his association with pirates, as once acquitted he could not be tried agan for the same offence. After Nicholas Simmons [**doc. 48**] *and his companions recaptured the* John and Mary *from Shipton's piratesand carried her to Rhode Island they were tried, not to discover their guilt, but to prove that they were innocent. This explains, for example, the court's willingness to move from the Sessions House to one tavern and then another to accommodate the sick Jonathan Barlow.*

At a Special Court of Admiralty for the Tryal of Piracys Felonys and Robberys held at the Town House in Newport in the Colony of Rhode Island and Providence Plantations the 24th Day of February in the Eleventh Year of his Majestys Reign Anno Domini 1724

PRESENT

The Hon: Samuel Cranston Esqr: Govr: of his Majestys Colony of Rhode Island and President of the Court.

The Hon: William Tayler
The Hon: Adam   Esqrs: of the Council of his
Winthrop   Majts Province of the
The Hon: Jonathan   Massachusets Bay
Dowse
The Hon: Thomas Palmer

John Menzies Esqr: Judge of the Court of Vice Admiralty

Thomas Lechmere Surveyor Genll: of North America

Nathaniel Kay Esqr: Collector of his Majestys Customs in Rhode Island

First Proclamation was made commanding silence upon Pain of Imprisonment whilst the Act of Parlament and his Majts: Commission for the Tryal of Piracys Felonys and Robberys were reading

Then the sd court was solemnly and publickly opened and proclaimed.

Then the Hon: Samuell Cranston Esqr: President took the Oath directed in Act after which his Honour administered the same Oath to the other Commissioners aforenamed.

Then the Court appointed and swore Richard Ward Notary Publick of his Majts: Colony of Rhode Island Register and Arthur Savage Esqr: Provost Marshall of sd Court.

Then a Warrant was Issued out to the Provost Marshall to bring the Prisoners into court tomorrow Morning.

Then the Cryer made Proclamation for all Persons that could give Evidence for the King against ye Prisoners to be tried to Come into Court and they should be heard.

Then the Court adjourned to the 25th Instant at Nine of the Clock in the Morning.

February 25th 1724. A.M.

The Court met according to Adjournmt: and opened by Proclamation.

Present

The Hon: Samuel Cranston Esqr: President

The Hon: William Tayler

The Hon: Adam Winthrop   Esqrs: of the Council of the Massachusets Bay

The Hon: Jonathan Dowse

The Hon: Thomas Palmer

John Menzies Esqr: Judge of the Vice Admiralty

Thomas Lechmere Esqr: Surveyor Genll: etc

Nathaniel Kay Esqr: Collector of Rhod Island etc

Then Matthew Parry, William Nathaniell Brown, Edwd: West, Francis Mozley, James Pidgeon, John Richmond, Benjm: Mellens and Smales Lewis were brought to the Barr and arraigned upon an Article of Felony exhibited against them.

The Register read the Article in the Words following.

At a Court of Admiralty for the Tryal of Piracys Felonys and Robberys on the Seas held in Newport in ye Colony of Rhode Island on the 24th Day of Febr: A.D. 1724.

An Article of Felony Exhibited then and there against Matthew Parry, William Nathaniell Brown, Edward West, Francis Mozley, James Pidgeon, John Richmond, Benjamin Mellens and Smales Lewis.

You stand here accused of Felony.

For that You the sd: Matthew Parry, William Nathaniell Brown, Edward West, Francis Mozley, James Pidgeon, John Richmond, Benjamin Mellens and Smales Lewis with diverse other on or about the 27th Day of December last in the Lat: of 17 Degrees North or thereabout off of the Island of Bonacca with Force and Arms on the High Seas within the Jurisdiction of the Admiralty Court of Great Britain on Board the Ship *John and Mary* Feloniously did kill and murder Thomas Ramage and Bryan Matthews two of the subjects of our sd Lord the King.

Which Felony aforesd was by you and each of you done and Committed in Manner aforesd contrary to the Statutes and Laws in such Cases made and Provided.

Robt: Auchmuty Advt: Genll:

To which Article the sd Mathew Parry with the other Prisoners before mentioned brought to the Barr severally pleaded not Guilty.

Mr Advocate Genll: opened and stated the Case of the Prisoners at the Barr to the Court in a very handsom Speech.

And the Register read against the Prisoners their Examination which was taken by and before the Honll: Samuell Cranston Esqr: and Nathaniel Kay Esqr: Two of the Commissioner for the Tryal of Piracys Felonys and Robberys which was as followeth. That on the 27th of December last they belonged to the Ship *John and Mary* of Boston, Thomas Glen Master, and sailed from the Island of Jamaica for the Bay of Hondoras and that on the 22d Day of sd December being under Turneff in Company with a Sloop one Ebenezer Kent Master they were taken by a Crew of Pirates in a Periauga one Shipton their Commander who took away their Master Thomas Glen and put five of his Crew on Board them being Voluntary Pirates who very much abused the Mate and wounded him in the head and bound him. And the same Night he Came on Board them again and took two of the Voluntary Men and put on board Nicholas Simonds and

Jonathan Barlow Two Men that they forced to go with them who the next Morning told the Mate they were very willing and desirous to free the Ships from the Pirates if the Ships Company would Consent and Assist. The Mate opened the Buisness to William Nathaniell Brown who was willing to the same and more especially when he overheard the sd Simonds and Barlow as they were discoursing in the Cabbin say that if the Ships Company would agree and Consent with them they would lose their Lives upon the spott or kill the Pirates upon which they Communicated the Design to the whole Company who agree to it but had no Opportunity to do it till they came to an Anchor at Bonacca on the 27th of sd December in the afternoon when the sd Shipton came on board them again and plundered the Ship of several Goods and Merchandize and took away with Them one of the voluntary Men and at Seven of the Clock in the Evening Jonathan Barlow gave to the Mate one Pistol in order to begin and sd Let us go on in God's Name who snap'd at one of the Pirates and the Pirate drew a Pistol from his side and snap'd at the Mate who retreated upon which Nicholas simonds who was with the other Pirate in the Cabin came out into the Stearage with a Pistol shot the Pirate through the Body and kill'd him at which Instant Jonathan Barlow and ye rest of the Ships Company jump'd down into the steerage and seized the other Pirate and knocked him down wth an axe and some other weapons and Cut their Cables and made the best of their way to Sea.

After this Examination was read the Prisoners at the Barr were told if they had any thing to say in their own Defence they should be heard.

All the Prisoners said they had nothing further to say than what they had declared upon their Examination and that what they had there said was the Truth of the whole Affair

Then Mr Advocate General summ'd up the Case of the Prisoners to the Court very handsomely and Elegantly.

Then the Prisoners were taken away from the Barr and the Court was cleared and in Private.

After the Court had duly and Maturely weighed and Considered the Cause of the Prisoners they unanimously voted that the sd Prisoners Matthew Parry, William Nathaniell Brown, Edward West, Francis Mozley, James Pidgeon, John Richmond, Benjamin Mellens and Smales Lewis were not guilty of the Article exhibited against them whereupon the Prisoner were brought to the Barr again and the President pronounced them not guilty.

Then Nicholas Simonds was Brought to the Barr and arraigned for Piracy Felony and Robbery.

The Register read the Articles in the words following.

Articles of Piracy Felony and Robbery Exhbited then and there against Nicholas Simonds.

You stand here acused of Piracy Robbery and Felony.

First for that you the sd Nicholas Simonds with Diverse others on or about the 22d Day of December under Turneff in the Lat. Of 17 Degree and 10 Minutes North or thereabout by Forc and Arms upon the High Seas within the Jurisdcton of the Admiralty of Great Britain Piraticall and Feloniously did surprise sieze and take the ship *John and Mary* burthen thirty Tuns or thereabouts whereof Thomas Glen was then

Commander or Master belonging to his Majt good Subjects and out of her then and there within the Jurisdiction aforesd Feloniously and Piratically did take and Carry away Goods Wares and Merchandize to the Value of Ten pounds or thereabouts being of the Property of his Majt Good Subjects.

Secondly, for that you the sd Nicholas Simonds with diverse others on or about the 27th Day of December aforesd in the Lat. of 17 Degrees North of the Island of Bonacco by Force and Arms on the Hgh Seas within the Jursdiction of the Admiralty Court of Great Britain Piratically and Feloniously did sieze hold and keep the Possession of the sd Ship *John and Mary* and then and there did kill and murder Thomas Ramage and Bryan Matthews two od the Subjects of our sd Lord the King.

All which aforesd Piracys Felonys and Robberys were by you done and Committed in manner as aforesd contrary to the Statutes and Laws in such Cases made and provided.

Robt: Auchmuty Advt: Genll:

Then the Register asked the sd Nicholas Simonds whither he was guilty of the articles exhibited against him or not guilty.

And the sd Nicolas Simonds pleaded not guilty, Whereupon the Register bid the sd Simonds attend to his Tryal.

Then the Kings Witnesses were called and sworn, Matthew Parry being sornd saith that on the 22d of December last ear Turneff a Crew of Pirates in a Periauga one Shpton commander took the Ship *John and Mary* whereof Thomas Glen was Master and the Deponent Mate, and put two of his Crew on Board hee took away the Master wounded the Deponent in the head in two Places and left him bound on board and that night Shpton came on board again and took out two of the Men he had put on board before and put Nicholas Simonds and Jonathan Barlow on board who were Men that had been forced to go with the Pirates some Time before and that Simonds came to him and unbound him and bid him be easy for he hoped to get clear of them ere long and that Simonds and Barlow told him that if the Ships Company would assist they would knock the Pirates on the Head and clear themselves and on the 27th of sd December being at anchor under Bonacca Shipton came on Board again and took out one of the Pirates then Simonds and Barlow with the Ships Crew agree to kill the Pirates and Barlow gave the Mate a Pistol loaded in order to begin the attack. And that about 7 of the Clock at Night the Mate went down into the Steerage and taking his Oppportunty he pull'd out his Pistol and presented at the Pirate but snap'd and as he was repeating the Pirate Drew out one of his Pistols and Snapped at him but by th Providence of God it did not go of[f] upon which Nicholas Simonds who was in the Cabbin with the other Pirate came into the Steerage and Shot the Pirate down and told the other f he stirr'd he was a Dead Man and the same Barlow with the Rest of the Shps Crew jump'd down into the Steerage and knock'd the other Pirate Down with an ax and killed him. And that neither Simonds nor Barlow ever took away any thing of the Ships Cargo.

William Nathaniell Brown, Edward West, Francis Mozley, James Pidgeon, John Richmond and Benjamin Mellens Marriners belonging to the ship *John and Mary* being all sworn deposed the same in substance as Matthew Parry the mate did and no other wise.

Then the Prisoner was bid to say what he could in his own Defence, Who said I belonged to a Ship one MacFashion Commander and was taken off of the West end of Hispaniola by one Spriggs a Pirate in a Ship of twenty two Guns who tooke me on board and asked me to sign the Artcles, I refused and he told me he would make me sign and sent to two Candles in a Plate and made me eat them, and then bid me go to the Devil for he wou'd force no Man then I see some of them with sticks in their Hands and Needles though the End of them. I asked Jonathan Barney a Prisoner on Board what they were for he told me to make me run around the Mast and prck me as I ran. This caused me to jump overboard rather choosing to die than suffer such Punishment. I was taken up by the Boat and put on Board the sloop that said Barney was taken in, one Shipton being the Commander who Compelled me to take charge of the Vessell as a Navgator in his absend they havng no other on board but himself. From thence they went down to the Bay and took the ship *York* but would not suffer me to go on shore there. The *Diamond* Man of War came down which parted them and Spriggs, and as they were going out of the Bay they took a ship and burnt her and sent away the Prisoners in a Bay Craft. The majr Part of the Company agreed to go to the Northward and as they were proceeding to the Northward at the Pitch of Cape Florida the sloop was cast away. Shipton and several of the Pirates went away in the Periauga and I with Jonathan Barlow and one Pirates went away to sea for fear of the Indians in a small craft and at the North Keys wee met with Shipton again who forced us with him to the West End of Cuba and in bad Weather turn'd us adrift. The third Day following we fetch'd Cape Catoach where wee saw the sd Pirate go by then we lay hid 7 days and went or the Bay in hopes to get clear of them all. About ten Leagues to the Eastward of the Bay wee met them again, the next day wee anchored at Camegul with them where they Discovered two Vessels the one was a sloop one Kent Master and the other a ship Commanded by Captain Glen which they took and put me and Jonathan Barlow, who was forced to go with me or be shot, on board the ship. I soon told the Mate if he and the ships Company would stand by me I would clear her of the Pirates who redily assented and on the 27th the Mate attacked one of the Pirates with a Pistol he had of Barlow which snapped whereupon I ran out of the Cabin into the steerage and shot him through and with the assistance of Barlow and the ships Company we kill'd the other.

Mr Advocate Genll made a very handsom conclusion.

The Prisoner being taken away from the Barr and all being withdrawn but the Register

The Court after due Consideration of ye Evidence and the Prisoners Case by a unanimous Vote found the Prisoner not Guilty of the article exhibited against him.

And the Prisoner being brought to the Barr the President pronounced him not guilty.

The Provost Marshall making Return to the Court that Jonathan Barlow one other Prisoner articles against was sick that he could not be brought into Court but that the Doctor thought he might be move to the Sloop Tavern without any great Danger.

The Court adjourned to the Sloop Tavern to three of the Clock in the afternoon.

And then opened according to Adjournment by Proclamation and the Doctor declaring the sd Barlow was very ill of a Malignant Feaver that it was impracticable to move him without Imminent Danger.

Whereupon the Court adjourned to the Three Mariners Tavern and opened by Proclamation.

Then the Register bid Jonathan Barlow to attend to the Articles exhibited against him for Piracy Felony and Robbery and the Rgiser read them in the same Words as they were read to Nicholas Simonds, to which Articles Jonathan Barlow pleaded not guilty.

Mr Advocate opened the Charge agt the Prisoner in an eloquent Oration.

The Kings Evidences were called and sworn. Nicholas Simonds being sworn saith that ye Prisoner Jonathan Barlow was on Board Spriggs when he was taken and the Prisoner shed Tears and wept to him aboundently and told him he was a forc'd Man and the Prisoner and he agreed to get away the first opportunity they had, and several of the Pirates said he was a forced Man also and that he was never at the taking of any other Vessel as he knew but the ship *John and Mary* and that he Prisoner and he as soon as ever they came on board the ship *John and Mary* agreed to retake her from the Pirates if the ships Company would assist and that Barlow del'd[303] one Pistol to the Mate to begin the attack and that Barlow and the ships Company assisted in killing the Pirates.

Matthew Parry mate of the sd ship *John and Mary* being swon deposed that Jonathan Barlow was very civil to him

---

[303] delivered

during the Time of his being on board the ship *John and Mary* and that he with Nicholas Simonds told him if the ships Company wou'd stand by they wou'd clear the ship of the Pirates and that Barlow thereupon gave him a Loaded Pistol to begin the attack with and assisted in killing the Pirates.

Wm Nathaniell Brown, Edward West, Francis Mozley, James Pidgeon, John Richmond and Benjamin Mellens Marriners all belonging to the sd ship *John and Mary* being sworn deposed and said the same in substance as Matthew did and no otherwise.

Smales Lewis being sworn deposed he was sick all the sd Time.

After the Evidene were severally examined the Court bid the Prisoner to speal what he had to say in his own Defence.

Who delivered in writing what he had to say which was read by the Register and was in substance as followeth,

That he was taken by Low the Pirate last summer on Board the ship *Delight* Capt. Hunt Commander who used him very Barbarously thretning to cut of one of his fingers for a Ring he had on and Low beat out one of his Teeth and thretned to Pistol him if he would not sign their articles but he still refused but was by the Fright and their ill Usage drove into a Fit of sickness for about thee Months together. In that Time the Pirates had differed amongst themselfs and Turn's Low away with two hand in a Fench sloop they had taken off of St. Lucia and the Company made one Shipton their Commander who went down to Ruby to Careen and thre met with Spriggs in the ship *Delight* that had been given him by Low and a sloop he had taken from Jonathan Barney who was along with Spriggs (and could not get away) where

341

Shipton burnt the ship he was in and with the Company went on boad Barney's sloop and took the sd Barlow with him. From thence they went down to the West End of Hispaniola where they took Capt. MacFashion and Nicholas Simonds out of him and that he was with Simonds from that Time till his arrival in this Harbour and that he and Simonds agree to kill the Pirates on Board the ship *John and Mary* if the ships Company wou'd assist and thet he gave the Mate one Loaded Pistol to begin the attack wth and assisted in killing the Pirates and that he never plundred any Vessell or Person whilst he was among the Pirates.

Mr Advocate Genll concluded with a very pithy Discourse.

Then the Court being in Private after they had thoroughly and deliberately weighed and considered the Evidence against the Prisoner unanimously Voted the Prisoner not guilty of the Articles exhibited against him.

And the President pronounced the Prisoner not Guilty accordingly.

5. MISCELLANEOUS DOCUMENTS

There exists, in addition to the testimoniesof pirates, forced men and pirates'victims, a large bank of written evidence composed by people who, while not pirates themselves, were one way or another involved in or with piracy. Adam Baldridge, an employee of merchant Frederick Phillipse, may have been a pirate at one time of his life, but during the time with which **doc. 63** is concerned was a trader who encountered numerous pirates at his trading post in Madagascar, and John Vickers [**doc. 68**] also witnessed pirates arrive at his island home, but with less hospitality. Three accounts of pirate battles [**docs 64, 72,** and **75**], written by people on the other ship, are included, along with a number of lists [**docs 67, 69, 71, 74,** and **76**] which shed light on pirate practice.

63. Adam Baldridge

Deposition of Adam Baldridge, 5 May, 1699. CO 5/1042, no. 30ii, printed in Jameson Privateering and Piracy, pp. 206-212

Adam Baldridge's tale is fairly well-told in the following document. It has been suggested that he was formerly a buccaneer who fled the Caribbean after committing a murder, but there s little evidence to establish the truth of this. He arrived at St. Mary's Island, Madagascar, employed as a factor by New Yok merchant Frederick Phillipse, who undertook to supply him with Western commodities and supplies that could be exchanged for slaves and pirate goods, which would be sent back to Phillipse at New York. The establishment of Baldridge's fortified trading post next to one of the most defensible natural harbours in the world provided pirates cruising in the Indian Ocean with a base to which they could return between cruises, and had a huge effect on the pattern of Anglo-American piracy in the region. Prior to Baldridge's arrival pirates sailed from their home ports, usually in the American colonies, raided in the Indian Ocean for periods of a few months at a time, and then had to return to their home ports to resupply and realise the value of their plunder, but once the trading post was established pirates could remain in the region indefinitely, in some cases up to ten years, raiding continually with only short breaks to return to St. Mary's. Baldridge was diven from the island by the local Malagasy whom he outraged by selling some of their people into slavery. Others attempted to continue Baldridge's work and there remained a trading post at St. Mary's until the early eighteenth century, but by that time the great wave of piracy in the Indian Ocean had all but ended. This document was reprinted in Jameson's Privateering and Piracy, *but is of such importance to the history of piracy that it is included again here.*

1. July the 17th 1690. I, Adam Baldridge, arrived at the Island of St. Maries in the ship *fortune*, Richard Conyers Commander, and on the 7th of January 1690/1 I left the ship, being minded to settle among the Negros at St. Maries with two men more, but the ship went to Port Dolphin and was Cast away, April the 15th 1691, and halfe the men drownded and halfe saved their lives and got a shore, but I continued with the Negros at St. Maries and went to War with them. Before my goeing to War one of the men dyed that went a shore with me, and the other being discouraged went on board againe and none continued with me but my Prentice John King. March the 9th they sailed for Bonnovolo on Madagascar, 16 Leagues from St. Maries, where they stopt to take in Rice. After I went to war six men more left the Ship, whereof two of them dyed about three weeks after they went ashore and the rest dyed since. In May 91 I returned from War and brought 70 head of Cattel and some slaves. Then I had a house built and settled upon St. Maries, where great store of Negros resorted to me from the Island Madagascar and settled the Island St. Maries, where I lived quietly with them, helping them to redeem their Wives and Children that were taken before my coming to St. Maries by other Negros to the northward of us about 60 Leagues.

2. October 13, 1691. Arrived the *Batchelors delight*, Captain Georg Raynor Commander, Burden 180 Tons or there abouts, 14 Guns, 70 or 80 men, that had made a voyage into the Red Seas and taken a ship belonging to the Moors, as the

men did report, where they took as much money as made the whole share run about 1100 l. a man. They Careened at St. Maries, and while they Careened I supplyed them with Cattel for their present spending and they gave me for my Cattel a quantity of Beads, five great Guns for a fortification, some powder and shott, and six Barrells of flower, about 70 barrs of Iron. the ship belonged to Jamaica and set saile from St. Maries November the 4th 1691, bound for Port Dolphin on Madagascar to take in their provision, and December 91 they set saile from Port Dolphin bound for America, where I have heard since they arrived at Carolina and Complyed with the owners, giving them for Ruin of the Ship three thousand pounds, as I have heard since.

3. October 14th 1692. Arrived the *Nassaw*, Captain Edward Coats Commander, Burden 170 Ton or there about, 16 Guns, 70 men, whereof about 30 of the men stayed at Madagascar, being most of them concerned in taking the Hack boat at the Isle of May Colonel Shrymton over, the said Hack boat was lost at St. Augustin. Captain Coats Careened at St. Maries, and whilst careening I supplyed them with Cattel for their present spending, and the Negros with fowls, Rice and Yams, and for the Cattel I had two Chists and one Jarr of powder, six great guns and a Quantity of great Shott, some spicks and nails, five Bolts of Duck[304] and some Twine, a hogshead of flower. The ship most of her belonged to the Company, as they said. Captain Coats set saile from St. Maries in November 92, bound for Port Dolphin on Madagascar, and victualed there and in December set saile for New-York. Captain Coats made about 500 l. a man in the red Seas.

---

[304] Canvas

4. August 7th 1693. Arrived the Ship *Charles*, John Churcher master, from New York, Mr. Fred. Phillips, owner, sent to bring me severall sorts of goods. She had two Cargos in her, one Consigned to said Master to dispose of, and one to me, containing as followeth: 44 paire of shooes and pumps, 6 Dozen of worsted and threed stockens, 3 dozen of speckled shirts and Breaches, 12 hatts, some Carpenters Tools, 5 Barrells of Rum, four Quarter Caskes of Madera Wine, ten Cases of Spirits, Two old Stills full of hols, one worme, Two Grindstones, Two Cross Sawes and one Whip saw, three Jarrs of oyle, two small Iron Potts, three Barrells of Cannon powder, some books, Catechisms, primers and horne books,[305] two Bibles, and some garden Seeds, three Dozen of howes, and I returned for the said goods 1100 pieces 8/8 and Dollers, 34 Slaves, 15 head of Cattel, 57 barrs of Iron. October the 5th he set sail from St. Maries, after having sold parte of his Cargo to the White men upon Madagascar, to Mauratan to take in Slaves.

5. October 19, 1693. Arrived the ship *Amity*, Captain Thomas Tew Commander, Burden 70 Tons, 8 Guns, 60 men, haveing taken a Ship in the Red Seas that did belong to the Moors, as the men did report, they took as much money in her as made the whole share run 1200 l. a man. They Careened at St. Maries and had some cattel from me, but for their victualing and Sea Store they bought from the Negros. I sold Captain Tew and his Company some of the goods brought in the *Charles* from New York. The Sloop belonged most of her to

---

[305] Horn book, a simple primer usually consisting of the alphabet and Lord's Prayer, used to teach reading. Their inclusion in the stock of goods sent to Baldridge raises some interesting questions about the pirate community.

Bermudas. Captain Tew set saile from St. Maries December the 23d 1693, bound for America.

6. August, 1695. Arrived the *Charming Mary* from Barbados, Captain Richard Glover Commander, Mr. John Beckford marchant and part owner. The most of the ship belonged to Barbados, the Owners Colonel Russel, Judge Coats, and the Nisames. She was burden about 200 Tons, 16 Guns, 80 men. She had severall sort of goods on board. I bought the most of them. She careened at St. Maries and in October she set saile from St. Maries for Madagascar to take in Rice and Slaves.

7. August 1695. Arrived the ship *Katherine* from New York, Captain Tho. Mostyn Commander and Super Cargo, Mr. Fred. Phillips Owner, the Ship Burden about 160 Tons, noe Guns, near 20 men. She had severall sorts of goods in her. She sold the most to the White men upon Madagascar, where he had Careened. He set saile from St. Maries for Mauratan on Madagascar to take in his Rice and Slaves.

8. December 7th 1695. Arrived the Ship *Susanna*, Captain Thomas Weak[306] Commander, burden about 100 Tons, 10 Guns, 70 men. They fitted out from Boston and Rhoad Island and had been in the Red seas but made noe voyage by reason they mist the moors fleet. They Careened at St. Maries and I sold them part of the goods bought of Mr. John Beckford out of the *Charming Mary* and spaired them some Cattel, but for the most part they were supplyed by the Negros. They stayed at St. Maries till the middle of April, where the Captain and Master and most of his men dyed. The rest of the men that were left alive after the Sickness Carried the Ship to St.

---

[306] Usually spelled 'Wake'

Augustin, where they left her and went in Captain Hore for the Red Sea.

9. December 11th 1695. Arrived the Sloop *Amity*, haveing no Captain, her former Captain Thomas Tew being killed by a great Shott from a Moors ship, John Yarland master, Burden seventy Ton, 8 Guns, as before described, and about 60 men. They stayed but five dayes at St. Maries and set saile to seek the *Charming Mary* and they met her at Mauratan on Madagascar and took her, giveing Captain Glover the Sloop to carry him and his men home and all that he had, keeping nothing but the ship. They made a new Commander after they had taken the ship, one Captain Bobbington. After they had taken the ship they went into St. Augustine Bay and there fitted the ship and went into the Indies to make a voyage and I have heard since that they were trapaned[307] and taken by the Moors.

10. December 29 1695. Arrived a Moors Ship, taken by the *Resolution* and given to Captain Robert Glover and 24 of his men that was not willing to goe a privateering[308] upon the Coasts of Indies, to carrie them away. The Company turned Captain Glover and these 24 men out of the Ship, Captain Glover being parte Owner and Commander of the same and Confined prisoner by his Company upon the Coast of Guinea by reason he would not consent to goe about the Cape of good hope into the Red Sea. The ship was old and would hardly swim with them to St. Maries. When they arrived there they applyed themselves to me. I maintained them in

---

[307] entrapped

[308] In the case of this document, privateering refers to piracy. It was widely, though unofficially, accepted that piracy committed against non-Christians was a much lesser offence than piracy committed against Christians.

my house with provision till June, that shiping arrived for to carry them home.

11. January 17th 1696/7. Arrived the Brigantine *Amity*, that was Captain Tew's Sloop from Barbadoes and fitted into a Brigantine by the Owners of the *Charming Mary* at Barbados, Captain Richard Glover Commander and Super Cargo. The Brigantine discribed when a Sloop. She was laden with severall sorts of goods, part whereof I bought and part sold to the White men upon Madagascar, and parte to Captain Hore and his Company. The Brigantine taken afterwards by the *Resolution* at St. Maries.

12. February the 13th 1696/7. Arrived Captain John Hor's Prize from the Gulph of Persia and three or four dayes after arrived Captain Hore in the *John and Rebeckah*, Burden about 180 Tons, 20 Guns, 100 men in ship and prize. The Prize about 300 Ton Laden with Callicoes. I sold some of the goods bought of Glover to Captain Hore and his Company as likewise the white men that lived upon Madagascar and Captain Richard Glover.

13. June the ---- 1697. Arrived the *Resolution*, Captain Shivers[309] Commander, Burden near 200 Tons, 90 men, 20 Guns, formerly the ship belonged to Captain Robert Glover but the Company took her from him and turned him and 24 more of his men out of her by reason they were not willing to goe a privateering into the East Indies. They met with a Mosoune[310] at sea and lost all their masts and put into Madagascar about 10 Leagues to the Northward off St. Maries and there masted and fitted their ship, and while they

---

[309] See **doc. 6**
[310] Monsoon

lay there they took the Brigantine *Amity* for her watter Casks, Sailes and Rigeing and Masts, and turned the Hull a drift upon a Rife.[311] Captain Glover promised to forgive them what was past if they would Let him have his ship again and goe home to America, but they would not except he would goe into the East Indies with them. September the 25th 97 they set saile to the Indies.

14. June 1697. Arrived the ship *Fortune* from New York, Captain Thomas Mostyn Commander, and Robert Allison Super Cargo, the Ship Burden 150 Tons or there abouts, 8 Guns, near 20 men, haveing severall sorts of goods aboard, and sold to Captain Hore and Company and to the White men upon Madagascar.

15. June ---- 1697. Arrived a Ship from New York, Captain Cornelius Jacobs Comander and Super Cargo, Mr. Fred. Phillips owner, Burden about 150 Ton, 2 Guns, near 20 men, haveing severall sorts of goods a board, and sold to Captain Hore and his Company and to the White men on Madagascar, and four Barrells of Tar to me.

16. July the 1st 1697. Arrived the Brigantine *Swift* from Boston, Mr. Andrew Knott Master and John Johnson Marchant and parte owner, Burden about 40 Tons, 2 Guns, 10 men, haveing severall goods aboard. Some sold to Captain Hore and Company the rest put a shore at St. Maries and left there. A small time after her arrivall I bought three Quarters of her and careened and went out to seek a Trade and to settle a forraign Commers and Trade in severall places on Madagascar. About 8 or 10 dayes after I went from St. Maries the Negros killed about 30 White men upon

---

[311] reef

Madagascar and St. Maries, and took all that they or I had, Captain Mostyn and Captain Jacobs and Captain Hor's Ship and Company being all there at the same time and set saile from St. Maries October 1697 for Madagascar to take in their Slaves and Rice. Having made a firm Commerse with the Negros on Madagascar, at my return I met with Captain Mostyn at sea, 60 Leagues of St. Maries. He acquainted me with the Negros riseing and killing the White men. He perswaded me to return back with him and not proceed any further, for there was noe safe goeing to St. Maries. All my men being sick, after good consideracion we agreed to return and goe for America.

The above mentioned men that were killed by the Natives were most of them privateers that had been in the Red Seas and took severall ships there, they were cheifly the occasion of the natives Riseing, by their abuseing of the Natives and takeing their Cattel from them, and were most of them to the best of my knowledge men that came in severall Ships, as Captain Rainor, Captain Coats, Captain Tew, Captain Hore, and the Resolution and Captain Stevens.

64. The battle between the *Dorrill* and the *Mocha*

William Reynolds to Sir John Gayer, A Large Account of the Action of the ship Dorrill *with the Pirate Ship* Mocha, *28 August, 1697*. Reprinted in Grey, *Pirates of the Eastern Seas*, pp. 138-143

Merchant ships, though usually armed, rarely had the capacity to withstand attack by a pirate vessel, and it was rarely in the crew's

352

interest to risk their lives in defence of somebody else's investment. Likewise, pirates tried to avoid battle on the whole with any ship of equal or superior strength, partly out of self-preservation and partly because they did not always have the facilities to repair a badly damaged vessel. Battles between prates and merchantmen were therefore relatively rare occurrences, and surviving accounts of pirate battles rarer still. Mackra's account of the battle between the Cassandra *and pirates under Edward England's overall command* [**doc. 55**] *is one such account, in which the pirates wee ultimately victorious. To redress the balance, the pirates were less successful in the following vivid account, written by the supercargo of the East-Indiaman* Dorrill. *See also* **docs 72** *and* **75**.

These presents truly representeth a scheme of what misfortune befell us as we were going through the Straits of Mallacca in pursuance of our pretended voyage. Vizt, Wednesday the 7th June at 5 o'clock in the morning we espied a ship to windward; as soon as it was well light, we preserved her to bear down upon us. We thought at first she had been a Dutchman, bound for Achin or Bengall until wee preserved she had taken down all her galleries,[312] and did then suppose her to be what to our dreadful sorrow we afterwards found her. Wee got our ship into the best posture of defence that such emergent necessity would permit of, and kept looking out expecting to see an Island called Pulo Verello,[313] but as then, saw it not. About eight of the clock the ship came fairly within shott.

---

[312] External structures, the removal of which could add considerably to a ship's speed and handiness. It was a common practice for pirates to 'streamline' their ships for maximum performance.

[313] Pulau Baralha, Malaysia

Then wee saw that in room of her galleries there were large sally ports in each of which was a large gun, seemingly of brass. Her taffrail was likewise taken down. Wee, having done what wee possibly could do to prepare ourselves, fearing wee might suddenlie bee sett upon sent all our people to their respective quarters for action, and now hoisted our colours whiche the Captain desired nailed to the staffe in sighte of the enemy; which was immediately done. As soon as they perceived oure colours, they hoisted theirs which were the Union Jack, and let fly a Broad Red Pendant, at their masthead.

The Pirate being now in little more than half pistol shott,[314] wee colde discerne abundance of men whiche went forward to the quarter deck as wee supposed, to consult. They stood as wee stood but wee spoke neither to the other. At noone it fell so calme that wee were afraid that wee shoulde by the sea, bee hove one on the other. At noone sprung up a gale. The Pirate kept as we kept. At three o'clocke the Pirate backt her saile and they went from us. Wee kept close hauled, the wind being contrary for Mallacca. When about seven miles distant from us the Pirate tacked and again stood after us with all sail.

At six in the evening wee saw the lookt for Island at whiche time the Pirate came up on oure starboard side within shott. Wee saw he kept a man at each topmast head looking out till it was dark then he hauled off a little from us, though keeping company all night. Att eight in the morning he drewe near us by whiche time wee had brought up oure other four guns that were in the hold, and were now in the best posture of defence

---

[314] A little over 15 yards or so away

wee coulde desire. Hee drawing nere to us and seeing that if we woulde wee colde nott get from him, hee far outsailing us bye and large, oure Captain resolved to see what the Rogue woulde do, so ordered us to hand oure small sailes, and furl oure mainsail.

Hee, seeing this, did the like, and as wee came back to him, beat his drum and sounded his trumpets, and then haled us foure times before wee woulde answer him. At last it was thought fitting to see what he woulde say, soe the Boatswaine spoke to him as ordered whiche was that wee came from London. Then he enquired, was it peace or war with France. We answered that itt was universal peace throughout Europe at which he pawsed a little, and then answered 'That's well.' He further enquired had wee touched at Achin; we said a boate came off, but came not neare us by seven miles. Further he enquired oure Captain's name and whither bound. We answered to Mallacca to which they replied, they also, and would oure Captain come aboard for a glass of wine?

Wee declining, said they 'Shall meete you at Mallaca.' Then again he called to us to lie bye and he woulde come aboard us. Our answer was 'Too late.' He said 'True, it is late for China' and enquired whether wee should touch at the Water Islands for water. Wee said wee shoulde. Then saide hee 'So shall wee.' After he had asked us all these questions wee desired to know who hee was and whence hee came. Hee saide from London, theire Captain's name Collyford,[315] the ship the *Resolution*, bound for China. Wee knew this Collyford had been Gunner's mate at Madras and run away with the Josiah Ketch. Thus passed the 8th July. Friday the 9th

---

[315] See **doc. 17**

hee being some distance from us, wee coulde discern a fellow on the Quarter deck wearing a sword.

As they drewe nearer this hellish Imp cried, 'Strike, you Doggs,' which we preserved was nott by general consent for he was called away. Now oure Boatswaine, unknown to the Captain, in a fury, ran upon the poop and answered wee shoulde strike to noe suche dogs telling him the Rogue Every[316] and all his gang were hanged, as hee shoulde bee. Oure Captain was angry that he spoke thus without order, but again ordered the Boatswaine to hail and ask why he dogged us. One stept forward upon the forecastle and said, 'Gentlemen, we want nott your ship, but onlie youre monie.' Wee told them wee had none for them, bidding them come alongside and take whatever they coulde get.

Then the parcel of Bloodhound Rogues clasht their cutlasses and said they woulde have oure money or oure hearts' blood saying 'do you not know us to be the *Mocha*?' Our answer was 'Yes Yes.' Thereupon they gave a great shout and all retired oute of sight, and wee also to our quarters. They were about to hoist colours but their halliards broke seeing which oure people gave a greate shoute. As soone as they coulde bring their chase guns to bear on they fired them, so keeping on oure quarter.[317] Oure guns could not bear for a short time, but as soon as did hap, we gave the Pirates better than they did like.

---

[316] Henry Every, see docs **2-5, 36**. Every had not, in fact, been hanged, though some of his crew had.
[317] That is, the *Mocha* was sailing to one side and somewhat behind the *Dorrill*, and was able to bring her forward-facing chase guns to bear before the *Dorrill's* broadside could be used

His second shott caried away oure sprit sayle yard. About half an hour after or more he carried on and came alongside after which wee both continewed powering oure fire, wee giving sometimes single guns, and sometime broadsides of three or four, as opportunity presented, and could bring them to doe best service. He was going to lay us athwart the hawse, but by good fortune Captain Hide frustrated his attempt by powering in a broadside which made him give back and goe astarne where he lay without firing for a small space. Then he fired one gun which shot came through oure Roundhouse window though without damage.

He now filled[318] and bore away, and when about a quarter mile off fired another gun which wee answered. Aboute an houre after he tacked and came up with us we making no sayle, but lying bye to wait him. The distance at most in all our firing was never more than two ships' lengths, the time of our engagement from half an hour after eleven till three in the afternoon. At this time he lay aloof and made no sign to renew the engagement. When wee came to see what damage we had sustained wee found our chiefe mate Mr Smith wounded in the leg close up by the knee with a piece of chaine, and the barber's mate two fingers shott off as hee was sponging a gun.

The Gunner's boy had his legg shott off when in the waist. Oure Quartermaster John Amos, had his leg shott off when att the helm, the Boatswaine's boy, a lad of thirteen, shott in the thigh going right through and splintering the bone, John Osbourne, in the roundhouse, wounded in the temple, the Captain's boy on the Quarter deck, his skull raised by a shott.

---

[318] Trimmed sails to catch the most wind for maximum speed.

William Reynolds his boy, his hat shot off and his hand sore wounded and John Blake, half his calf shott away.

The shipps damage is the mizzen maste shott away in the cap ('twas a miracle it stood so long), all oure rigging save one rope only shott to piece, our mainemast ten feet from the deck cut eight inches deep by great shott, a great shot through the Roundhouse, one on the quarter deck, two in the forecastle, two in the bread room, which cawsed us to make much water and damaged the greater part of our bread. They dismounted two of our guns in the stearidge, two in the waist, one in the Roundhouse and one in the forecastle with abundance more damage 'twould be tedious to relate. Their small shot was mostly tin and tutenagle[319] and they fired pieces of glass bottles, teapots, chains, stones and what not, which we found on our decks.

We observed abundance of our great shott pass through the Rogue's sayles and our hope is to have done him such damage as will now make him shun any Europe ship. At night wee preserved and kept close to their lights, and in the morning they made off as far as wee coulde discerne. We knotted and spliced our rigging and in the morning made all haste to repair our damage. At the beginning our men seeing the Pirates stand after us wee coulde perseve their countenances to bee dejected. Wee cheered them what wee coulde, and the Captain and wee, oute of our own proper money, gave to every man and boy three dollars each which animated them, and wee further promised them if wee took the Pirate ship for every prisoner, five pounds, besides a gratuity from oure Gentleman employers.

---

[319] pewter

At 9 o'clock July 10th wee perseved the Rogue make from us, so gave the Almighty our most condign thanks that hee had delivered us from the worst of oure enemies, for, truly the Pirate was very strong having at least 100 Europeans aboarde, besides 10 patereroes[320] and two small mortars in the forecastle head, his lower tier being, we judged sixteen, and eighteen pounders. The 12th July, died the Boatswaine's boy, George Mopp, Friday the 16th, died the Gunner's boy, Thomas Matthews, Sunday the 18th died the barber, Andrew Miller, Sunday the 25th, died the Chiefe mate, Mr. John Smith. The other two are yet in a deplorable condition and wee are ashore here to refresh ourselves. The Chinese report that these Rogues careened at the Maldives, where they gave an end to their Commanding Rogue, Ralph Stout, who they murdered for attempting to run away.

65. A pirate's widow seeks her inheritance

Ann Canterell to Adam Baldridge, 25 March, 1698. HCA 1/98, f. 92

This letter from Ann Canterell, widow of the pirate John Read, to Adam Baldridge is interesting firstly because of the light it sheds on pirate practices and secondly because of the genealogical possibilities that it, and its accompanying documents, raise. John Read died leaving his wife and two children, a son and daughter destitute. The name of the daughter, christened at the Bristol Church of St. Augustine the Less, was Mary. This Mary Read, of whom no firm trace has yet been found after the date of this letter, was born around the right time to fit with the supposed life of Mary

---

[320] Small swivel guns

Read, the notorious female pirates of the 1720s, and the details of the early life of Mary Read of Bristol coincide on multiple occasions with the early life of Mary Read the pirate as it is related by the sometimes-unreliable Charles Johnson. Both women were born to a seaman's wife, both lost their fathers at a young age, both had one brother. It would be delightful if Mary Read the pirate was also the daughter of a pirate, but it is unlikely ever to be proven.

Capt. Baldridge,

I have been Informed yt my late husband John Read dyed at Maligascar, and left a Considerable sume of mony in yor hands for my selfe and his Children. This goes by my friend Mr John Powell, whome I have Impowere wth a letter of Attorney to Receive wt Monys or other things my said late husband John Read left in yr or any other Persons Custody wch I desire you to pay him, and doubt not but he will be very carefull in bringing or sending it, yt it may come safe to my hands, if there be any thing I hope you will be so kind, as to pay it, for my selfe and family are in a very poor Condition, and in great want thereof.

I have also sent a Certificate by Mr Jno Powell yt I was ye true Wife of John Read, I take leave and Rest, Yor Humb Servant, Ann Cantrell

66. A letter to a pirate

Sarah Horne to Jacob Horne, 5 June, 1698. HCA 1/98, f. 118

This letter is perhaps the most poignant of the documents included here, a simple letter from wife to husband, passing on family news and expressing her love for her husband half a world away. It also sheds some interesting light on the possibility for international correspondence with pirates: this is the third of Sarah Horne's letters to her husband, and she had received one reply from him.

My Dear Deare Jacob Horne this with my Kind Love and harty Respects Remembered to you Hopeing to God that these few Lines will find you in Good Bodely helth as they Leave mee att this present time praysed bee God for it

Deare Jacob, haveing opertunyty I was willing to Imbrace It and let you heare How It is with mee and Your Children: they are well, Margrett presents her Duty to you, your Son I have put out according to your Desire to oure Couson Isack Tayler till you com home againe. Pray Bee so Kind if you have opertunity as to Lett us hear from you if possible how it is with you all for wee here abundance of flying news Concerning you – but Glader if it should please God that I should [see] your face once more. Oure Relations and friends are all well and Give theyr loves to you. I have sent you two letters before this and have Receved One, no more att present But Giving my prayers to ye Almyty for your Helth and happiness so I Rest your true and faithfull Wife till Death.

Sarah Horne xx

Denis Holdren and wife are alive and well and Remembur theyr Kind love to you and theyr Dear son willing.

67. Prices of Pirate Supplies

A List of the Prices that Capt. Jacobs sold Licquors and other Goods att, at St. Mary's, 9 June, 1698. HCA 1/98, f. 142

The following list of prices for goods shipped to the trading post at St. Mary's Island, Madagascar [**doc. 63**] *was drawn up at the instigation of Frederick Phillipse on the information of Captain Jacobs who had shipped and sold them.*

Rumme: At first by the Barrill for 3 pc of 8[321] a Galln, afterward 3 ½ pc of 8 and at Last 4 and 5 pc of 8 a Galln.

Wine: By the whole Barril att 3 pc of 8 a Galln, but most retailed at a pc of 8 the Bottle

Beer: One barril was sold at 60 pc of 8. All the Rest retailed by the Tancker at a pc of 8 the Tancker, which held about ⅓ of a Galln. But had been the same price if it had held but a quarter.

Lime Juice was sold att 4 pc of 8 a Galln.[322]

Suggar att 4 Ryales a lb.

Tarr att 24 pc of 8 a barril.

Salte att 10 pc afterward 12 pc of 8 a ½ barril.

Peace,[323] att first 12 and afterwards 15 pc of 8 a ½ barril.

---

[321] Pieces of eight

[322] Note that until the very end, when rum reached the price of 5 pieces of eight per gallon, lime juice was the most expensive drink

[323] Peas (dried)

Writing Paper 1 pc of 8 a quyor.

Hatts 12 pc of 8 a pc.

Pumps 3 pc of 8 a paire.

Tobacco Pipes 6 Ryales a dosen.

68. John Vickers describes the arrival of the pirates at New Providence, Bahamas

Calendar of State Papers, Colonial series, 1716-1717, item. 240.i

John Vickers was an inhabitant of the Bahamas when it became a focal point for pirates operating the Caribbean. Hs account of the arrival of early members of the Flying Gang (so named in this document) paints a vivid picture of a neighbourhood going downhill at the arrival of bad elements.

Deposition of John Vickers; late of the Island of Providence. In Nov. last Benjamin Hornigold arrived at Providence in the sloop *Mary* of Jamaica, belonging to Augustine Golding, which Hornigold took upon the Spanish coast, and soon after the taking of the said sloop, he took a Spanish sloop loaded with dry goods and sugar, which cargo he disposed of at Providence, but the Spanish sloop was taken from him by Capt. Jennings of the sloop *Bathsheba* of Jamaica. In January Hornigold sailed from Providence in the said sloop *Mary*, having on board 140 men, 6 guns and 8 pattararas, and soon after returned with another Spanish sloop, which he took on the coast of Florida. After he had fitted the said sloop at Providence, he sent Golding's sloop back to Jamaica to be

363

returned to the owners: and in March last sailed from Providence in the said Spanish sloop, having on board near 200 men, but whither bound deponent knoweth not. About 22nd April last, Capt. Jenings arrived at Providence and brought in as prize a French ship mounted with 32 guns which he had taken at the Bay of Hounds, and there shared the cargo (which was very rich consisting of European goods for the Spanish trade) amongst his men, and then went in the said ship to the wrecks where he served as Comodore and guardship. There are at Providence about 50 men who have deserted the sloops that were upon the wrecks, and committ great disorders in that Island, plundering the inhabitants, burning their houses, and ravishing their wives. One Thomas Barrow formerly mate of a Jamaica brigantine which run away some time ago with a Spanish marquiss's money and effects, is the chief of them and gives out that he only waits for a vessell to go out a pirating, that he is Governor of Providence and will make it a second Madagascar,[324] and expects 5 or 600 men more from Jamaica sloops to join in the settling of Providence, and to make war on the French and Spaniards, but for the English, they don't intend to meddle with them, unless they are first attack'd by them; nevertheless Barrow and his crew robb'd a New England brigantine, one Butler master, in the harbour of Providence and took a Bermuda sloop, beat the master and confined him for severall days, but not finding the said sloop fitt for their purpose, discharged her. About a year ago one Daniel Stillwell formerly belonging to Jamaica, and lately settled on Isle Aethera,[325] went in a small shallop, with John Kemp,

---

[324] See **doc. 63**
[325] Eleuthera

Matthew Low, two Dutchmen, and Darvell to the coast of Cuba and there took a Spanish lanch having on board 11,050 pieces of eight, and brought the same into Isle Aethera; and Capt. Thomas Walker of Providence having received advice thereof from the Governor of Jamaica, seized Stillwell and his vessell, but upon the coming of Hornigold to Providence, Stillwell was rescued and Capt. Walker threatned to have his house burned for offering to concern himself, Hornigold saying that all pirates were under his protection. It is common for the sailors now at Providence (who call themselves the flying gang) to extort money from the inhabitants, and one Capt. Stockdale who came passenger with deponent to Virginia was threatned to be whipp'd for not giving them what they demanded, and just upon his coming from thence he payed them 20sh. for which the aforementioned Barrow and one Peter Parr gave him a receipt on the publick account. Many of the inhabitants of that Island had deserted their habitations for fear of being murdered. Sometime about the beginning of March one Capt. Farnandez, an inhabitant of Jamaica, in the sloop *Bennet* mounted with 10 guns and with about 110 men took a Spanish sloop with about three millions of money as it was reported and silks and cochenile to the like value and brought the sloop into Providence and there divided the money and goods among the men and is returned to the North side of Jamaica to try whether he may go home in safety and if he found he could not he gave out that he would return to Providence and settle amongst the Rovers.

John Vickers.

69. Pirates surrender to Captain Pearse

A List of the Names of such Pirates as Surrender'd themselves at Providence, 3 June 1718, ADM 1/2282

Captain Vincent Pearse and his ship, HMS Phoenix, were stationed at New York when news of the 1717 Proclamation of Pardon reached the American colonies. Determined that the Bahamas pirates should hear of the pardon as soon as possible, he sailed to New Providence and distributed copies of the proclamation. Though he had no authority to actually grant pardon he agreed to make a note of all those pirates who surrendered to him, as an act of good-will on both sides. In all, 209 pirates submitted their names for his list, and though several of them returned to piracy, even before Pearse had left the Bahamas, many do not appear again in the annals of piracy so presumably took full advantage of the offered pardon.

Note. Those that are marked thus **+** before their Names are gone out a Pirating againe.

No	Persons Names	No.		Persons Names	No.		Persons Names
	Picker Adams			John Clarke			Peter Mallet
	Arthur Allen		+	Richd. Bishop			William Titso
	James Coates			Henry Barnes			John Arterile
	Jno. Dalrymple			Davd. Champion		+	John Mounsey
5	Benj. Hornigold	5		John Rowall	5		John Johnson
	Josiah Burgess			William Willis			John Pyley
	Francis Lesley[326]			Trustram Wilson			John Furrow
	Thomas Nichols[327]			Daniel Jones			Samuel Addy
	Palsgrave Williams			Philip Calvorley			John Magness
10	John Lewis	80		James Brown	150		Thomas Trouten

[326] See **doc. 20**
[327] See **doc. 20**

	Rich. Nowland			John Sutton			Edw. Miller
	John Martin			Geo. Raddon			Davd. Swoord
	William Conner			Adam Forbes			Richd. Earle
	Thos. Grahame			Cornelius Mahon			Anthony Kemp
5	Thomas Terrill	5		Tho. Pearse	5		John Caryl
	John Ealling			David Ross			Robt. Shear
	Robt. Wishart		+	Jacob Johnson		+	Jno. Mitchell
	James Gratricks			Wm. Bridges		+	Edw. Rogers
	Edward Stacey			Robt. Brown			Michl. Rogers
20	John Tennet	90		Rt. Moggridge	160		John Kemp
	John Hunt			Henry Shipton			John Sipkins
	John Pearse			John Cullemore			Othenias Parr
	James Bryan			Peter Johnson			Wm. Pinfold

	Henry Berry		Charles Morgan		Pearse Wright
5	Thomas Lamb	5	John Auger	5	Jacob Roberts
	John Allen		William South		Wm. Williams
	Martin Carrill		Marmadke. Gee		Edwd. Wells
	Thomas Clies		James Mowat		Jno. Cockram
	Jno. Hipperson		Benjn. Turner		Joseph Fryers
30	Jno. Charlton	100	John Mutlow	170	Geo. Rouncifull
	Fras. Charnock		John Stout		John Creigh
	+ Davd. Merredith		Tho. Reynolds		Wm. Roberts
	+ Edward Nowland		James Wheeler		Mathw. Reveire
	+ James Goodsir		Alexr. Lyell		Joseph Michelbro
5	Denis McCarthy	5	William Rouse	5	Robert Bass
	Rowld. Harbin		Joseph Clapp		James Kerr

		George Gater		+	Peter Goudet			Edward Kerr
		George Mann			Mark Holmes		+	Tho. Williamson
		Richd. Richards			Danl. Stillwell[328]		+	Thos. Chandler
40		Anthony Jacobs	110		Jno. Edwards	180	+	Samuel Moodey
		Nabel Clarke			Chas. Garrison			Wm. Spencer
		Henry Hawkins			Joseph Pearse			William Hunt
		Danl. White			Wm. Grahame			Nathl. Hudson
		Edwd. Savory			Alexr. Campbell			William Smith
5		Peter Marshall	5		James Nevill	5		Adonijah Stanbury
	+	Archd. Murry			James Tasset			Edward Bead
		Daniel Hill			Edw. Berry			Edw. Parmyter
		William Davey			Jno. Andrews		+	Tho. Stoneham
		Richard		+	David		+	John Crew

[328] See **doc. 68**

		Tayler			Nearne		
50		Martn. Townsend	120		Garrt. Peterson	190	Wm. Edmundson
	+	Michl. Swernstone			Richd. Divelly		Richd. Hawks
		Saml. Richardson		+	Charles Veine[329]		Andrew Daws
		Robert Brown			Rogr. Houghton		Thomas Pearse
		Henry Chick			Rd. Valentine		Richd. Ward
5		Robt. Hunter	5		Samuel Boyce	5	Henry Glinn
		James Moodey			Richd. Legatt		Legh Ashworth
		Richd. Kaine			Rd. Rawlings		Domink. Dwoouly
		Tho. Birdsell			Darby Connelly		Geo. Chissem
		Robt. Drybro			Arthr. Van Pelt		David Turner
60	+	Danl. Carman	130		Jno. Richards	200	Clois Derickson
	+	John Dunkin			Saml. Beach		Tho. Bradley

[329] See **doc. 52**

		Geo. Feversham		Wm. Peters			Thomas Emly
		John Barker		John Smith			Nichs. Woodall
		Thomas Codd		Geo. Sinclair			Edward Hays
5		William Roberts	5	Wm. Hasselton	5		Chrisr. Peters
		John Waters		Wm. Harris			John Jackson
		Wm. Austin		William Chow			Chas. Whitehead
		Fras. Roper		Abra. Adams			Edw. Arrowsmith
		Griffith Williams		Joseph Thompson	209		John Perrin
70		Edw. German	140	James Peterson			

70. Certificate of Pardon

CO37/10, f. 21

Like Vincent Pearse [doc.69]*, Governor Bennet of Bermuda was keen to see pirates surrender, and sent his own son to convey the news of the Proclamation of Pardon to the pirates in the Bahamas,* *but unsure of the exact mechanism by which the pardons were to be granted. He therefore drew up an interim certificate to testify to a pirate's voluntary surrender under the terms of the proclamation until such time as their pardon could be formalised.*

By His Excelly Benja Bennet Esqr Capt General Govr and Comr in Chief of these Islands and Vice Adml of these Seas

To all to whom these presents may Concern

Whereas His most sacred Majesty George, King of Great Britain France and Ireland by His Royal Proclamation bearing Date the fifth day of Septr 1717 and in the fourth year of His Majesty's Reign hath been graciously pleased to declare that if any Pirate and Pirates shall by the time therein limitted surrender him or themselves to one of His Majesty's Principal Secrys of State in Great Britain or Ireland or to any Govr or Deputy Govr of his said Majesty's Plantations or Dominions every such Pirate and Pirates so surrendering him or themselves as afordsd should have His most gracious Pardon of and for such his or their Piracy and Piracyes by him or them Comitted as more fully and at large appears by the said Proclamation.

These are Therefore to Certifye till His Majesty's Pardon can be made out that [blank] hath this day arrived in these His Majesty's sd Islands of Bermuda and surrendered himself to me the Govr and Vice Admiral aforesaid Accordingly.

Given under my Hand and the Publick seale of these Islds this [blank] day of [blank] in the fourth year of His Majesty's Reign Anno Dom 1717/18

71. Inventory of a pirate sloop

Minutes of the Provincial Council of Pennsylvania, vol. III (Philadelphia, 1852), pp. 52-53

The following document is the inventory of the pirate sloop recaptured by Richard Appleton and others and is more or less a companion piece to **doc. 39**.

At a Council held at Philada[lphia], the 11th of August, 1718.

The Governour putting the Board in mind, that at their Last meeting at which those persons, who had brought a Sloop into this Port, lately in Possession of the Pirates, were Examined. The Governr had then assured the Board he wou'd take no steps in Relation to that affair without their knowledge & approbacon, thought now fit to Inform them that Capt. Hardy, whom at the Sloops first arrival he had Commissionated to take her under his Care, was now attending, with an Inventory of what was found on board her, which is as follows:

10 Great Guns & Carriages,	4 Spunges,
2 Swivle Guns,	2 Crows,
3 Pateraroes,	10 Organ Barrels,
4 Chambers,	7 Cutlasses,
80 Musketts,	5 Great Gun Cartridge Boxes,
5 Blunderbusses,	8 Cartridge Boxes for small arms.

5 Pistols,

6 Old Pateraroes,

4 Old Chambers,[330]

20 Guns Tackles,

10 Breechins,[331]

2 Guns, Worm and Ladle,

53 hand Granadoes,

200 Great Shot,

2 Barrl. Powder,

4 Caggs of Partridge,

2 Powder Horns.

ACCT. OF SAILS, RIGGING & STORES, etc.

1 Main sail,

1 Fore sail,

1 Jib,

2 Flying Jibbs,

1 Top Sail,

1 Sprit Sail,

1 Square Sail,

1 boat Main Sail & Fore Sail,

22 Spare Blocks,

1 main Sheet,

1 Topmast Stay,

1 Fore halliards,

1 Jib halliards and Down hall,

2 Runners & Tackles,

a Small Quantity of tallow, and Tobacco,

3 Compasses,

1 Doctors Chest,

1 black flagg,

1 Red flagg,

2 Ensignes,

2 pendants,

1 Jack,

8 Stoppers,

1 fflying Jibb halliards,

1 Top Sail Halliards,

1 main Halliards,

---

[330] Probably chambers for breech-loading swivel guns, archaic by the eighteenth century, but certainly not uknown.

[331] Ropes for fastening the guns against the bulwarks of the ship.

1 Topping Lift,	1 main Down hall,
2 Grinding Stones,	1 Jib Sheet, the other for Bow fast.
24 Water Casks,	1 Flying Tack,
1 barl. of Tar & a piece,	1 Fish Hook & Pendant,
30 barr. of Powder,	2 pump Spears,
7 Dead Eyes,	1 Broad Ax,
1 Kittle,	1 Wood Ax,
2 Iron potts,	1 hand Saw,
3 Anchors,	1 pair of Canhooks,
1 Cable,	1 hammer,
1 old piece of Junk,	1 Augur,
13 planks,	1 plain,
2 Top Sail Sheets,	Some Iron work and Lumber.
1 Boom Tackle,	18 bbr. of Beef & pork.

72. The end of Blackbeard

Mr Maynard to Mr Symonds,[332] 17 December, 1718. Printed in *The Weekly Journal, or British Gazetteer*, 25 April, 1719.

When a number of North Carolina residents approached Governor Spotswood of Virginia for help dealing with the notorious Blackbeard, Captain Ellis Brand of HMS Pearl, *sent Lieutenant*

---

[332] Lieutenant, HMS *Phoenix*.

Robert Maynard to intercept the pirate by sea while he himself led a small expedition overland. Maynard, with two small unarmed sloops under his command, cornered Blackbeard at his base on Ocracoke island and there ensued a battle in which Blackbeard was killed, along with several others from both sides. Maynard's unofficial account of the action was written for his brother-officer, Lieutenant Symonds of HMS Phoenix [**doc. 69**] *and later made public in the press.*

Sir,

This is to acquaint you, that I sail'd from Virginia the 17th past, with two Sloops, and 54 Men under my Command, having no Guns, but only small Arms and Pistols. Mr. Hyde[333] commanded the little Sloop with 22 men, and I had 32 in my Sloop. The 22d I came up with Captain Teach, the notorious Pyrate, who has taken, from time to time, a great many English Vessels on these Coasts, and in the West-Indies; he went by the name of Blackbeard, because he let his Beard grow, and tied it up in Black Ribbons. I attack'd him at Cherhock[334] in North Carolina, when he had on Board 21 Men, and nine Guns mounted. At our first Salutation, he drank Damnation to me and my men, whom he stil'd Cowardly Puppies, saying, He would neither give nor take Quarter. Immediately we engag'd, and Mr. Hyde was unfortunately kill'd, and five of his Men wounded in the little Sloop, which, having no-body to command her, fell a-stern, and did not come up to assist me till the Action was almost over. In the mean time, continuing the Fight, it being a

---

[333] A midshipman
[334] Ocracoke

perfect Calm, I shot away Teach's Gib, and his Fore halliards, forcing him ashoar, I boarded his Sloop, and had 20 Men kill'd and wounded. Immediately thereupon, he enter'd me with 10 Men; but 12 stout Men I left there, fought like Heroes, Sword in Hand, and they kill'd every one of them that enter'd, without the loss of one Man on their side, but they were miserably cut and mangled. In the whole, I had eight Men kill'd, and 18 wounded. We kill'd 12, besides Blackbeard, who fell with five Shot in him, and 20 dismal Cuts in several parts of his Body. I took nine Prisoners, mostly Negroes, all wounded. I have cut Blackbeard's Head off, which I have put on my Bowspright, in order to carry it to Virginia. I should never have taken him, if I had not got him in such a Hole, whence he could not get out, for we had no Guns on Board; so that the Engagement on our Side was the more Bloody and Desperate.

73. Captain Davis on the African Coast

The Weekly Packet, 12 December, 1719.

This account of Howell Davis' activities on the African coast was probably a digest of numerous previous newspaper articles detailing individual incidents.

An Account of what Vessels have been taken by the Pirates on the Coast of Africa, from their first Beginning to appear on that Coast.

One Capt. Davis, with 9 Men, went out from the Island of Providence in a Long-Boat, and took a Sloop with 9 Hands, and all Hands joining, came to the Cape Devere's Islands,[335] where they met with a Leverpool Ship at the Isle of May, and took her; she had on Board about 20 Men, all whom he forc'd with him, quitted his old Sloop, and call'd the Ship the *King James*. After that he went into the Gambo River, where he took one French and two English Ships, and getting most of their Hands, mounted 20 Guns. He then took Gambo Fort,[336] brought the Guns away, and mounted the largest on Board. As he came out of the River's Mouth he met a Brigantine, who fir'd at him and hoisted Pirates Colours, and they doing the same, met and join'd: which Brigantine also first began in the West Indies, and most of the Men also came from Providence, who had been before Pirates, but were pardon'd. They both went into the River Seration[337] where they took the *Bird Galley*, Capt. Snelgrove, and the *Sarah Galley* of London, shut up their Decks, and made Pirates of them; the *Jacob and Jael* of London, one Thompson Commander, and a Brigantine, one Bennet Commander, both which they burnt; the *Queen Elizabeth* and *Dispatch*, both of London; and two more Ships of Liverpool; the *Guineamen Sloop*, and one Elliot, both of Barbadoes. They lay in the River about three Weeks, in which time they fitted their Ships and mann'd them, and took also the Company's Fort, and destroyed the Place; and likewise did great Damage to most of their Ships, throwing overboard most of their Cargoes, and went out from Seration. These three Pirates, the *King James*, the *Bird*, call'd

---

[335] Cape Verde Islands
[336] Fort James, Kunta Kinteh Island, near the mouth of the Gambia river.
[337] Sierra Leone

the *Speakwell*, mounting 26 guns, and the *Sarah*, call'd the *Ormond*, mouting 22 Guns, at Cape Mount; took two Ships, one a Glascow Pink and the other of Whitehaven, and went on and off Duslin and took a French Ship, and throw'd all her Cargo overboard, and a Liverpool Snow, and a little after, a Snow belonging to Glascow; and going further along Shore, took several Canoes and kill'd the Blacks; after they parted , the *Speakwell* and *Ormond* staid behind,[338] and the *King James* made all sail down the Coast, and at Cape Appelona met with a large Ostend Ship, with the Emperor's Commission, and bound to the South Seas, they both engag'd, but the Pirate soon took her; she had above 20 Guns, they made her also a Pirate, and threw all her Cargo overboard, which some of them said cost above 8000 Pounds; still going down, they took a Long-Boat of the African Company's, and so came down to Anamaboe, where they took the *Royal Hind, Hall*, and *Prince Plumb*, all of London, and the *Morris Sloop*, Capt. Fen, of Barbadoes, and went on and off Mumford, took a Dutch Ship, and after pundering her discharg'd some of the Men. The *King James*, and his Consort, the other Ship, as they made a Pirate, call'd the *New King James*, with the *Prince Plumb*, went down towards Widaw, and a Day after came down the other two Pirate, *Speakwell* and *Ormond*, and took off the Salt Ponds the *Condrade*, and a large Ship of Barbadoes, and made her a Pirate; she came down again, and retook the *Royal Hind* and *Hall*, with what Men was left on Board, cut the Rigging, and took his Sails and all his Stores, did what Mischief they could, and left her at wreck; so went down, and all met at the River Walta; then went down to Widdaw, where were three

---

[338] See **docs 41** and **44**

Frenchmen, three Portugueze, and the *Heroin Galley*, of London, Capt. Blincks; two of the French Ships cut and run away, and got clear; meanwhile they took the other, and one of the Portuguese Ships; they burnt and made great Destruction with the rest, for they wanted Men and larger Ships to be stronger, to go on the Coast of Brazil, and then to the South Sea; they said they would do all the Mischief they could, for they knew they should have another Pardon sent to call them in, and then they would go into Providence, to their old Friend Johnny Rogers, and lay down their standard, which they hoisted topmast head, with a Gun and Sword, which they call'd Johnny Rogers,[339] and when all was spent, take it up and begin again; they said they knew of 8 or 10 Sail more, besides themselves, that were out upon the same Account, and they reckon'd among their ships to have above 500 men, and increasing.

74. Lists of ships taken by pirates

These two newspaper articles almost certainly represent earlier articles in digest form, and are included as probably the best attempt by contemporaries to enumerate the losses of shipping to pirates.

---

[339] This is the earliest reference to the term 'jolly roger' or a variant. It is also the only explanation of many for the origin of the term that is supported by a contemporary source.

The London Journal, 17 February, 1722.

The Names of all the Ships taken by the Pyrates for five Years last Past, with a particular Account of every one that has been destroy'd by them, or otherwise treated in any extraordinary and barbarous Manner:

The *Widdah*.[340] The *Kent*. The *George*. The *Dolphin*, destroy'd by the Pyrates. The *Ludlow*. The *Mary*. The *Henry and John*. The *Weymouth*. The *Sea Nymph*. The *Ann Galley*. The *Dover*. The *Berkley*. The *Tanner Frigate*, this they stript of all her Goods and Ship Materials, as Guns, Anchors, Cables, etc. murthered some of her Men, and set the Ship on Fire, and left her burning. The *Sarah Sloop*. The *Samuel*. The *Buck Sloop*, this was carry'd off by the Pyrates, and burnt on the Coast of Guinea. The *Betsey*. The *Margaret*. The *Emperor*. The *Neptune*. The *Minerva*. The *Bridge Town*. The *Kingston*. The *Eagle*. The *Pearle*. The *Mary*. The *Alexander*. The *London*. The *Crowne*. The *King of Prussia*. The *Protestant*. The *Colston*. The *Society*. A Sloop. Two Sloops. The *Charlotta*. The *John Galley*. The *Victory*, burnt on the Coast of Guinea. The *Peterborough*. The *Temperance*, sunk by the Pyrates on the Coast of Guinea. The *Mercury*. The *Sea Nymph*. The *Essex*. The *Fame*, destroy'd on the Coast of Guinea. The *Indian Queen*.[341] The *Mediterranean*. The *Experiment*,[342] burnt on the Coast of Guinea. The *Comrade*.[343] The *Queen Mary*. The *Mary and Elizabeth*. The *Success*. The *Queen Elizabeth*. The *Prince Eugene*. The *Morrice*, destroy'd by the Pyrates at Guinea. The *Guinea Hen*. The *Tarlton*. The

---

[340] **Doc. 21**
[341] **Docs 41** and **55**
[342] **Docs 24** and **53**
[343] **Docs 41, 44** and **73**

Princess. The *Leopard.* The *Dove*, the *Sarah Galley*, both destroy'd on the Coast of Guinea. The *Royal Hind.* The *Elizabeth and Katherine.* The *Jacob and Jael.* The *Westberry.* The *Onslow.* The *Martha.* The *Robinson.* The *Sarah*, burnt by Pyrates on the Coast of Guinea. The *Sierra Leon*, destroy'd on the Coast of Guinea. The *Robert and Jane*, destroy'd in Sierra Leon River. The *Dragon*, burnt. The *Heroine.*[344] The *Edward and Steed.* The *Society.* The *Margaret.* The *Loyalty*, burnt at Guinea. The *Frederick.* The *Katherine*, sunk at Newfoundland. The *Expectation*, sunk also. The — Capt. Square, sunk also. The — Capt. Russel, his Masts and Rigging cut down and plunder'd. The *Willing Mind.* The *Commerce*, burnt at Newfoundland.

In July 1720, a Pirate Sloop with 30 or 40 Hands came to Newfoundland, and besides the Ships above-named destroyed and plundered most of the Ships that were on the Bankcs, and the Northern Harbour of Newfoundland. The *Martha and Mary*, burnt in the Road of St. Christophers. The *Cassandra.*[345] The *Lloyd Galley*,[346] burnt near Jamaica. The *Norman.* The *Two Sisters.* The *Samuel.* The *Kittey.* The *Queen Ann Galley*, taken near New England, they cut down her Masts and Plundred her, and then turned her a drift. The *Irwin*, sunk near Martinico. The *Belfast Merchant.* The *Don Carlos.* The *Hamilton Galley*,[347] Burnt near Antegoa. *Bumper Galley*,[348] bound from London to Guinea etc in the African Company's Service, the Seamen being joined by some Soldiers, put the Master ashore on the Coast of Guinea, and

---

[344] **Docs 41 and 73**
[345] **Docs 55-56**
[346] **Doc 58**
[347] **Docs 43 and 61**
[348] **Doc. 28**

turned Pirates. The *Sarah*, bound from Bristol to Guinea, etc, the Seamen turning Pirates, set the Master ashore, and went off with her. The *Morning Star*.[349] The *Nassaw*. Four Sloops. -— Capt Bull. A Sloop. The *Expedition*. Two Sloops. The —, Capt. Farmer, bound from Jamaica to New York, taken twice in his Way by Pirates, and stript of all his Goods. A Snow. The *Dispatch*, Taken by the Pirates, who flung away the Goods, cut away the Masts and Rigging, and left her, but for want of her Masts run ashore and stranded. Five Sloops, taken by them and stranded. The —, Capt. Colston, from Antegoa, for Philadelphia, taken and plundered by the Pirates. Three Sloops. The *Greyhound*. The *Bird Galley*, burnt by them. The *Duke of York*. The *Samuel*. The *Palmer*. The *St. Ann*. The *Experiment*. The *Eagle*. The *West River Merchant*. The *Blessing*. The *Dolphin*. The *John*. The —, Capt Codd, Bound from Leverpool to Pensilvania, taken by Pirates, who flung her Goods overboard, and turned her adrift. The *Crawley*. The *Ruby*. The *Merry-thought*. The *D[uke] of York*.

The London Journal, 24 February, 1722.

A List of the Vessels which have been taken by Pirates on the Coast of South-Carolina, or bound to or from that Place, from the year 1717 to 1721.

The *Tanner*, 300 tons, Capt. Samuel Stoneham, from Jamaica to London, taken in the Windward Passage, plundered and put into Carolina, by a Pirate Ship of 30 Guns and 250 Men, commanded by one Bellamy. The *Dove* Sloop, Capt. John

---

[349] **Docs 29, 42, 43, 46**, and **61**

Stoneman, from Carolina to Jamaica, taken near Jamaica, and burnt, by a French Pirate Sloop of 10 Guns and 80 Men, one Martell, Captain. *Mary* Sloop, 70 tons, Capt. Jos. Palmer, from Barbados to Carolina, taken off the Bar of Carolina, and burnt: and the *Dolphin*, 80 tons, Capt. John Porter, bound from New England to Carolina, taken off the Bar of Carolina, and plundered; both by a Pirate Sloop of 10 Guns and 80 Men, called the *Royal James*, alias, the *Revenge*, commanded by one Bonnett. *Providence* Sloop, 40 tons, Capt. Neale Walker, bound from Providence to Carolina, taken off the Bar of Carolina, and plundered, by the same Pirate Sloop as the two former. *Amity* Sloop, 80 tons, Capt. Tho. Palmer, bound from Dartmouth to Carolina, taken in the Latitude of 32 Deg. 45 Min. and plundered, by a French Pirate Ship of 30 Guns and 250 Men, one Lebous, Commander. *Crowley*, 180 tons, Capt. Rob. Clarke, bound from Carolina to London, taken off the Bar of Carolina and plundered. *Ruby*, 140 tons, Capt. Isaac Craige, bound from Carolina to London, taken off the Bar of Carolina, and plundered. *John and Thomas*, 140 tons, Capt. Napper Reeves, bound from London to Carolina, taken off the Bar of Carolina and plundered. The *Artemesia*, 140 tons, Capt Tho. Dornford, bound from London to Carolina, taken off the Bar of Carolina, and plundered. *Neptune*, 130 tons, Capt. Tho. Mason, bound from New England to Carolina, taken off the Bar of Carolina, and plundered. *Thomas* Sloop, 30 tons, Capt. Thomas Smith, bound from South Carolina to North Carolina, taken off the Bar of Carolina, and plundered. *Morning Star*, 90 tons, Capt. John Bedford, bound from Guinea to Carolina, taken off the Bar of Carolina, and plundered. These seven taken by three Pirate Vessels, one a Ship of 40 Guns, called the Queen

Anne's Revenge,[350] 350 Men, and two Sloops, one of 10 Guns and 90 Men, the other of 8 Guns and 50 Men, all under the Command of one Thatch, commonly called Black beard, who rode at Anchor with their black Flags flying four Days, in sight of Charles Town, having all their Prizes then in Possession. The Pirates had the Insolence to send ashore to the Governour, and demand a Chest of medicines, which was accordingly sent them, they having threatened, on refusal, to burn all their Prizes, and murder the Men. The *Sea-flower*, 50 tons, Capt. Isaac Gill, bound from Barbados to Carolina, taken off the Bar of Carolina, and plundered. *Fontaine*, 110 tons, Capt. William Cook, bound from Antegoa to Carolina, taken off the Bar of Carolina, and plundered. *Dorothy*, 90 tons, Capt. William Thompson, bound from Guinea to Carolina, taken off the Bar of Carolina, and plundered. *Neptune*, 150 tons, Capt. John King, bound from Carolina to London, taken off the Bar of Carolina, carried off and afterwards sunk. *Emperor*, 180 tons, Capt. Arnold Bowers, bound from Carolina to London, taken off the Bar of Carolina, and plundered. *William and Andrew*, 70 tons, Capt William Adams, bound from Curaso to Carolina, taken off the Bar of Carolina, carried off, all six by a Pirate Brigantine of 12 Guns and 120 Men, commanded by one Vane. *Ludlow*, 170 tons, Capt. Arthur Lone, bound from Carolina to London, taken on the Banks of Newfoundland, and plundered. *Glascow*, 140 tons, Capt. Delapp, bound from Glascow to Jamaica, taken in the Latitude of Bermudas, plundered and put into Carolina, these Three [sic] by a Pirate Ship of 36 Guns and 300 Men, commanded by a Frenchman named Louis Lebore.[351] *Neptune*, 80 tons, Capt. John

---

[350] See **doc. 22**

Masters, bound from Carolina to Jamaica, taken off the crooked Islands, and plundered, by a Pirate Sloop of 10 guns and 90 Men, commanded by one Burgess. *Eagle*, 150 tons, Capt. Roberts Staples, bound from London to Virginia, taken off the Capes of Virgina, retaken and brought into Carolina, by a Pirate Sloop of 9 Guns and 30 Men, one Wooley, commander. *Mediterranean*, 200 tons, Capt. Arthur Lone, bound from Guinea to Carolina, taken on the Coast of Guinea and carried off. The *Carteret*, Capt. Tho Lynche, bound from Guinea to Carolina, taken on the Coast of Guinea and burnt, these two by three Pirate Ships, one of 20, one of 26, and the other of 30 Guns, all under the Command of one England. The *Sarah*, 170 tons, Capt. Benjamin Austin, bound from London to Carolina taken off the Bar of Carolina, and carried off, by a Spanish Pirate Sloop of 8 Guns and 70 Men. *Minerva*, 140 tons, Capt. John Smyter, bound from Madera to Carolina, taken off the Bar of Carolina, and plundered. *Atalantis*, 170 tons, Capt. Rumsey bound from New England to Carolina, taken off the Bar of Carolina, and plundered. *Sea-flower*, 80 tons, Capt. Jeremiah Brown, bound from Rhode Island to Carolina, taken off the Bar of Carolina, and carried off, these Three by a Pirate Ship of 30 Guns and 200 Men, commanded by one Moody. The *Mermaid* Sloop, 60 tons, Capt. John Ramp, bound from Barbados to Carolina, taken among the Leward Island, and carried off by a Spanish Pirate. *Adventure* Sloop, 50 tons, Capt. John Donuist, bound from Carolina to Jamaica, taken off Jamaica, and carried off by a Spanish Pirate. *Fortune* Sloop, 60 tons, Capt. Thomas Read, bound from Pensilvania to Barbados, taken off the Capes of Pensilvania, retaken and brought to Carolina.

[351] La Buse

Frances Sloop, 70 tons, Capt. Peter Manns, bound to Antegoa, taken off the Capes of Pensilvania, retaken and brought to Carolina, by a Pirate Sloop of 10 Guns and 70 Men, commanded by one Boune, afterwards taken and brought into Carolina. *Andrew and William*, Sloop, Capt. Jos. Stollard, bound from Carolina to Newfoundland, and plundered by a Pirate Ship of 36 Guns and 250 Men, commanded by one Roberts. *Belfast*, 150 tons, Capt. Macphedries, bound from Carolina to London, taken at Newfoundland, and plundered by a French Pirate Ship of 20 Guns. *Morning Star*, Brigantine, Capt. Poole, bound for Guinea and Carolina, taken in the Leeward Islands, and carried off by a Pirate of 40 Guns, commanded by one Roberts.

N.B. The Damage which the Province of South Carolina sustain'd by these Depredations of the Pirate, obliged that Government in the Year 1718, to fit at their own Cost and Charge 2 Sloops under the Command of Capt. William Rhett of that Province, who took and brought into Carolina a Pirate Sloop called the *Royal James* alias the *Revenge* of 10 Guns and 70 Men, commanded by one Bennett, and after an obstinate Resistance of 2 Hours, and at the same Time retook 2 Vessels, who had been taken by the said Pirates. Robert Johnson Esq, late Governour of Carolina, soon after, with a Ship and 2 Sloops under his Command took and brought into Carolina, a Pirate Sloop of six Guns and 30 Men, commanded by one Richard Worley, and called the *New York Revenge*, and also retook a Ship called the *Eagle*, which had been before taken by the said Pirate near the Capes of Virginia. Of which Pirates about 40 were executed in Carolina.

75. The end of Bartholomew Roberts

Capt. Chaloner Ogle to the Admiralty, April 5, 1722. ADM 1/2242. Also printed in *The London Gazette*, 4 September 1722.

Bartholomew Roberts and his company were, to some extent, victims of their own success when their very extensive depredations caused the Admiralty to send HMS Weymouth *and HMS* Swallow *to hunt them down. By the time Roberts was found HMS* Weymouth *had been so ravaged by sickness that she had had to abandon the chase, and HMS* Swallow *was alone. The battle, or rather series of battles, that followed was sharp and bloody and ended with 52 of Roberts' company hanging by the shore at Cabo*

Corso. For the destruction of the last of the big pirate bands of the 'golden age', Ogle received a knighthood

Sir,

In mine bearing Date the 6th of November last I gave you an Account that His Majties Ship's Company under my Command were on Recovery, and that I intended in a few Days to ply to Windward and Cruise between Cape Palmas and Cape Three Points, I sail'd accordingly the 10th D[itt]o, the *Weymouth* I left here (most of the men being sick) with Orders, when she was in all respects fit for the sea to proceed and Cruise between Cape Mount and Cape Three Points till the 30th of December.

On the 20th of November I spoke with a Ship belonging to the African Company come from London, from whom I receiv'd Yours Dated the 3d of August, Wherein you acquaint me that their Lordships had Order'd me three Months Provisions and Wine in Proportion to be sent out for the Use of His Majties Ships Here, the Master of the said Company ship inform'd me he had the Proportion of Beef, Pork, and some of the Bread aboard, and that the Other Provisions with the Wine I might expect very soon by a ship that was to leave England soon soon [sic] after he sail'd. The 7th of January I return'd hither in hopes to find the said Provisions and Wine all Arriv'd, but was disappointed, for Neither the Wine nor Dry Provisions were come.

The sickness Aboard the *Weymouth* was not at all Abated, but the Dry Season being come hinder'd her being further supply'd with Water at this Place, so that Captn Herdman[352] with his small Number of Men that were in Health, and some soldiers borrow'd from this Castle, ply'd up to Windward to Water at Cape Three Points. I took in a Month's Beef, pork and Bread which with the Provisions I had on Board completed me to Three Months of all Species, pease and Oatmeal excepted.

On the 10th D[itt]o the Governr here received Advice from the Dutch that on ye 6th Instant Two Pyrate ships had taken a French ship off of Axim. I lodged Orders here for Captn Herdman at his return with His Majesty's Ship the *Weymouth* to cruise (as soon as he was in a Condition for the Sea) between Cape Three Points and Cape Palmas till the 25th of March, and I forthwith got under sail, and ranged Down the Coast for Whydah, but could gain no Intelligence of the Pyrates 'till I arriv'd there tho' I met with several ships trading on the Coast in my Passage down.

On my Arrival at Whydah I was inform'd that two Pyrate ships, One of 40 and Another of 24 Guns[353] commanded by one Roberts had been there and had sail'd About 36 Hours before, I found 10 sail of ships in the Road, Two of which were English, Three French, and five Portuguese, they all Ransom'd at the Rate of Eight Pound Wt of Gold each except One English ship for refusing to Ransom they burnt with a Considerable Number of Negroes aboard, the Pyrates being inform'd that One of the ships sail'd well and had formerly been a Privateer out of St. Maloes, did notwithstanding a Ransom paid for her carry her Away with a Design to fitt her for their service and quit their 24 Gun ship. Therefore I

---

[352] Mungo Herdman acted as President of the Vice-Admiralty Court that tried the survivors of Roberts' company
[353] By comparison, HMS *Swallow* carried 50 guns.

judged they must go to some Place in the Bite to clean and fit the French ship , before they would think of Cruising again, Which occasion'd me to stretch away into the Bite and look into those places which I knew had Depth of Water sufficient for His Majties Ship.

On the 5th of February at Daylight I saw Cape Lopus[354] bearing WSW about 3 Leagues and at the same time discover'd three ships at Anchor under the Cape, which I believed to be the Pyrates, Two of 'em having Pendants flying, I was Oblig'd to Hawl off NWt and WNWt to clear the Frenchman's Bank the Wind at SSEt and in less than an Hour one of the Three got under sail and gave me Chace, and I to give her a fairer Opportunity of coming up with me without being Discover'd kept on the same Course, with the same sail abroad I had when I first saw her, about 11 that Morning she got within Gun shott of me, and fir'd several Chace Guns, under English Colours and a black Flag at her Mizon Peak, soon afterwards being come within Musquett shott, I starboard my Helm and gave her a Broadside, and in an Hour and a Half Time she struck and call'd for Quarters, having Disabled her very Much and shot down her Maintop Mast. She prov'd to be the French ship they had taken out of Whydah Road, and had Mounted 32 Guns and a hundred twenty three Men, Twenty three of which was Blacks, she had kill'd and wounded Twenty six Men, her Captn's Name was Skyrm who had one Leg shot off. The Prisoners inform'd me that the Two ships they left at Anchor under the Cape were Roberts in ye 40 Gun ship and the Other 24 Gun ship they had that morning quitted for ye Prize. The 6th

---

[354] Cape Lopez

392

D[itt]o in ye Night I left the Prize having put her into the best Condition for sailing so short a time would allow of, and order'd her away to the Island Princes[355] I made the best of my way to Windward again in Order to descry the two ships that remained at Anchor under Cape Lopus. On the 9th D[itt]o in the Evening I made the Cape and saw two ships stretching in under the land about 5 Lgs distance, but not having Day-light Enough I was oblig'd to stand off and on all Night and in the morning I stretched in under the Cape where I saw at Anchor three Ships, the Biggest of 'em with Jack, Ensign and Pendant flying, whom I lay up with till I got within Random shott[356] when the wind took her a-head and I made two Tripps in which time he slipp'd and had got under sail and came down upon me with English Ensign and Jack, and a Black Pendant flying at her Maintopmast Head, and I shewing him a French Ensign when he came within Pistoll shott[357] I hoisted my proper Colours, and gave him a Broadside which he return'd, and endeavour'd to get from me by making all the sail he could, but in less than two Hours I shot his Mainmast down and then he struck, his Mizon top mast being shot away some time before. The Captn, whose name was Roberts was kill'd, this Prize (formerly call'd the *Onslow* and since by the Pyrates the *Royal Fortune*) had 40 Guns mounted and 152 Men 52 of which were Negroes.

The next day I ply'd back again for the Cape in Order to take out the 24 Gun ship the Pyrates had quitted, and to restore to the third (wch was a ship Freighted by the African Company – Hill Commander) such Provisions as the Pyrates had

---

[355] Principe
[356] Extreme cannon range, around 1,800 yards
[357] Less that 30 yards

robbed him of, together with his Surgeon and four Men, Roberts having seized her the Day before I took him, as she was coming-to under the Cape to water, but anchoring again under the Cape ye 12th D[itt]o I found there only the Pyrate ship of 24 Guns without any body aboard her, all the Men's chests being broke open and Rifled, which Occasions me to believe that by the speedy sailing of the Above said Company's hired ship, which had but a very small Quantity of Water or Provisions a-board two days before that they must have Robbed her, otherwise could not possibly have sail'd so soon. The Pyrates inform'd me that they had left in their Chests aboard considerable Quantity of Gold but not above ten Oz were found aboard her, the Quantity of Gold I have got out of all the Prizes will amount to about £3000, and I beg their Lordships will be pleased to use their Good Offices with His Majty that the Prizes may be shared among the Captors.[358] The 18th of Febry I compleated Watering and sail'd for Princes from whence I took out the Prize and then proceeded directly for Cape Corse. The three Prizes lost Company with me in a Tornado near St. Thomas.

The 15th of March I arrived here where I found the Dry Provisions and part of the Wines which arriv'd not here before the latter end of February, and according to the Bills of Lading saw there should be fifty Pipes, whereas no more than thirty four were here, the Mastr pretending he was so stow'd with Goods from England that he could not possibly take in more.[359] The 26th D[itt]o the Weymough Anchored

---

[358] In fact, the Admiralty awarded a total prize fund to Ogle of £5,364 9s 9d, out of which he was expected to pay £1940 to the crew of HMS *Swallow*. However, it was not until 1725, after the matter had been exposed by Charles Johnson in the *General History of the Pyrates* that Ogle actually distributed the money.
[359] This complaint about the missing wine was not included in the *London*

here, and then proceeded to the trials of the Pyrates, Captn Herdman sitting as President of ye Court, I being Captor, disqualified me from sitting. The 3ʳᵈ of April the three Prizes arrived.

As soon as the Court has made an End of Trying the Pyrates I shall loose no time, but according to my Instructions shall proceed by the way of Barbadoes and Jamaica to Great Brittain.

PS. Since my last I buried my 1ˢᵗ Lieut. Mr Barton, who came out of England 2d.

76. Inventories of goods in the possession of Pierce and Andrew Cullen

Inventories, 22 January, 1723. HCA 1/17, ff. 163-164

Pierce and Andrew Cullen, members of Philip Roche's pirate company [doc. 31], were not typical Atlantic or Indian Ocean pirates in the manner of Blackbeard or Taylor, but such a list of pirates' possessions is unusual enough to warrant inclusion here. It is important to note that not all of the items in Pierce Cullen's possession are likely to have been for his own use: boots, spurs, 'riding spatterdashes' and a saddle pillion would not have served any purpose at sea, and the woman's stomacher suggests that at least some of the items listed were things Cullen had saved because of their resale value. Andrew Cullen's inventory is probably far more typical of a pirate's actual personl possessions.

Gazette's version of the letter.

An Acct of all the things marked and unmarked which are now in a Leather Portmanteau, which was brought up to Town by Warrant from the Amdty Board from His Maties Ship the *Lively* at Portsmouth as appertaining to Pierce Cullen now a prisoner in ye Marshalsea for Piracy and Murder.

Acct of the things marked wth their Marks.

5 white shirts marked P.B.C.
1 white shirt marked C.
1 napkin marked C.A. 1714
1 napkin marked w.j.

Acct of the things not marked
1 white shirt
5 blew and white shirts
1 old frise coat
1 worsted damask wastcoat and serge damask breeches
1 pair of silk damask breeches
2 flannell wastcoats
2 bob wigs
1 pair of sleeves
1 pair of boots and spurs
4 plain cravat stocks
2 night caps
2 muslin cravats
1 pair of black silk stockings, 2 pair of white cotton stockings
1 pair of worsted stockings
1 towell
1 thread sack

1 blew and white bag

1 white Fustian wastcoate

1 old handkerchief

1 razor and hoand[360]

pair of blew and white riding spatterdashes

1 mail pillion

1 silk quilted stommacher

All this I humbly certify having carefully examined the Contents of the above mentioned Portmanteau in the presence of Mr John Durridge who brought ye same from Portsmouth. Witness my hand this 22d of January 1722.

Robt: May

An Acct of the severall things which are in a Wallet, brought up from on board his Majestys Ship the *Lively* as belonging to Pierce Cullen: and allso a Copy of the note affixed to the said Wallet.

1 Arithmetick Book signed Andrew Cullen

3 paire of breeches

2 flannell wastcoats

2 blew and white shirts

1 white shirt

6 plain cravat stocks

1 Turneover

1 holland cravat

1/2 a yard of new holland

3 paire of yarn hose

---

[360] Sharpening stone

1 paire of worsted hose
2 Wollen Caps
1 paire of shoes
2 blew and white baggs
2 Razers
1 knife and fork
1 Glove

Copy of the Note fixed to ye Wallet.

This Bagg or Wallet Containes the wearing apparell and other Goods seizd in the Lodgins of Andrew Cullen when he fled on the hearing of his sd Brother's being Apprehended the particulars whereof are mentioned in a Schedule Referr'd to in the Examination of Ralph Glin date the 3d Novm 1722.

There is no marke on any of the above sd things. Witness my hand this 22d day of Janry 1722.

Robt: May

COMMON ABBREVIATIONS

Abd – aboard

Abt – about

Afosd/aforsd - aforesaid

Comp – company

Comr – commander

Dept – deponent

Exiate/exate – examinate

Govr/govnr – governor

Maty – majesty (his Majesty)

Mercht – merchant

Mstr/mr/mar – master (usually sailing master)

Onbd – onboard

Recd/recvd – received

Sd – said

Sevll – several

Wt – weight

Y – the

Yr – your

Yt - that

BIBLIOGRAPHY OF SECONDARY SOURCES

Anderson, John L. 'Piracy and World History, an Economic Perspective on Maritime Predation', in Pennell, *Bandits at Sea*, 82-106

Anderson, Olive. 'British Governments and Rebellion at Sea', *Historical Journal*, 3 (1960), 56-84

Appleby, John C. *Under the Bloody Flag. Pirates of the Tudor Age* (Stroud, 2009)

Arnold-Forster, F.D. *The Madagascar Pirates* (New York, 1957)

Baer, Joel. '"The Complicated Plot of Piracy": Aspects of English Criminal Law and the Image of the Pirate in Defoe', *Studies in Eighteenth Century Culture*, 14 (1985), 3-28

————'"Captain John Avery" and the Anatomy of a Mutiny', *Eighteenth-Century Life*, 18 (1994), 1-26

———— 'Bold Captain Avery in the Privy Council: Early Variants of a Broadside Ballad from the Pepys Collection', *Folk Music Journal*, 7 (1995), 4-26

————'William Dampier at the Crossroads: New Light on the "Missing Years," 1691-1697', *International Journal of Maritime History*, VIII (1996), 97-117

————*Pirates* (Stroud, 2007)

Beal, Clifford. *Quelch's Gold, piracy, greed, and betrayal in colonial New England* (Westport, 2007)

Benton, Lauren. 'Toward a New Legal History of Piracy: Maritime Legalities and the Myth of Universal Jurisdiction', *International Journal of Maritime History*, XXIII (2011), 225-240

Bernhard, Virginia. 'Bermuda and Virginia in the Seventeenth Century: A Comparative View', *Journal of Social History*, 19 (1985), 57-70

Bialuschewski, Arne. 'Between Newfoundland and the Malacca Strait: a Survey of the Golden Age of Piracy, 1695-1725', *Mariner's Mirror*, 90 (2004), 167-186

—— 'Daniel Defoe, Nathaniel Mist, and the General History of the Pyrates', *Papers of the Bibliographical Society of America*, 98 (2004), 21-38

——'Pirates, Slavers and the Indigenous Population in Madagascar, c. 1690-1715', *International Journal of African Historical Studies*, 38 (2005), 401-425

—— 'Pirate Voyages in History and Fantasy', *Global Crime*, 7 (2006), 256-259

—— 'Pirates, Markets and Imperial Authority: Economic Aspects of Maritime Depredations in the Atlantic World, 1716-1726', *Global Crime*, 9 (2008), 52-65

——'Black People under the Black Flag: Piracy and the Slave Trade on the West Coast of Africa, 1718-1723', *Slavery and Abolition*, 29 (2008), 461-475

Black, Clinton V. *Pirates of the West Indies* (Cambridge 1989)

Botein, Stephen, Jack R. Censer, Harriet Ritvo. 'The Periodical Press in Eighteenth-Century English and French Society: A Cross-Cultural Approach', *Comparative Studies in Society and History*, 23 (1981), 464-490

Bromley, J.S. *Corsairs and Navies, 1660-1760* (London, 1987)

Burg, B.R. 'Legitimacy and Authority: A Case Study of Pirate Commanders in the Seventeenth and Eighteenth Centuries', *American Neptune*, 37 (1977), 40-51

——*Sodomy and the Pirate Tradition* (New York, 1984)

Burgess, Douglas R. *The Pirates' Pact* (New York, 2008)

Burl, Aubrey. *Black Barty: Bartholomew Roberts and his Pirate Crew 1718-1723* (Stroud, 2006)

Chapin, Howard M. *Privateer Ships and Sailors, the First Century of American Colonial Privateering* (Toulon, 1926)

Cordingly, David. *Life Among the Pirates, the Romance and the Reality* (London, 1995)

———*Heroines and Harlots, Women at Sea in the Great Age of Sail* (London, 2001)

Course, Alfred George. *Pirates of the Eastern Seas* (London, 1966)

———*Pirates of the Western Seas* (London, 1969)

Craton, Michael. *A History of the Bahamas* (London, 1962)

Davis, Ralph. *The Rise of the English Shipping Industry in the Seventeenth and Eighteenth Centuries* (Newton Abbot, 1972)

Dow, George, and John Edmonds. *Pirates of the New England Coast* (Mineloa, 1999)

Earle, Peter. *Sailors. English Merchant Seamen, 1650-1775* (London, 1998)

———*The Pirate Wars* (London, 2004)

Fuller, Basil, and Ronald Leslie-Melville. *Pirate Harbours and Their Secrets* (London, 1935)

Furbank, P.N. and W.R. Owens. 'The Myth of Defoe as "Applebee's Man"', *The Review of English Studies*, New Series, 48 (1997), pp. 198-204

Fury, Cheryl A. *Tides in the Affairs of Men: the social history of Elizabethan seamen, 1580-1603* (Westport, 2002)

Fury, Cheryl A. (ed.) *The Social History of English Seamen, 1485-1649* (Woodbridge, 2012)

Gilje, Paul A. *Liberty on the Waterfront, American maritime culture in the Age of Revolution* (Philadelphia, 2004)

Gilje, Paul A., and William Pencak (eds). *Pirates, Jack Tar, and Memory: New Directions in American Maritime History* (Mystic, 2007)

Gosse, Philip. *The Pirates' Who's Who* (New York, 1924)

Grey, Charles. *Pirates of the Eastern Seas 1618-1723: a Lurid Page of History* (London, 1933)

Hay, Douglas, Peter Linebaugh, John G. Rule, E.P. Thompson, and Cal Winslow. *Albion's Fatal Tree: Crime and Society in Eighteenth Century England* (New York, 1975)

Hill, Christopher. 'Radical Pirates?', in Jacob, *Anglo-American Radicalism*, 17-32

———*Liberty Against the Law* (London, 1997)

Jacob, Margaret C. and James R. Jacob (eds), *The Origins of Anglo-American Radicalism* (London 1984)

Kemp, Peter, and Christopher Lloyd. *Brethren of the Coast, the British and French Buccaneers in the South Seas* (London 1960)

Kinkor, Kenneth J. 'Black Men under the Black Flag', in Pennell, *Bandits at Sea*, 195-210

Konstam, Angus. *Blackbeard: America's Most Notorious Pirate* (Hoboken, 2006)

Lee, Robert E. *Blackbeard the Pirate: a Re-appraisal of his Life and Times* (Winston-Salem, 1974)

Leeson, Peter T. 'An-arrgh-chy: The Law and Economics of Pirate Organization', *Journal of Political Economy*, 115 (2007), 1049-1094

———*The Invisible Hook. The Hidden Economics of Pirates* (Princeton, 2009)

———'The Calculus of Piratical Consent: the myth of the myth of the social contract', *Public Choice*, 139 (2009), 443-459

Linebaugh, Peter, and Marcus Rediker. *The Many Headed Hydra: The Hidden History of the Revolutionary Atlantic* (London, 2000)

Lizé, Patrick. 'Piracy in the Indian Ocean: Mauritius and the *Speaker*', in Skowronek and Ewen, *X Marks the Spot*, pp. 81-99

Lusardi, Wayne R. 'The Beaufort Inlet Shipwreck Artefact Assemblage' in Skowronek and Ewen, *X Marks the Spot*, pp. 196-218

Lydon, James. *Pirates, Privateers, and Profits* (Upper Saddle River, 1970)

McLynn, Frank. *Crime and Punishment in Eighteenth-Century England* (New York, 1989)

Morgan, Kenneth. 'Bristol and the Atlantic Trade in the Eighteenth Century', *English Historical Review*, 107 (1992), 626-650

———*Slavery, Atlantic Trade and the British Economy, 1600-1800* (Cambridge, 2000)

Oberwittler, Dietrich. 'Crime and Authority in Eighteenth Century England: Law Enforcement on the Local Level', *Historical Social Research*, 15 (1990), 3-34

Pennell, C.R. (ed.). *Bandits at Sea, a Pirates Reader* (New York, 2001)

Pérotin-Dumon, Anne. 'The Pirate and the Emporer, Power and the Law on the Seas, 1450-1850', in Pennell, *Bandits at Sea*, 25-54

Pringle, Patrick. *Jolly Roger* (Mineola, 2001)

Rediker, Marcus. '"Under the Banner of King Death": The Social World of Anglo-American Pirates, 1716-1726', *The William and Mary Quarterly*, Third series, 38 (1981), 203-227

———*Between the Devil and the Deep Blue Sea: merchant seamen, pirates, and the Anglo-American maritime world, 1700-1750* (Cambridge, 1987)

———*Villains of all Nations: Atlantic Pirates in the Golden Age* (London, 2004)

Ritchie, Robert C. *Pirates: myths and realities* (Minneapolis, 1986)
————*Captain Kidd and the War Against the Pirates* (Cambridge, Mass., 1986)
Rodger, N.A.M. *The Wooden World, an Anatomy of the Georgian Navy* (London, 1988)
————*Command of the Ocean, a Naval history of Britain, 1649-1815* (London, 2004)
Rogozinski, Jan. *Honor Among Thieves: Captain Kidd, Henry Every, and the Pirate Democracy in the Indian Ocean* (Mechanicsburg, 2000)
Sanders, Richard. *If a Pirate I Must Be* (London, 2007)
Sherry, Frank. *Raiders and Rebels. The Golden Age of Piracy* (New York, 1986)
Skowronek, Russell K. and Charles R. Ewen (eds). *X Marks the Spot: The Archaeology of Piracy* (Gainesville, 2006)
Starkey, David J. (ed.). *British Privateering Enterprise in the Eighteenth Century* (Exeter, 1990)
Pirates and Privateers: new perspectives on the war on trade in the eighteenth century (Exeter, 1997)
———— 'Pirates and Markets', in Pennell, *Bandits at Sea*, 107-124
————'The Origins and Regulation of Eighteenth-Century British Privateering', in Pennell, *Bandits at Sea*, 69-81
———— 'Voluntaries and Sea Robbers: A review of the academic literature on privateering, corsairing, buccaneering and piracy', *Mariners Mirror*, 97 (2011), 127-147
Thomson, Janice. *Mercenaries, Pirates, and Sovereigns: State-Building and Extraterritorial Violence in Early Modern Europe* (Princeton, 1994)
Turley, Hans. *Rum, Sodomy and the Lash* (New York, 1999)

Vickers, Daniel, and Vince Walsh. 'Young Men and the Sea: the sociology of seafaring in eighteenth century Salem, Massachusetts', *Social History*, 24 (1999), 17-38

————*Young Men and the Sea: Yankee seafarers in the age of sail* (New Haven, 2005)

Williams, Crystal. 'Nascent Socialists or Resourceful Criminals? A Reconsideration of Transatlantic Piracy', in Gilje and Pencak, *Pirates, Jack Tar and Memory*, 31-50

Williams, Daniel E. 'Puritans and Pirates: A Confrontation between Cotton Mather and William Fly in 1726' *Early American literature*, 22 (1987), 233-251

Witt, Jann M. 'Mutiny and Piracy in Northern Europe Merchant Shipping: Forms of Insurrection on board British and German Merchant Ships in the Late 17th and 18th Centuries', *Northern Mariner*, 18 (2008), 1-27

Woodard, Colin. *The Republic of Pirates* (Orlando, 2007)

Lightning Source UK Ltd.
Milton Keynes UK
UKOW04f1851151015

260632UK00001B/73/P